TAX POLICY AND THE ECONOMY 5

edited by ***David Bradford***

National Bureau of Economic Research
The MIT Press, Cambridge, Massachusetts

Send orders and business correspondence to:
The MIT Press
55 Hayward Street
Cambridge, MA 02142

In the United Kingdom, continental Europe, and the Middle East and Africa, send orders and business correspondence to:
The MIT Press Ltd.
14 Bloomsbury Square
London, WC1A 2LP
ENGLAND

ISSN: 0892-8649
ISBN: hardcover 0-262-02295-8
       paperback 0-262-52158-X

Library of Congress number 91-61074

Copyright Information
Permission to photocopy articles for internal or personal use, or the internal or personal use of specific clients, is granted by the copyright owner for users registered with the Copyright Clearance Center (CCC) Transactional Reporting Service, provided that the fee of $5.00 per copy is paid directly to CCC, 27 Congress St., Salem, MA 01970. The fee code for users of the Transactional Reporting Service is: 0892-8649/91 $5.00. For those organizations that have been granted a photocopy license with CCC, a separate system of payment has been arranged.

©1991 by The National Bureau of Economic Research and The Massachusetts Institute of Technology.

NATIONAL BUREAU OF ECONOMIC RESEARCH

Officers:
George T. Conklin, Jr., *Chairman*
Paul McCracken, *Vice Chairman*
Martin Feldstein, *President*
Geoffrey Carliner, *Corporate Secretary and Executive Director*
Charles A. Walworth, *Treasurer*
Sam Parker, *Director of Finance and Administration*

Directors at Large:

John J. Biggs	Martin Feldstein	Robert T. Parry
Andrew Brimmer	George Hatsopoulos	Peter G. Peterson
Carl F. Christ	Lawrence R. Klein	Robert V. Roosa
George T. Conklin, Jr.	Franklin A. Lindsay	Richard N. Rosett
Kathleen B. Cooper	Paul W. McCracken	Bert Seidman
Jean A. Crockett	Leo Melamed	Eli Shapiro
George C. Eads	Michael H. Moskow	Donald S. Wasserman
Morton Ehrlich	James J. O'Leary	

Directors by University Appointment:

Jagdish Bhagwati, *Columbia*
William C. Brainard, *Yale*
Glen G. Cain, *Wisconsin*
Franklin Fisher, *Massachusetts Institute of Technology*
Jonathan Huges, *Northwestern*
Saul H. Hymans, *Michigan*
Marjorie B. McElroy, *Duke*
James L. Pierce, *California, Berkeley*
Andrew Postlewaite, *Pennsylvania*
Nathan Rosenberg, *Stanford*
Harold T. Shapiro, *Princeton*
Craig Swan, *Minnesota*
Michael Yoshino, *Harvard*
Arnold Zellner, *Chicago*

Directors by Appointment of Other Organizations:

Rueben C. Buse,
American Agricultural Economics Association
Richard Easterlin,
Economic History Association
Gail Foster,
The Conference Board
A. Ronald Gallant,
American Statistical Association
Robert S. Hamada,
American Finance Association
David Kendrick,
American Economic Association
Ben E. Laden,
National Association of Business Economists
Rudolph A. Oswald,
American Federation of Labor and Congress of Industrial Organizations
Dean P. Phypers,
Committee for Economic Development
Douglas D. Purvis,
Canadian Economics Association
Charles A. Walworth,
American Institute of Certified Public Accountants

Directors Emeriti:

Moses Abramovitz	Thomas D. Flynn	George B. Roberts
Emilio G. Collado	Gottfried Haberler	Willard L. Thorp
Frank W. Fetter	Geoffrey H. Moore	William S. Vickrey

Since this volume is a record of conference proceedings, it has been exempted from the rules governing critical review of manuscripts by the Board of Directors of the National Bureau (resolution adopted 8 June 1948, as revised 21 November 1949 and 20 April 1968).

CONTENTS

Introduction: *David Bradford*   vii

Acknowledgments   xiii

THE ROLE OF TAX RULES IN THE RECENT RESTRUCTURING OF U.S. CORPORATIONS   1
Myron S. Scholes and Mark A. Wolfson

TAXATION AND THE COST OF CAPITAL: THE "OLD" VIEW, THE "NEW" VIEW, AND ANOTHER VIEW   25
Hans-Werner Sinn

GENERATIONAL ACCOUNTS: A MEANINGFUL ALTERNATIVE TO DEFICIT ACCOUNTING   55
Alan J. Auerbach, Jagadeesh Gokhale, and Laurence J. Kotlikoff

THE INCIDENCE OF MANDATED EMPLOYER-PROVIDED INSURANCE: LESSONS FROM WORKERS' COMPENSATION INSURANCE   111
Jonathan Gruber and Alan B. Krueger

IS THE GASOLINE TAX REGRESSIVE?   145
James M. Poterba

INTRODUCTION

David Bradford
Princeton University and NBER

The 1980s were a time of substantial change for tax policy in the United States. Although it represented continuation of a trend that began at least as early as 1978, the 1981 Tax Act was notable for sharp reductions in the effective rate of tax on certain forms of investment. In particular, accelerated depreciation and investment tax credits favored investment in structures and equipment, and the exclusion from the base of 60% of capital gains encouraged corporate investment supporting equity claims ("equity-financed" investment). The Tax Reform Act of 1986 apparently balanced less accelerated depreciation, the elimination of the investment tax credit, and the removal of the capital gains exclusion with reduced tax rates at both the corporate and individual level. The objective of the 1986 law was to even the investment playing field, to subject all forms of investment to lower but more uniform levels of taxation. In the process, windfall gains were generated for many taxpayers (for example, those on the verge of retirement, who paid lower than anticipated taxes on pension benefits), whereas others (notably investors in real estate) experienced windfall losses. In addition, both the 1981 and the 1986 Acts brought about some strong incentive side-effects that were poorly anticipated.

In their paper, "The Role of Tax Rules in the Recent Restructuring of U.S. Corporations," Myron S. Scholes and Mark A. Wolfson take up some important issues. They emphasize the unintended consequences, especially for the choice of business form and financial structure, of the shifts in the taxation of corporate equity, *relative* to debt or noncorporate capital, between the 1981 and the 1986 laws. Indeed, in 1986 for the first time the rate of tax on corporations was set above the rate applicable to high-income individuals. The combination of this change and the reduction in the tax advantage of capital gains resulted in significant shifts in incentives. Scholes and Wolfson argue that whereas the 1981 Act encouraged mergers and acquisitions among U.S. corporations, the 1986 Act discouraged them. Furthermore, the opposite incentives were set up with respect to takeovers of U.S. companies by foreign corporations. Recognizing that it is difficult to demonstrate causal relationships in a world that is changing in many respects at the same time, they show that their analysis offers an explanation of the historical record of merger and acquisition activity, of both domestic and foreign firms.

Considerable political attention and a large body of law have been directed toward the regulation of phenomena such as mergers and acquisitions and the issue of junk bonds. Currently, concerns about the takeover of U.S. businesses by foreign firms is a subject of political concern. The lessons that Scholes and Wolfson have to teach about the fundamentals that underlie these oftentime puzzling economic effects are well worth our close attention and may help us avoid imposing rules that unnecessarily address symptoms rather than causes.

Hans-Werner Sinn's contribution to this volume represents something of a departure from the usual pattern in that his focus is on a conceptual rather than an empirical issue. The subject of his paper, "Taxation and the Cost of Capital: The "Old" View, the "New" View, and Another View," is the effect of tax rules on the pretax rate of return required on corporate investment. This is a topic on which Bureau researchers have contributed frequently over the past decade and more. Although no one will be surprised that there is much that remains to be learned of an empirical nature about the influence of taxes on corporate behavior, it may be less obvious that the conceptual framework for the analysis is incomplete. This is exactly Sinn's argument, however.

The key point at issue is the well-known "double taxation" of corporate equity, once at the level of the corporation and again at the level of the shareholder, either on distribution in the form of dividends or on realization of capital gains generated by the corporate-level investment. At the heart of the matter is the fact that we do not yet have a fully convincing theory of corporate financial structure. Putting the matter simply, under existing rules it seems clear that corporations should be financed essentially entirely from debt. To the extent that equity financing does occur (for example, because of the historically inherited corporate financial structure or because a debt-finance project pays off more than can be distributed as interest) the associated distributions to shareholders should certainly not (at least in the United States) be in the form of dividends. Instead, funds should be distributed out of the corporate sector through share repurchase or its functional equivalent, cash acquisition of other corporations.

There are many explanations for the observed facts that contradict these (oversimply stated) predictions of economic theory, but none of the explanations has yet proven fully satisfactory. Yet predictions about the effect of, say, dividend taxation depend on the determinants of corporations' use of equity finance. In the absence of a unifying theory, tax analysts resort to assumptions, for example, a fixed ratio of debt and equity. In the course of a broad overview of the conceptual issues, Sinn argues in his paper that our view of the effect of tax rules has been marked by a too-restrictive set of assumptions about corporate financial behavior. Enlarging the set in a very plausible way reveals the likelihood that mature companies can greatly moderate the distorting effects that would be implied by very rigid financial behavior, but that the discouragement of new firms is probably greater than has been generally recognized.

In a series of papers, Laurence Kotlikoff has asserted that the budgetary accounting tools currently employed to express the government's economic choices are flawed to the point of being useless. In particular, he has argued that the budgetary concepts of taxes and transfers are based on arbitrary conventions and have no economically meaningful foundation. The economic content of "budget deficit" refers to the degree to which fiscal policy shifts burdens toward future generations. Current budgetary conventions carry no reliable indication of this incidence effect. Consequently, current budgetary measures of deficit or surplus are poor indicators of economic policy, and they may even give the wrong sign to the directions of policy change.

Although Kotlikoff's critique has attracted some support, until now we have lacked more than the most rudimentary quantitative version of accounts that are economically meaningful in the terms he has set out. The paper, "Generational Accounts: A Meaningful Alternative to Deficit Accounting," by Alan J. Auerbach, Jagadeesh Gokhale, and Laurence J. Kotlikoff, in this volume presents the first attempt at a comprehensive accounting for the intergenerational effect of fiscal policy of the entire U.S. governmental sector (federal, state, and local). The results are revealing in a great many respects. One is naturally attracted first to their quantitative conclusion that the present path of fiscal policy implies a burden on future generations that is 10 to 17% larger than that facing those born today. More important is the fleshing out of a framework within which to debate and evaluate the myriad assumptions about the economy and about the future that are necessary to an economically meaningful assessment of fiscal policy. A nice example is provided by the alternative consequences calculated by the authors of the federal budget agreement reached in the fall of 1990. Depending on the degree of permanence of the tax and spending changes embodied in the agreement, the estimated reduction from a baseline 17% excess burden on future generations ranges from 1 to 13%.

The measurements developed by Auerbach, Gokhale, and Kotlikoff are erected on a structure of assumptions that will certainly be subject to challenge and controversy. In my view, however, their contribution to advancing the cause of meaningful accounting for government will be a lasting one.

The last two papers in the volume contain empirical analyses with clear connections to ongoing policy concerns.

The paper by Jonathan Gruber and Alan B. Krueger deals with another area of policy that is much influenced by the weaknesses in our system of accounting for government. One of the ways that government may influence the distribution of benefits and the allocation of resources is through the simple mandating of certain programs. Generally, a mandated program is economically equivalent to a combination of tax and spending rules, but it does not appear in a government budget. Thus, a requirement that schools provide adequate access for the physically handicapped is economically equivalent to a government grant to schools to cover the cost of constructing the required facilities combined with a tax on schools in the same account.

Mandating employer provision of health insurance benefits has attracted increasing attention as a policy option. In "The Incidence of Mandated Employer-Provided Insurance: Lessons from Workers' Compensation Insurance," Gruber and Krueger assess the incidence of a similar program that has existed for some time. They take advantage of the considerable variation across time and across states in the costs of providing workers' compensation insurance to identify the degree to which the cost of the program is shifted to employees through wage adjustments. They interpret the weight of the evidence as suggesting that changes in employers' costs of workers' compensation insurance are largely shifted to employees.

The federal budget package enacted in 1990 incorporated a small increase in the per gallon tax on gasoline. If the current strong interest in matters of energy conservation is sustained, this and similar tax instruments are likely to receive continuing consideration. James Poterba's paper, "Is the Gasoline Tax Regressive?" takes up an important dimension of this tax policy issue, the distribution of burdens it implies between rich and poor.

Poterba points out that frequently encountered claims of regressivity of gasoline taxes rely for evidence on annual surveys of consumer income and expenditures. These surveys show that gasoline expenditures are a larger fraction of income for very low-income households than for middle- or high-income households. His paper argues that annual *expenditure* provides a more reliable indicator of household well-being than annual income.

This point is a general one, and would apply to any incidence analysis (for example, of the income tax). Poterba focuses on the particular case of the gasoline tax. Using data from the Consumer Expenditure Survey, he reassesses the claim that gasoline taxes are regressive by computing the share of total expenditures that high-spending and low-spending households devote to retail gasoline purchases. This alternative approach shows that low-expenditure households devote a smaller share of their budget to gasoline than do their counterparts in the middle of the expenditure distribution. Although households in the top 5% of the total spending distribution spend less on gasoline (as a fraction of spending) than those who are less well off, the share of expenditure devoted to gasoline is much more stable across the population than the ratio of gasoline outlays to current income. The conclusion, which appears to be typical when a consumption basis for analysis is used, is that the gasoline tax is far less regressive than conventional analyses suggest.

ACKNOWLEDGMENTS

The authors and I are indebted to the people who made this volume and the conference on which it is based possible. Since the conference's inception five years ago, NBER President Martin Feldstein and Executive Director Geoffrey Carliner have wholeheartedly supported this effort to communicate widely the results of economic policy research. Candace Morrissey assisted in every stage of this project. Kirsten Foss Davis and Ilana Hardesty did their efficient job of handling the conference logistics as usual. I am especially grateful to the authors of the papers presented here for their responsiveness to my editorial requests.

David Bradford

THE ROLE OF TAX RULES IN THE RECENT RESTRUCTURING OF U.S. CORPORATIONS

Myron S. Scholes
Stanford University and NBER

Mark A. Wolfson
Stanford University and NBER

U.S. tax reforms in the 1980s have changed substantially the relative attractiveness of operating in partnership form relative to corporate form. They have also changed the desirability of debt financing relative to equity financing, both of domestic operations and of foreign subsidiaries. And whereas the 1981 Tax Act encouraged mergers and acquisitions among U.S. corporations, the 1986 Act discouraged such transactions. Moreover, these Acts had the *opposite* effect on incentives of foreign companies to acquire U.S. businesses. In this paper, we attempt to show that these apparently disparate claims are all implied from a common (and simple) framework. Moreover, we present empirical evidence to support the claims.

I. CORPORATIONS VERSUS PARTNERSHIPS

To a degree that is historically unprecedented, the corporate form of organization was made tax disfavored relative to partnerships in the United States with the passage of the 1986 Tax Act. Corporate tax rates were set above the rate that applies to high-income individuals on ordinary income (the tax rate that individuals face on partnership income). Moreover, the United States imposes tax at two levels on corporate income, but only one level on partnership income. The second level of tax, at the shareholder level, was increased dramatically with the 1986 Tax Act, relative to ordinary tax rates. This was done by making capital gains taxable at the same rate as ordinary income is taxed (whereas capital gains had previously been taxed at favorable rates) and by eliminating some important opportunities to postpone the shareholder-level tax (such as by eliminating the ability to postpone tax through the use of installment sales of publicly traded securities).

The United States is out of sync with most of the rest of the world in taxing corporate income so heavily relative to noncorporate income. In most other countries, corporate income is taxed more favorably either by allowing shareholders to take a tax credit for corporate taxes they pay indirectly as shareholders, by imposing low shareholder-level tax rates, or by imposing relatively low corporate-level tax rates.

To illustrate the tax-disfavored nature of investing in corporations relative to partnerships in the United States, suppose the corporate tax rate is 35% and the personal tax rate on partnership income, dividend income, and capital gains, is 30%. Then each dollar of income earned at the partnership level yields a tax obligation of 30¢, whereas, the same dollar of income earned at the corporate level yields corporate tax of 35¢, enabling a 65¢ dividend or capital gain to be "distributed" to the shareholders. This 65¢ dividend or capital gain in turn will trigger an additional 19.5¢ in personal tax, so the total tax burden on the dollar of corporate income becomes 54.5¢.

To put into perspective the significance of the tax disadvantage of the corporate tax treatment, the corporate project must earn 54% *more* before tax to yield the same after-tax return to shareholders as the same investment undertaken in partnership form provides to partners. This can be seen by noting that the after-tax returns are equal when

$$R_c(1-t_c)(1-t_s) = R_p(1-t_p)$$

or

$$\frac{R_c}{R_p} = \frac{1-t_p}{(1-t_c)(1-t_s)}$$

For $t_p = 30\%$, $t_c = 35\%$, and $t_s = 30\%$, $(1-t_p)/[(1-t_c)(1-t_s)] = 1.54$, so R_c must exceed R_p by 54% to yield the same after-tax return to investors.

The example above overstates the degree to which corporations are tax disfavored relative to partnerships under the 1986 Tax Act. First, unless all corporate profits are distributed to shareholders each period as dividends, the shareholder-level tax can be deferred until shareholders sell their shares. This reduces the present value of the shareholder-level tax. Second, if shareholder tax rates vary over time, shareholders may time their stock sales to coincide with periods of low tax rates. Third, certain shareholders may be able to avoid the shareholder-level tax on capital gains by holding their shares until death or by making a charitable contribution of their shares (although such gifts may trigger the alternative minimum tax). Fourth, shareholders may anticipate that capital gains tax rates will be reduced in the future at a time preceding the date at which they will have sold their shares. And fifth, equity financing is not the only type of financing available to corporations. Many of the financing alternatives reduce the entity-level tax by permitting tax-deductible distributions to capital suppliers. These include debt, employee compensation, leases, and royalties. We will return to this point later.

II. DEFERRAL

To illustrate the importance of deferral, suppose the corporation were to pursue a policy of paying no dividends, reinvesting after-corporate-tax profits in the firm. Suppose further that investors were to hold their investment positions for a period of 10 years before selling and triggering a capital gains tax on 10 years of share appreciation. Finally, suppose that the pretax return available on partnership projects is 10%, so that, after tax, partnership investments yield 7%. Then the required before-tax rate of return on corporate projects would become 40% above the required return on partnership projects. This is down from a 54% required premium when the shareholder-level tax was paid each period. One way to calibrate the magnitude of the deferral benefit is to note that paying the shareholder-level tax at a 30% rate at the end of ten years is equivalent to paying the tax at a 23.2% rate each year.[1]

If the shareholders' investment horizon were to increase to 20 years, the required corporate pretax premium would drop further to 31%. On the other hand, there may be nontax costs associated with extending the investment horizon. To the extent that there are, we overstate the value of tax deferral, and this increases the require premium on corporate projects even further.

---

[1] This can be seen by noting that $R_c/R_p = (1-t_p)/[(1-t_c)(1-t_s)]$, substituting values of 1.4 for R_c/R_p, 30% for t_p, 35% for t_c, and solving for t_s.

III. FAVORABLE CAPITAL RATES TAX RATES

If the shareholders' investment horizon were 10 years, but the capital gains tax rate were only 70% of ordinary tax rates (that is, 30% of capital gains were excluded from taxable income), the required rate of return on corporate projects would still be 28% above the required rate on partnership projects. This is down from a 40% premium when capital gains are subjected to a full tax at ordinary rates.

The calculations above assume that shareholders receive all of their return in the form of capital gains. The required premium on corporate projects increases considerably with the dividend yield. The reasons for this include an increase in the fraction of income taxed at ordinary tax rates (rather than favorable capital gains tax rates) and an acceleration of the *payment* of the tax (reduced value of deferral).

IV. FOREIGN INVESTORS

It is worth noting that the tax disadvantage of the corporate form does not apply to all investors. Certain foreign investors, for example, actually find corporations to be the tax-favored organizational form through which to invest in the United States.

To illustrate, suppose a foreign investor faces a home-country tax rate on ordinary income of 50% and a home-country capital gains tax rate of 0%. The home country taxes ordinary income from U.S. partnerships as the income is earned and grants a tax credit for any U.S. taxes paid. If a partnership generated a pretax return of 10% on invested capital, a foreign investor in the U.S. partnership would earn 10% (1–50%) or 5% after tax.[2]

What pretax rate of return would a nondividend-paying U.S. corporation have to earn to provide the same 5% after-tax return that the U.S. partnership provides? Since the United States exempts capital gains earned by foreign investors, and since there is no U.S. withholding tax when the corporate profits are distributed to foreign investors by way of a sale of stock, the after-tax return to the foreign investor becomes $R_c(1 - t_{c,US})$. Here, $t_{c,US}$ denotes the U.S. corporate tax rate and is assumed to be equal to 35%. Then R_c need only be equal to 5%/(1 − .35) or 7.69% to yield the required 5% after-tax return to our foreign investors. So, the

---

[2] Since the home country credits any U.S. taxes paid, it does not matter to the foreign investor whether the U.S. tax was paid or not.

foreign investor would require the U.S. corporation to generate a pretax profit that is 23% *less* than would be required of a partnership at the same time that a U.S. investor might require the corporation to earn substantially more than a partnership earns. Note how this phenomenon sows the seeds for conflict in desirable investment strategies among various classes of shareholders.

V. COMPARISON OF CORPORATIONS AND PARTNERSHIPS BEFORE THE 1986 TAX ACT

Corporate equity investments were not always so tax disfavored relative to partnerships as they appear to be in the United States today. For example, prior to the 1986 Tax Act, the top personal tax rate on ordinary income was 50%, the corporate tax rate on ordinary income was 46%, and long-term capital gains were taxed at 40% of ordinary taxes, a maximum rate of 20%. If we once again assume that partnership projects yielded 10% before personal taxes, and that shareholders defer the shareholder-level tax on capital gains for 10 years, then corporate projects would have to earn only 11% more pretax profit than partnership projects to yield the same after-tax return to high-income investors.

Or consider the situation in the 1960s for investors facing personal tax rates on ordinary income of up to 70%, a capital gains tax rate of up to 35% (or half of the ordinary tax rate), and a corporate tax rate of 48%. Here we find the required return on corporate projects to be *below* that on partnership projects. To provide the same after-tax return as a 10% partnership project, the corporation would only need to earn 8.34% before corporate tax. This is 17% *less* than the required return on partnership projects.

VI. TAX INCENTIVES INTRODUCED BY THE 1986 TAX ACT

Two types of tax-planning incentives follow from the fact that corporate equity investments are tax disfavored relative to investments that avoid an entity-level tax following the 1986 Tax Act: to undertake activity in the non(regular) corporate form, and to finance corporate activities in ways that avoid as much entity-level tax as possible.

As for the first of these incentives, it is worth noting the explosion of so-called S-Corporation elections (where the corporation chooses to have taxable income passed through to the tax returns of its owners without the payment of an entity-level tax) surrounding year-end 1986. S-

Corporations are limited liability corporations that are not taxed at the entity level so long as a number of restrictive conditions are met. For all practical purposes, large corporations cannot avail themselves of this status. Whereas 75,000 of such elections were made throughout 1985, *three times* this number of elections (or 225,000) were made in the 5 weeks surrounding year-end 1986.

Despite the tax advantages of doing so, the vast majority of corporations did not restructure their businesses in ways that would allow them to avoid facing an entity-level tax. There are a host of nontax factors that make this a sensible strategy.

The nontax advantages of operating in corporate form include liquidity, more clearly defined property rights under law, and a more efficient market for organizational control to discipline nonowner management. Moreover, there are both tax and nontax costs to change an entity's legal organizational form. In this respect, there is an important distinction to be drawn between tax planning for a new firm and tax planning for a seasoned firm.

Given a strategy of operating in regular corporate form, there are clear tax implications for corporate capital structure. Note, for example, that if all corporate pretax profit could be distributed to investors in the form of tax-deductible interest, rather than nondeductible dividends and capital gains, the required return on corporate projects would be equal to that on partnership projects. The reason, of course, is that the entity-level tax would be eviscerated under such a capital structure policy.

It should be noted, however, that the tax advantages of debt financing disappear for firms that are unprofitable. For such firms, the interest on debt yields no current tax benefits. It is typically better for such firms to issue securities that are tax favored in the hands of investors, like common or preferred stock. Such securities yield *implicit* tax deductions to the issuer, because investors are willing to accept lower risk-adjusted expected returns for these tax-favored securities.

VII. MITIGATING ENTITY-LEVEL TAXATION THROUGH INVESTMENT STRATEGIES

Myriad investment projects yield tax deductions and tax credits that allow the statutory tax to be postponed or eliminated altogether. Examples of such investments include research and development projects, capital intensive projects that yield accelerated depreciation, and oil and gas exploration projects. Because such tax-favored investments bear *implicit* tax, however, they generally will not result in elimination of an entity-level tax. For example, if fully taxable investment projects yield 10% pretax, while tax-favored investment projects of equal risk that yield no corporate-level taxable income yield 7% pretax, then the corporation bears an implicit tax at the rate of 30% on pretax corporate profits. To the extent this implicit tax rate is less than the statutory corporate tax rate, investment in tax-favored assets can succeed in *mitigating* the entity-level tax on corporate equity investments. But the presence of implicit taxes prevents the entity-level tax from being eliminated.

In fact, the presence of implicit taxes makes it impossible to eliminate the entity-level tax by adjusting the capital structure. For example, debt financing no longer succeeds in distributing corporate profits in a way that avoids the corporate-level tax in the presence of implicit tax. The reason is identical to why debt financing is not desirable when the corporation is unprofitable: that is, interest deductions yield tax benefits only when entity-level *taxable* income is positive. But when the corporation pursues tax-favored investments, income is not fully (explicitly) taxed. This prevents interest from yielding tax deductions that lead to a full corporate tax reduction.

If the corporation invests in tax-favored assets that bear no explicit tax and only implicit tax, shareholders cannot avoid double taxation. Ignoring nontax factors that influence the desirability of issuing debt, this implies that corporations should avoid investing in tax-favored assets even when they face higher tax rates than other investors in the marketplace.

To see this, note that investing in explicitly taxed assets yielding pretax return R_c, financed with debt bearing interest equal to the pretax income on these investments, yields the following return to investors:

Corporate return before interest and taxes	R_c
Corporate interest expense	(R_c)
Corporate return after interest expense	0
Corporate tax	0
Personal interest income	R_c
Personal tax on interest income	$(R_c t_p)$
Total return to investors after tax	$R_c(1 - t_p)$

That is, the entity-level tax is avoided. By contrast, if the corporation invests in explicitly tax-exempt assets bearing implicit tax at rate t_I, corporate investors earn

$$R_c(1 - t_I)(1 - t_p)$$

This is lower than the return on a debt-financed investment in fully taxable assets by fraction t_1.

VIII. EFFECT OF LIMITS TO DEBT FINANCING

Although U.S. corporations cannot avoid, by issuing debt, the double taxation of returns on tax-favored projects that bear implicit taxes, this does not imply that tax-favored investments should be avoided by corporations. After all, there are both tax and nontax limitations on debt financing. On the tax side, there is the question of whether the taxing authority will permit unlimited deductibility of interest on debt. In other words, there is always a risk that debt will be recharacterized as equity by the taxing authority (Code Section 385).

As for nontax factors, the secondary market for debt securities is much less liquid than the secondary markets for equity securities. As a consequence, debtholders may require an illiquidity premium to be induced to lend funds to the corporation. Debt may also give rise to significant bankruptcy or workout costs. Although debt financing can also yield nontax benefits relating to management incentives, it is clear that the costs are perceived by corporate managers to overwhelm the benefits at high ratios of debt as a fraction of total capitalization.

IX. EVIDENCE ON DEBT FINANCING

Net new borrowings by the U.S. corporations exploded in the 1980s. From less than half a trillion dollars of outstanding corporate bonds at year-end 1980, corporate bonds outstanding increased to nearly 600 billion dollars by year-end 1983, to nearly 800 billion dollars by year-end 1985, and to nearly $1,400 billion by year-end 1988.

At the same time, there was a dramatic reduction in the supply of equity securities. Share repurchases averaged $37 billion per year from 1984 to 1986 and amounted to $54 billion in 1987. This compares with only $5 billion per year from 1978 to 1983. Other equity retirements by way of corporate acquisitions from $15 billion per year from 1980 to 1983 to $75 billion per year from 1984 to 1986.

It is interesting to note that the trend toward greater debt financing that occurred in the United States in the 1980s was much less dramatic elsewhere around the world. This is consistent with our argument that the corporate form of organization is simply not (very) tax disfavored in countries other than the United States.

X. INCENTIVES OF U.S. MULTINATIONALS TO INCREASE DEBT FINANCING OF FOREIGN OPERATIONS

The 1986 Tax Act also encouraged U.S. multinational companies to increase their debt financing of foreign subsidiaries. The 1986 Tax Act made the United States a tax haven relative to many other countries. Because the United States credits foreign taxes paid only up to the U.S. tax rate, the 1986 Tax Act caused many U.S. multinationals to face binding foreign tax credit limitations. This means that U.S. multinationals began to pay tax on foreign income at a rate above the U.S. rate in many circumstances. Just as debt financing of U.S. corporations allows some corporate profits to avoid an entity-level tax, so debt financing of foreign operations allows some foreign profits to avoid being taxed locally at tax rates above the U.S. corporate rates.

XI. THE EFFECTS OF THE 1981 AND 1986 TAX ACTS ON MERGERS AND ACQUISITIONS

The 1981 Tax Act encouraged mergers and acquisitions in several ways. The introduction of the accelerated-cost-recovery-system (ACRS) depreciation provided incentives to "step up" the basis of depreciable assets and to change depreciation schedules to ones that were much more highly accelerated than existed previously. In addition, the Installment Sales Revision Act passed in October of 1980 promoted asset sales by making installment notes a more effective way of reducing the tax costs relating to depreciation recapture and capital gains than previously was the case.

The introduction of ACRS depreciation in conjunction with making investment tax credits more generous in 1981 also gave rise to an increase in net operating loss and tax credit carryforwards on corporate balance sheets. This along with very high interest rates encouraged mergers and acquisitions. High interest rates are relevant because carryforwards diminish in value when discount rates are high.

In contrast to the 1981 Act, the 1986 Tax Act discouraged asset sales among domestic taxpayers (but did *not* discourage such transactions between domestic sellers and foreign buyers as we will see later) in a number of important respects:

- by reducing tax rates, thereby reducing the size of the potential gains from stepping up asset basis;

- by eliminating the so-called General Utilities doctrine, thereby eliminating the opportunity to avoid a corporate-level tax on capital gains in the event of corporate liquidation;
- by introducing less generous depreciation schedules;
- by introducing more stringent rules regarding the availability of net operating loss and other tax attribute carryforwards in the event of merger;
- by increasing the capital gains tax rate at both the corporate and personal levels;
- by reducing substantially the ability to use installment sales to postpone taxes; and
- by increasing the amount of ordinary income that must be recaptured in a corporate liquidation.

As for the evidence, Table 1 displays annual merger and acquisition activity between 1970 and 1987 in three ways: in nominal dollars, in constant 1986 Consumer Price Index (CPI) dollars, and in dollars of constant 1986 Standard & Poor's (S&P) 500 index of stock prices. Note the near doubling of activity between 1980 and 1981 despite weakness in the U.S. economy around this time. This increase in activity is especially impressive given that the Act was not signed into law until August 1981 and the President's proposal was not made until March 1981.

In fact, the activity in the first quarter of 1981 was no greater than that in the fourth quarter of 1980. But there was a doubling in the dollar value of activity in the second quarter and another 40% increase in the third quarter.

Note further that the average level of activity increased fivefold in nominal dollar terms between 1970–1980 and 1981–1986. The increase in constant CPI dollars was threefold, and there was a doubling in volume even after adjusting for the increase in the level of stock prices.

Whereas the 1981 Tax Act is associated with an increase in merger activity, the 1986 Act should have discouraged transactions among U.S. businesses. However, taxpayers were given a one-quarter window of opportunity to undertake transactions prior to the effective date of the 1986 Tax Act.

Table 2 shows two things. First, there was a bulge in activity during the fourth quarter of 1986. The volume was a record in nominal, real, and S&P 500-adjusted dollars for at least the preceding 50 years. The volume of activity exceeded the average over the eight surrounding quarters by 85%. Second, the table reveals a decline in activity over the four quarters of 1987 relative to the four quarters preceding the passage of the 1986 Act by 20% in nominal dollars, 23% in constant CPI dollars, and 38% in

TABLE 1
Merger and Acquisition Values: Nominal Dollar, Constant Dollar, and Constant Stock Index Amounts: Annual Figures, 1968–1987

Year	Nominal dollar value of M&A activity ($billions)	Constant 1986 dollar value of M&A activity ($billions)	Constant 1986 S&P 500 index value of M&A activity ($billions)
1968	43.61		
1969	23.71		
1970	16.42	42.48	86.90
1971	12.62	31.15	58.44
1972	16.68	39.62	64.93
1973	16.67	37.42	76.01
1974	12.47	25.75	77.32
1975	11.80	22.23	53.33
1976	20.03	35.77	73.12
1977	21.94	37.09	86.28
1978	34.18	53.93	126.15
1979	43.54	63.06	135.66
1980	44.35	58.88	104.36
1981	82.62	100.04	204.46
1982	53.76	61.52	109.57
1983	73.08	80.45	121.59
1984	122.22	129.02	191.36
1985	179.77	183.23	212.97
1986	201.37	201.37	201.37
1987	174.99	168.77	166.30
Avg 1970–1980	22.79	40.67	85.68
Avg 1975–1980	29.30	45.16	96.48
Avg 1981–1986	118.80	125.94	173.55
1981–86/1975–80	4.05	2.79	1.80
1981–86/1970–80	5.21	3.10	2.03

Sources: W.T. Grimm (*Mergerstat*) for 1968–1985 nominal values; *Mergers & Acquisitions* for 1986–1987 nominal values; 1985 *Economic Report of the President Industry Week* for consumer prices; 1985–1987 Ibbotson Associates (*Stocks, Bonds, Bills and Inflation*) for S&P 500 index values.

constant S&P 500 dollars. Moreover, Table 2 ignores the secular trend in merger and acquisition activity. If the series is detrended using data in the 1970s, the decline in activity in 1987 becomes 37% in nominal dollars, 32% in constant CPI dollars, and 45% in constant S&P 500 dollars.

The decline in merger and acquisition activity in 1987 is all the more impressive given that it includes leveraged buyouts. Given the enhanced tax advantages of debt financing introduced by the 1986 Tax Act,

TABLE 2
Merger and Acquisition Values: Nominal Dollar, Constant Dollar, and Constant Stock Index Amounts Quarterly Figures: 1985-4 through 1987-4

	Transactions between U.S. companies only					
Quarter	Nominal amount ($billions)	Rank excl 86-4	Constant 87-4 CPI amount ($billions)	Rank excl 86-4	Constant 87-4 S&P amount ($billions)	Rank excl 86-4
1985-4	45.93	1	48.60	1	57.26	1
1986-1	29.97	7	31.65	7	32.75	5
1986-2	44.55	2	47.15	2	45.97	2
1986-3	34.86	4	36.65	3	38.67	3
Sum	155.31	14	164.05	13	174.65	11
Avg	38.83		41.01		43.66	
1986-4	64.65		67.44		68.03	
1987-1	21.66	8	22.38	8	18.78	8
1987-2	32.97	6	33.63	6	27.20	6
1987-3	33.66	5	33.96	5	26.04	7
1987-4	35.82	3	35.82	4	35.82	4
Sum	124.11	22	125.79	23	107.84	25
Avg	31.03		31.45		26.96	
Prob[1]		.1714		.1000		.0286

[1] Prob denotes the probability that the sum of the ranks in the four quarters preceding 1986-4 could be as low or lower than the sum of the ranks in the four quarters succeeding 1986-4 by chance alone.

Sources: *Mergers & Acquisitions* for nominal values; *Industry Week* for consumer prices; Ibbotson Associates (*Stocks, Bonds, Bills and Inflation*) for S&P 500 index values.

the incidence of leveraged buyouts would not necessarily be expected to fall. Indeed, the resurgence of acquisition activity in 1988 is heavily weighted toward highly leveraged transactions. But another important component of acquisition activity that has been on the rise since 1986 is foreign acquisitions of U.S. businesses. As explained next, this is quite consistent with the incentives provided by the 1986 Tax Act.

XII. INVESTMENT AND REPATRIATIONS POLICIES FOR MULTINATIONAL CORPORATIONS FACING WORLDWIDE TAX SYSTEMS

Although tax systems around the world have a great deal in common, they also differ from one another along a variety of dimensions: marginal tax rates can vary from essentially 0% in certain tax haven countries to well over 60% in certain high-tax countries; the definition of income can vary dramatically from country to country; the use of nonincome taxes can vary substantially; taxpayers may be taxed only on domestic income or on worldwide income.

To avoid double taxation of income (once in the host country and once in the home country), countries that tax worldwide income also provide a tax credit for foreign taxes paid. But countries differ in their generosity regarding foreign tax credits. Moreover foreign tax credits typically apply only to *income* taxes. Value added taxes, for example, are not refundable via foreign tax credits in most countries, including the United States. Instead, any value added tax paid is allowed only to be taken as a tax deduction, and as a result, only the fraction of the nonincome tax paid equal to the taxpayer's marginal income tax rate will effectively be refunded. Just as with value added taxes, *implicit taxes* paid in a foreign tax jurisdiction on tax-favored investment are often not refundable. By implicit taxes, we mean the reduced level of pretax return the investor earns by investing in tax-favored assets that result from competition for the right to own such assets.

For example, a tax-sheltered investment made by a foreign investor in the United States prior to the 1986 Tax Act might result in no payment of explicit tax to the U.S. Treasury Department. Competition for the right to hold such assets would cause the pretax return available on the investment to be less than that available on less tax-favored assets. The reduced pretax return represents an implicit tax paid by the investor. On repatriation of U.S. earnings back to the tax home of the foreign investor, the foreign investor may be subjected to taxation on the income earned in the United States, but since no explicit U.S. tax was paid, the investor would receive no foreign tax credit. On the other hand, the implicit tax paid will imply a reduced level of income available for repatriation and therefore a reduced level of home-country taxable income. As such, the implicit tax will give rise to a tax deduction (but not a credit) in the home country.

Prior to the Tax Reform Act of 1986, the availability of generous investment tax credits and highly accelerated depreciation made many investments in the United States highly tax favored. As a result, such investments bore a high level of implicit taxes. Moreover, U.S. marginal tax rates were roughly of the same order of magnitude as most other industrialized countries over this period of time. To the extent that implicit taxes are not completely recoverable from their home country on repatriation of profits from U.S. investment, foreign investors were disadvantaged relative to U.S. investors during the 1981–1986 period. This is explained more fully below.

The 1986 Tax Act favors foreign investment in the United States in several ways. It taxes many U.S. investments much less favorably relative to ordinary income-producing assets, such as bonds, thereby eliminating much of the implicit tax on active investments. The Act also reduced U.S. tax rates relative to those in most of the other industrialized countries. Finally, foreign investors in many countries do not face double taxation of corporate profits as we illustrated earlier. Since the 1986 Tax Act increases the shareholder-level tax to U.S. investors by more than it increases the shareholder-level tax to many foreign investors (recall that the United States does not tax capital gains from the sale of corporate stock by foreign investors), foreigners should find U.S. investments relatively attractive now.

Because income from foreign passive investments, like interest income, often escapes taxation in the foreign country, whereas income from active investments, like operating a business, does not, the pretax return on passive investments is typically less sensitive to local tax rates than is the pretax return on active investments. This means that in countries where the statutory tax rate is low, marginal investments by local residents will typically be in passive assets since the rate available on them will exceed the pretax rate on active assets in such countries.[3] In addition, the ability of foreigners to invest in active assets at a low marginal tax rate, until profits are repatriated to the home country, will cause foreign investors to be the marginal players in active assets.

The primer that follows develops optimal investment and reinvestment policies for multinational firms facing a worldwide tax structure similar to that in existence in the United States. To keep things simple, only two tax jurisdictions are considered, so issues relating to country-by-country versus worldwide foreign tax credit limitations do not arise. In addition, only two kinds of assets are considered: active and passive.

Suppose that you can invest abroad to earn at the rate of R_f pretax. The local tax rate is t_f. Each unit of capital invested abroad then grows at rate $R_f(1 - t_f)$ or r_f each year before considering any additional home-country tax on repatriation.

The home-country tax rate is t_d. Assume that $t_d > t_f$. Taxable income earned abroad will be taxed in the home country on repatriation (that is, a worldwide tax system is assumed), but a foreign tax credit will be allowed for foreign taxes paid. On repatriation, then, the foreign invest-

---

[3] Naturally, to avoid arbitrage possibilities, this requires an inability to effect costlessly short sales of active assets in the low-tax country for which an ordinary tax deduction can be taken on any losses from holding the short position.

ment will attract additional tax at the rate of $t_d - t_f$ on all taxable income generated abroad.

If home-country investment yields R_d pretax each period, under what conditions is investing abroad preferred to investing in the home country? This can be determined as follows.

After-tax accumulation from investing n periods abroad, followed by repatriation to the home country (per unit of domestic currency invested):

1. Local after-tax accumulation in n years: $\quad [1 + R_f(1 - t_f)]^n = (1 + r_f)^n$
2. Total foreign taxable income $\quad [(1 + r_f)^n - 1]/(1 - t_f)$
   - Except for initial investment, each unit of after-tax income is the result of generating $1/(1 - t_f)$ units of taxable income.
3. Additional domestic tax on repatriation $\quad (t_d - t_f)[(1 + r_f)^n - 1]/(1 - t_f)$
   - All taxable income will be taxed at rate t_d less a foreign tax credit at the rate t_f.
4. After-tax accumulation, after tax on repatriation: (1) − (3) $\quad \dfrac{(1 + r_f)^n(1 - t_d)}{(1 - t_f)} + \dfrac{(t_d - t_f)}{(1 - t_f)}$
5. How does this compare with domestic investment for n years? $\quad [1 + R_d(1 - t_d)]^n = (1 + r_d)^n$

For $n = 1$, foreign investment yields [substituting into (4) and noting that $r_f = R_f(1 - t_f)$]:

$$1 + R_f(1 - t_d)$$

whereas domestic investment yields

$$1 + R_d(1 - t_d)$$

Over such a short investment horizon, R_f must exceed R_d to favor investment abroad.

For example, suppose an investment of $6 million can be made in one of two mutually exclusive projects, one foreign and one domestic. The foreign project is expected to return 25% after local tax, where the tax rate is also 25%. The domestic project is expected to earn only 20% after domestic tax, where the tax rate is 40%. If the investment is made abroad, assume that all profits and the investment will be repatriated at the end of 1 year. Which project is preferred?

Our calculations above reveal that the decision should be based on whether pretax return R_f exceeds pretax return R_d. If so, foreign investment is preferred:

$$R_f = \frac{r_f}{1 - t_f} = \frac{.25}{1 - .25} = 33\frac{1}{3}\%$$

$$R_d = \frac{r_d}{1 - t_d} = \frac{.20}{1 - .40} = 33\frac{1}{3}\%$$

As a result, it is a matter of indifference! To see this, note that the $6 million invested abroad yields taxable income of $2 million, tax of $0.5 million, and after-tax income of $1.5 million. This results in a repatriation of ($6 + $1.5 or) $7.5 million. The repatriation triggers additional domestic tax of (40% − 25% or) 15% on the taxable income of $2 million or $0.3 million. This leaves ($7.5 − $0.3 or) $7.2 million after repatriation tax. This is equal to a 20% after-tax increment on the $6 million investment, exactly the same as would result from investment in the domestic project.

Now suppose that the investment horizon increases. In fact, let us consider the other extreme (permanent investment abroad versus domestically). Foreign investment is favored when expression (4) $> (1 + r_d)^n$. As n becomes large, this condition is satisfied if, and only if, $r_f > r_d$. Recall that for $n = 1$, the required condition was $R_f > R_d$. So as the investment horizon lengthens, we can have $R_f < R_d$ (that is, pretax rates of return abroad falling short of domestic pretax rates of return) and yet investment abroad will be preferred due to the opportunity to reinvest abroad at higher after-tax rates. This is the condition currently faced by many foreign investors vis-à-vis U.S. investment.

Returning to our earlier example, where $R_f = R_d = 33\frac{1}{3}\%$ and $t_f = 25\%$ and $t_d = 40\%$, an investment horizon of $n > 1$ years would favor foreign investment. Over a 5-year horizon, for example, the foreign investment would result in an after-tax repatriation of $15.85 million [substituting into expression (4)], whereas domestic investment would accumulate to $14.93 million after tax or nearly $1 million less on this $6 million investment.

XIII. Implicit Taxes and Foreign Investment Incentives: Example

Suppose you have $100 million to invest in one of two mutually exclusive projects: one at home and the other, of equal risk, located in a lower tax-rate foreign country:

	Tax rate	Pretax return	After (local) tax return
Home	55%	22%	9.9%[2]
Abroad	35%	20%[1]	13.0%[3]

[1] Implicit tax to invest abroad = 22−20/22 = 9.09%.
[2] 22% (1−55%) = 9.9%.
[3] 20% (1−35%) = 13.0%.

Why might there exist an implicit tax to investing abroad? There are both tax and nontax reasons. For tax reasons, competition for the right to undertake activity in a low-tax environment can naturally lead to the pretax return being lower in the low-tax-rate environment. As for nontax reasons, low tax rates are typically offered by the local government to lure business that would not otherwise be undertaken in the low-tax jurisdiction.

Where should you invest: at home at 22% pretax or abroad at 20% pretax? Note that if the investment horizon were 1 year, investment abroad followed by repatriation to the home country would yield an after-tax return of only 9.0%. This compares unfavorably with the 9.9% return available by investing at home. The reason is that the income earned abroad is taxed at the higher of the local tax rate and the home country tax rate, so all that matters is the *pretax* rate of return.

On the other hand, if profits can be reinvested abroad rather than repatriated at the end of 1 year, the repatriation tax of 20% (that is, 55% minus 35%) is postponed. This improves matters since the funds are reinvested abroad at 13% rather than at 9.9%. For sufficiently long time horizons, investing abroad dominates investing at home. So where you should invest is a function of the duration of the investment:

| Annual after-tax | Repatriate after (years) | | | |
rates of return	1	5	10	20
Home	9.90%	9.90%	9.90%	9.90%
Abroad	9.00%	9.62%	10.27%	11.15%

Now suppose the implicit tax abroad is made more generous (e.g., via investment tax credits or accelerated depreciation available only locally), holding local after-tax returns constant:

	Tax rate	Pretax return	After (local) tax return
Abroad$_2$	20%	16.25%	13%
Abroad$_3$	0%	13.00%	13%

Now the after-repatriation-tax returns become

	Horizon (years)			
	1	5	10	20
Abroad$_1$ (implicit 9.09%)	9.00%[1]	9.62%	**10.27%**	**11.15%**
Abroad$_2$ (implicit tax 26.14%)	7.31%	8.07%	8.91%	**10.15%**
Abroad$_3$ (implicit tax 40.91%)	5.85%	6.64%	7.59%	9.13%
Home	**9.90%**	**9.90%**	9.90%	9.90%

[1] Example: 20% (1–35%) – 20% (55% – 35%) = 20% (1–55%) = 9%.

Note that the attractiveness of investing abroad decreases as investment incentives are introduced abroad. What's going on? Whereas explicit taxes are eligible for foreign tax credit, refundable dollar for dollar by the home country, implicit taxes are *not*. Instead, implicit taxes, by reducing pretax income, give rise to tax *deductions* at home rather than to tax *credits*. At a 55% home-country tax rate, 45% of the implicit tax is not refunded. So it is expensive for foreign investors to invest in assets that yield a lot of *implicit* tax.

Whereas under implicit tax regime 1, investing abroad for 20 years beats investing at home by $168 million (in 20 years), investing abroad under implicit tax regime 3 loses to investing at home by $87 million! And this, despite the fact that foreign investments earn 13% after local tax under both regimes.

Now suppose that the home country is Japan. The foreign country in regime 1 is the United States after the 1986 Tax Act: the tax rate is roughly 35% and most operating assets in the United States do not bear much implicit tax compared to what they used to with investment tax credits and more rapid depreciation allowances. The foreign country in regime 3 is the United States following the 1981 Tax Act: investment tax credits and accelerated-cost-recovery-system (ACRS) depreciation made new investments largely tax exempt.

What does the foregoing analysis suggest about foreign investment incentives in the United States in 1981 and 1986? They were reduced and increased, respectively.

Next, we turn to empirical evidence to test whether foreign direct incentives to purchase U.S. interests increased following the introduc-

TABLE 3
Quarterly Merger and Acquisition Values: Nominal Dollar, Constant Dollar, and Constant Stock Index Amounts: 1985-4 Through 1987-4

Quarter	U.S. purchase by non-U.S. companies only					
	Nominal amount ($billions)	Rank excl 86-4	Constant 87-4 CPI amount ($billions)	Rank excl 86-4	Constant 87-4 S&P amount ($billions)	Rank excl 86-4
1985-4	2.13	8	2.25	8	2.66	8
1986-1	3.27	6	3.45	6	3.57	6
1986-2	2.87	7	3.04	7	2.96	7
1986-3	3.43	5	3.60	5	3.80	5
Sum	11.70	26	12.35	26	12.99	26
Avg	2.93		3.09		3.25	
1986-4	15.52		16.19		16.33	
1987-1	10.66	3	11.01	3	9.25	2
1987-2	10.98	2	11.20	2	9.06	3
1987-3	12.82	1	12.93	1	9.92	1
1987-4	9.43	4	9.43	4	9.43	4
Sum	43.89	10	44.57	10	37.66	10
Avg	10.97		11.14		9.42	
Prob[1]	.0143		.0143		.0143	

[1] Prob denotes the probability that the sum of the ranks in the four quarters preceding 1986-4 could be as high or higher than the sum of the ranks in the four quarters succeeding 1986-4 by chance alone.

Sources: Mergers & Acquisitions for nominal values; *Industry Week* for consumer prices; Ibbotson Associates (*Stocks, Bonds, Bills and Inflation*) for S&P 500 index values.

tion of the Tax Reform Act of 1986. In particular, we compare merger and acquisition activity between U.S. companies to that in which *non-U.S.* companies are represented on the buy side (see Table 3) around the time of the passage of the 1986 Act in the United States.

The dollar volume of acquisitions of U.S. firms by U.S. companies increased by 85% during the fourth quarter of 1986 relative to the average during the eight quarters surrounding this period. More precisely, it increased by 66% in the fourth quarter of 1986 relative to the average over the four preceding quarters. Then acquisitions dropped over the four quarters of 1987 to a level roughly 20% below that in the four quarters preceding 1986–4.

In comparison, the dollar value of U.S. acquisitions by non-U.S. companies in 1986–4 increased 430% to $15.52 billion relative to the average over the preceding four quarters of $2.93 billion.[4] The level of activity during the fourth quarter of 1986 alone exceeded by 39% the average *annual* dollar volume of such activity recorded by W. T. Grimm and Company in their annual *Mergerstat* volume for the 1981–1985 period.

Moreover, while the level of acquisitions activity declined over the four quarters of 1987, relative to 1986-4, to $11 billion per quarter, the level of acquisitions in the four quarters of 1987 was 3.74 times as high as during the four quarters preceding 1986-4.[5] Using a simple rank-sum test, the ranking differences (in nominal dollars, constant dollars, or adjusted for changes in the S&P 500 stock index) could have occurred by chance with probability equal to only .0143.

This evidence is quite consistent with the 1986 Tax Reform Act's having stimulated foreign demand for U.S. business. Moreover, the increase in foreign demand for U.S. businesses was approximately offset by the decrease in domestic demand for U.S. businesses. That is, whereas U.S. purchases of U.S. businesses dropped by roughly $8 billion per quarter over the eight quarters surrounding the passage of the 1986 Tax Act, non-U.S. purchases of U.S. businesses increased by roughly $8 billion per quarter. Absent a consideration of how changes in tax rules affected domestic and foreign investors differently, one might have concluded, incorrectly, that the 1986 Act was accompanied by only a transitory shift in demand for mergers and acquisitions during the fourth quarter of 1986.

The argument that the 1986 Tax Act should have increased foreign investment in the United States due to the elimination of tax preferences such as investment tax credits and accelerated depreciation runs in reverse in 1981. The Economic Recovery Tax Act (ERTA) of 1981 accelerated depreciation schedules sharply and liberalized investment tax credits somewhat. It is worth noting that foreign acquisitions dropped very sharply in the post-ERTA period, both in absolute dollar terms and relative as percentage of total acquisitions. Whereas foreign acquisitions of U.S. companies as a percentage of total acquisitions was less than 8% in the post-ERTA/pre-1986 Tax Reform Act period, it was over 20% of the total both immediately before ERTA and immediately after the 1986 Tax Act.

The analysis above ignores other factors that may have contributed to the surge in foreign acquisitions of U.S. businesses in the fourth quarter

---

[4] The increase is 424% in real terms and 402% adjusted for changes in the level of the S&P 500 stock index.

[5] Postreform activity was 3.61 times as high in constant dollar terms and 2.90 times as high adjusted for changes in the level of the S&P 500 stock index.

of 1986. For example, concern by foreign investors over increasing trade restrictions may have prompted acquisitions by foreign manufacturers that sell to U.S. consumers. Another factor is the changes in the magnitude of the trade deficit, although this is not entirely independent of the amount of foreign acquisitions. A related factor is currency exchange rates. Several recent papers document an association between foreign direct investment in the United States and the exchange rate between the dollar and other major foreign currencies.[6] In particular, foreign direct investment apparently increases when the dollar is relatively weak, and conversely, although this would not be expected in perfect capital markets.

What is particularly interesting is that the dollar was relatively very strong during the several years immediately following the passage of the 1981 Tax Act and was very weak in the period surrounding the 1986 Tax Act. Consequently, we are faced with an identification problem in sorting out the independent contribution of tax rule changes and exchange rate changes on acquisition behavior of foreign investors.

But it is also interesting to note that Froot and Stein (1989) find that the relation between exchange rates and foreign direct investments in the United States applies to the manufacturing sector but not the nonmanufacturing sector. Since it is the manufacturing sector where the investment tax credit and depreciation rule changes are most important, this lends further credence to the role of taxes.

In addition, the weakness of the dollar surrounding passage of the 1986 Tax Act began in 1985. The fact that such a dramatic shift in foreign acquisition activity began during the fourth quarter of 1986 rather than earlier is further evidence suggesting the importance of taxes.

It is also worth noting that Froot and Stein find that the relation between foreign direct investment and exchange rates is not significant for the United Kingdom, Canada, or Japan. And although it *is* significant for West Germany, the coefficient is only one-ninth as large as for the United States. The one indication in Froot and Stein that exchange rates are important in explaining foreign direct investment in the United States is that the relation holds strongly during the 1970s, where tax changes do not seem terribly significant in the United States.

[6] For example, see Caves, Richard E. (1988). "Exchange-Rate Movements and Foreign Direct Investments in the United States." Discussion Paper No 1383, Harvard Institute of Economic Research, May; Froot, Kenneth A., and Stein, Jeremy C. (1989). "Exchange Rates and Foreign Direct Investment: An Imperfect Capital Markets Approach." Unpublished working paper, February 19; Slemrod, Joel B. (1989). "Tax Effects on Foreign Direct Investment in the U.S.: Evidence from a Cross-Country Comparison." University of Michigan and NBER working paper, January; and Swenson, Deborah. (1989). Unpublished Ph.D. Dissertation, M.I.T. Department of Economics.

Recent evidence gathered by Deborah Swenson provides further support for our implicit tax hypothesis. Swenson shows that foreign direct investment in the United States occurs most in those industries where explicit tax rates are highest and hence implicit tax rates are lowest, exactly as our model predicts. She also shows that the relation between foreign direct investment and tax rates is stronger involving buyers from countries facing worldwide tax systems than those facing territorial tax systems, again as we would predict.

XIV. REINVESTMENT OF RETAINED EARNINGS

The analysis above considered whether new investment should be made abroad or domestically. On the other hand, suppose we have already made investments abroad. Assume further that our tax basis in the investment is $0 (e.g., we have already taken tax deductions for amounts equal to our original investment). Earnings of $1 have been generated, and local taxes of t_f have been paid, leaving retained earnings of $1-t_f$. Should $1-t_f$ be reinvested locally or repatriated?

(a) Reinvestment locally for n periods at pretax rate R_f per period yields:

$$(1 - t_f)\left[(1 + r_f)^n \frac{(1 - t_d)}{(1 - t_f)} + \frac{(t_d - t_f)}{(1 - t_f)} \right] - (t_d - t_f)$$

expression (4) — additional domestic tax on repatriation for the $1 of taxable income that gave rise to the $1-t_f$ in retained earnings to begin with.

Conveniently, this simplifies to:

$$(1 + r_f)^n (1 - t_d)$$

(b) Repatriation of $1-t_f$, after attracting additional domestic tax of $(t_d - t_f)$, invested domestically for n periods yields

$$[1 - t_f - (t_d - t_f)](1 + r_d)^n = (1 + r_d)^n (1 - t_d)$$

So here, the optimal policy is to repatriate, rather than reinvest abroad, if, and only if, $r_d > r_f$. Moreover, this is true whether n is small or large.

XV. REINVEST VERSUS REPATRIATE WITH SUBPART F-TYPE INVESTMENTS

The analysis above assumed that reinvestment abroad gave rise to domestic tax deferral on all income generated abroad until such income is repatriated. Passive (Subpart F) income is deemed to be repatriated as it is earned. Although this might appear to be disadvantageous relative to non-Subpart F income, this need not be so.

In particular, suppose that passive income earns the same pretax rate whether invested abroad or domestically (e.g., Eurodollar bonds abroad versus equally risky dollar-denominated bonds domestically). Then $1 pretax income abroad, reduced by t_f for local tax, and reinvested locally at rate R for n years (taxed each year domestically as Subpart F income) yields

(c) $\qquad (1 - t_f)[1 + R(1 - t_d)]^n - (t_d - t_f)$

Additional tax at time n on repatriation attributable to the $1 of taxable income that gave rise to the $1-t_f$ initial retained earnings.

By contrast, immediate repatriation of $1 - t_f$ gives rise to immediate domestic tax of $(t_d - t_f)$, such that $1 - t_d$ gets invested domestically for n periods:

(d) $\qquad (1 - t_d)[1 + R(1 - t_d)]^n$

Note that (d) can be expanded to

(d') $\qquad (1 - t_f)[1 + R(1 - t_d)]^n - (t_d - t_f)[1 + R(1 - t_d)]^n$

Comparing (d') to (c), we see that as long as $t_d > t_f$ (as we have assumed), (c) is larger by an n-period after-tax interest factor on the additional tax due on repatriation. In (d), the immediate repatriation strategy, the tax is paid immediately, whereas in (c), the local reinvestment strategy, it is paid (without accretions for interest) in n periods.

XVI. INVESTMENT AND REPATRIATION POLICY WHEN THE FOREIGN TAX RATE EXCEEDS THE DOMESTIC TAX RATE

In the analysis above, comparisons of foreign and domestic investment accumulations were complicated by the fact that repatriation of foreign earnings gave rise to an additional tax. When the foreign tax rate exceeds the domestic rate, repatriation triggers no additional tax (assuming that there is no foreign withholding tax). With these assumptions, it is straightforward to verify that foreign investment is preferred to domestic investment, for *any* length investment horizon, if and only if $r_f > r_d$. The *same* condition determines whether reinvestment abroad is preferred to repatriation of foreign retained earnings.

XVII. CONCLUDING REMARKS

U.S. tax reforms in the 1980s had profound consequences for optimal investment and financing strategies of both domestic and foreign investors. Evidence indicates that taxpayers can be quite responsive to a change in tax incentives. Although highly leveraged corporations have fallen from favor of late on Wall Street the incentive to distribute corporate profits to investors in tax deductible ways is very strong under the current tax regime. Unless the tax system is changed to make U.S. corporations less tax disfavored relative to partnerships, investment bankers and other organization designers will continue to search for ways to gut the corporate tax without introducing excessive nontax costs. If such strategies are deemed to exact substantial social costs, U.S. legislators might pause to wonder why their tax treatment of corporate profits is so out of step with the way such activities are taxed by the rest of the world.

TAXATION AND THE COST OF CAPITAL: THE "OLD" VIEW, THE "NEW" VIEW, AND ANOTHER VIEW

Hans-Werner Sinn
University of Munich and NBER

EXECUTIVE SUMMARY

This paper is a critical survey and discussion of the recent literature on the tax effects on corporate finance and investment decisions. It corrects a common misinterpretation of the "new" view, emphasizes the cushioning effect of financial optimization, dismisses the view that optimizing firms behave as if they maximized their cost of finance, studies the role of immature firms, questions the alleged support of the old view by the occurrence of share repurchases, comments on the U.S. budget compromise, and suggests the idea of a political Miller equilibrium.

I. INTRODUCTION

Economists agree that the cost of capital is an important analytical tool for predicting a country's intersectoral distortions, its growth perfor-

The paper has benefitted from very useful comments by David Bradford and Larry Goulder. It was written while the author was Research Scholar at the Center for Economic Policy Research, Stanford University, and Olin Visiting Fellow at the Woodrow Wilson School of Public and International Affairs, Princeton University. The paper is also part of the NBER's research program in Taxation. The support and hospitality of these institutions are gratefully acknowledged.

mance, or its attractiveness for international capital. However, there is no consensus as to how the tax influence on the cost of capital should be measured.

The cost of capital is defined as the minimum pretax rate of return an investment project must earn to be profitable. The controversy among tax economists is primarily concerned with the question of how the required rate of return is affected by personal and corporate income taxation, and the double taxation of dividends has received particular attention. While it is obvious that the double taxation creates a substantial tax burden for corporations, there is no agreement as to how much of the burden falls on marginal investment projects. The "old view" is that the total tax burden falls entirely on marginal investment projects and therefore implies a high cost of capital, far above the market rate of interest. By way of contrast, the so-called "new view" (which, in fact, is no longer so new) is that only the tax burden on retained earnings matters. The burden of the double taxation of dividends is seen to fall largely on inframarginal investment projects and is believed to have no effect on the cost of capital at the margin.

This note is an exposition and critical review of some of the arguments exchanged between the members of the two schools. It presents the basic theories, discusses the role of financial optimization, comments on immature firms, and includes an analysis of the role of share repurchases, attention to which has recently led to a revival of the "old" view among North American economists. It also presents the idea of a political Miller equilibrium.

The crucial reason for the different views on the way taxes affect the cost of capital is that authors make different assumptions about the firms' financial decisions, sometimes without explicitly mentioning them. The holders of the new view have pointed to the importance of these assumptions and they have emphasized that new share issues, debt, and, in particular, retained profits should be distinguished as alternative *sources of finance*. Three different cost of capital expressions are typically used by them, depending on which source of finance is assumed.

Equally important, however, is the distinction between alternative *uses of profits*. These uses are not only dividend and interest payments, as is usually assumed, but also profit retentions and share repurchases. The specification of the use of profits is as essential for the calculation of the cost of capital as the specification of the source of finance. Only when it is clear where an additional dollar used for investment comes from and where its returns are going, is it possible to calculate the tax burden on marginal investment and to find out which minimum pretax return is required to make this investment profitable.

TABLE 1.
Taxation and the Cost of Capital

SOURCE OF FINANCE	USE OF PROFITS			
	Dividends	Interest	Retentions	Share repurchases
New share issues	$i \dfrac{1}{1-\tau_d}$	—	$> \dfrac{i}{1-\tau_d}$ *	$i \dfrac{1-\tau_i}{(1-\tau_c)(1-\tau_r)}$
Retained earnings (dividend reductions)	$i \dfrac{1-\tau_i}{(1-\tau_c)(1-\tau_r)}$	—	$i \dfrac{1-\tau_i}{(1-\tau_c)(1-\tau_r)} - \dfrac{\dot{q}/q}{1-\tau_r}$	$i \dfrac{(1-\tau_d)(1-\tau_{dp})(1-\tau_i)}{(1-\tau_c)^2(1-\tau_r)^2}$
Debt	—	i	—	—

*Sufficient conditions derived in Sinn (1988b, 1990).

Distinguishing retained earnings, debt, and new share issues as marginal sources of finance and retentions, dividends, interest income, and share repurchases as marginal uses of profit in principle gives up to 12 different expressions for the cost of capital. However, since interest payments are the marginal use of profits only when the marginal source of finance is debt, the number reduces to 7. The possibilities are depicted in Table 1. As will be shown, not all of them will be equally relevant to an optimizing firm: however, they will turn out to be a useful guide in the course of this paper.

II. THE OLD VIEW

In the good old days economists distinguished just two financial alternatives: equity and debt, and equity was seen as being provided by the household sector. The term "old view" will be used to characterize this approach.

With equity finance, the conceptual experiment for determining the cost of capital was that shareholders inject an additional dollar into their firm by purchasing newly issued shares and compare the returns in the form of dividends with the returns they could have received by investing their money in bonds. Let π be the annual dividend from marginal investment of one dollar and i the annual rate of interest on bonds. Then, if there are no taxes, the shareholders would be willing to inject funds into their firm until, at the margin, $\pi = i$.

If taxes are levied, the decision is different. Suppose distributed earnings are subject to a corporate tax of rate τ_d and in addition to a personal tax of rate τ_{dp}, the frequently deplored "double tax." Assume that interest income on the other hand is taxed only once at the personal rate τ_i. In this case, the marginal investment project is determined by equality of the dividend net of all taxes and the net-of-personal tax interest rate: $\pi(1-\tau_d)(1-\tau_{dp}) = i(1-\tau_i)$. In all OECD countries except Norway the personal tax on dividends is the same as that on interest income: $\tau_{dp} = \tau_i$. The equation can therefore be simplified to $\pi(1-\tau_d) = i$ or, solving for π, to

$$\pi = \frac{i}{1 - \tau_d} \qquad (1)$$

The right side of this equation is the pretax rate of return the firm must earn—that is, its cost of capital. This is represented in the box in the first column and first row of Table 1.

If the formula were true, the cost of capital would exceed the rate of interest significantly. Before 1986, when the U.S. corporate tax rate was 46%, the cost of capital would have exceeded the interest rate by 85% and presently, with a corporate tax rate of 34%, it would exceed the interest rate by 52%.

Clearly this signals substantial economic distortions. Too much of the available aggregate stock of capital would be allocated to the noncorporate sectors or to countries that do not impose a corporate tax on dividends (such as Norway, Germany, or Italy). Aggregate output would be lower than in the case where all investment projects had to satisfy the same profitability requirements. This is the traditional or "old" view of the role of corporate taxation that can be attributed to Harberger (1962, 1966) and McLure (1979) and, in an international context, to MacDougall (1960), Kemp (1962, 1964), and Hamada (1966).

It was clear to these authors that the cost of capital would be lower if firms could escape the double taxation of equity returns by choosing debt as the source of finance. An early writer who emphasized this point was Oberhauser (1963, pp. 67–68). He argued that, because of the deductibility of debt interest, a debt-financed marginal investment project is not affected by the tax rates and the cost of capital is simply equal to the market rate of interest. For a debt financed investment project, the dividend net of interest payments and net of all taxes is $(\pi-i)(1-\tau_d)(1-\tau_{dp})$. Obviously, the taxes reduce this dividend when it is positive, but they do not make it negative. All investment projects which are worth being carried out in the absence of taxation therefore retain this property despite taxation and

$$\pi = i \qquad (2)$$

remains the marginal investment condition. This is the case captured by the box in the third row and second column of Table 1.

Debt financing is an important example of a situation where the corporate tax is a burden on inframarginal, but not on marginal, investment projects. Only inframarginal projects generate profits in excess of their interest cost; only they pay the tax. Marginal debt financed projects that just break even are tax exempt. This is the reason why, under debt finance, the set of profitable investment projects is not affected by the corporate tax and the cost of capital equals the interest rate. The neutrality of the corporate tax in the case of debt financing has been emphasized by many authors and is well accepted by holders of the "old" view of corporate taxation. Often the literature takes account of the role of debt financing by assuming that the cost of capital is a weighted average of equations (1) and (2).

III. THE NEW VIEW

One of the problems with the "old" view is that it rests heavily on the assumption that new share issues are the marginal source of equity finance. This assumption does not harmonize well with the empirical fact that most corporate equity capital is generated by internal investment rather than new share issues. For example, in the period from 1980 to 1985, an average 67.8% of gross investment by U.S. nonfinancial corporations was internally financed, 31.0% was debt financed, and only 1.2% was financed with share issues.[1] Contrary to the assumption of the holders of the old view, these data suggest that corporations are self-perpetuating enterprises that rarely rely on equity injections by shareholder households but generate the needed equity capital primarily through profit retentions.

Probably the first to analyze the cost of capital consistently in the case of profit retentions was King (1974a,b, 1977). His contributions initiated a new literature that includes the contributions of Bradford (1980, 1981), Auerbach (1979, 1983), Fullerton and King (1984), Edwards and Keen (1984), Sinn (1985), and many others. The common element of this literature, which soon was labeled the "new view," was that it allowed with-

---

[1] See *Survey of Current Business,* volumes 57 (July 1977, p. 24n.), 61 (1981, special supplement, p. 10), 63 (July 1983, p. 30), 66 (July 1986, p. 33); and *Federal Reserve Bulletin,* Volumes 55 (November 1969, p. A 71.4), 60 (October 1974, p. A 59.4), 64 (June 1978, p. 433), 65 (December 1979, p. A 44). For a more extensive record see Gertler and Hubbard (1990, Table 1).

held dividends to replace new share issues as a marginal source of equity finance.

The modification is important in all cases where the personal tax on capital gains differs from that on dividends and where different corporate tax rates are applied to retained and distributed earnings. Let τ_r be the corporate tax rate on retained profits, τ_d (as before) the corporate tax on distributed profits, and τ_c the personal capital gains tax rate. In the classical system of corporate taxation that prevails in the United States and a few smaller countries (Australia, Luxemburg, Netherlands, New Zealand, Switzerland), τ_r equals τ_d; there is only one corporate tax rate regardless of whether earnings are retained or distributed. However, in nearly all other OECD countries, τ_r exceeds τ_d because imputation systems are used which refund part of the corporate tax to shareholders. The statutory capital gains tax rate in the United States is currently—however, perhaps not for much longer—equal to the personal tax rate, but it is applied only to realized rather than accrued capital gains. It is a widely used approximation to model this preferential treatment by assuming an effective tax on accrued capital gains whose rate is smaller than the personal tax rate: $\tau_c < \tau_i$. A good guess is that, in the United States, τ_c is currently *half* the personal tax rate where the latter can be taken to be 28% for the typical shareholder.[2] In most other countries, the difference between τ_c and τ_i is even more pronounced for the simple reason that these countries do not have any personal capital gains tax rates worth mentioning. Currently, only one-third of the OECD countries impose personal taxes on capital gains that are realized after a holding period of more than one year!

Verbally deriving the cost of capital expression for the case where retained earnings is the source of finance is slightly more arduous than in the case where new share issues or debt are the sources of finance. Nevertheless the argument is straightforward. Consider a firm that decides to finance additional investment by retaining earnings and thus foregoing a potential dividend payment. From the shareholders' point of view, this policy is worthwhile if its rate of return on investment is sufficiently high to generate future dividends in excess of the interest income that they would have earned had they received the current dividend payment and invested it in bonds. The minimum pretax rate of return necessary to satisfy the shareholders is the cost of capital to the firm.

To calculate this cost of capital, it is important to realize that the

---

[2] In inflationary times, τ_c may, however, become larger, since nominal rather than real capital gains are taxed.

decision to retain more profits creates more capital gains and raises the shareholders' capital gains tax liability. Suppose, in toto, one dollar is given up by the shareholders in the form of additional capital gains taxes to be paid and net-of-tax dividends foregone. If all market participants know what is going on, this renunciation must be offset by an increase in the market value of shares by exactly one dollar. Thus the additional capital gains taxes equal τ_c and the foregone dividend net of the personal and corporate dividend taxes equals $1-\tau_c$. "Grossing up" the foregone dividend with the corporate and personal dividend taxes τ_d and τ_{dp} translates it into $(1-\tau_c)/[(1-\tau_d)(1-\tau_{dp})]$ units of before-tax profits or, after subtracting the corporate tax on retained earnings, into investable funds of size $(1-\tau_c)(1-\tau_r)/[(1-\tau_d)(1-\tau_{dp})]$. On the other side of the ledger, the flow of net-of-tax dividends resulting from this investment outlay has to be determined. If one additional dollar were invested in the firm, the resulting before-tax return would be π and the corresponding net-of-all-tax dividend flow would be $\pi(1-\tau_d)(1-\tau_{dp})$. In this case, however, the additional amount invested is not one dollar but $(1-\tau_c)(1-\tau_r)/[(1-\tau_d)(1-\tau_{dp})]$ dollars. Hence the resulting net-of-all-taxes dividend flow is $\{(1-\tau_c)(1-\tau_r)/[(1-\tau_d)(1-\tau_{dp})]\} \cdot \pi (1-\tau_d)(1-\tau_{dp})$ or simply $\pi(1-\tau_c)(1-\tau_r)$. Comparing this amount with the interest income that the shareholders could have earned by not giving up the dollar but investing it in the capital market results in the break even condition $\pi(1-\tau_c)(1-\tau_r) = i(1-\tau_i)$. The solution of this condition for π yields the expression for the cost of capital which was sought:

$$\pi = i \frac{1-\tau_i}{(1-\tau_c)(1-\tau_r)} \tag{3}$$

This is the value represented by the box in the second row and first column of Table 1.

With current U.S. tax rates of, say, $\tau_i = 0.28$, $\tau_r = 0.34$, and $\tau_c = 0.14$, the cost of capital implied by equation (3) would be 27% above the interest rate vs. 52% according to the old view. This still signals economic distortions, but, with the usual quadratic excess burden functions, the welfare loss from intersectoral distortions would only be one-fourth of that implied by the old view. Before 1986, when the maximum marginal personal tax rate (50%) exceeded the corporate tax rate (46%) and the effective tax rate on accrued capital gains may have been about one-fifth of the personal tax rate, it was even possible that $(1-\tau_c)(1-\tau_r) \approx 1-\tau_i$. With this constellation, the cost of equity finance would have equalled the interest rate under the "new" view, whereas, as argued above, it would have exceeded this rate by 85% under the "old" view.

In most OECD countries, including those in continental Europe, the practical nonexistence of capital gains taxes implies that equation (3) reduces to

$$\pi = i \frac{1-\tau_i}{1-\tau_r} \quad \text{(European case)}$$

and the relative magnitudes of the personal and corporate tax rates alone determine the cost of capital. In the special case where both tax rates are equal, the tax system operates like a pure Schanz–Haig–Simons tax[3] and the cost of capital equals the interest rate—*as if debt rather than retained earnings were the marginal source of finance.* Basically, this is the fundamental neutrality result that European tax economists call the *Johansson–Samuelson Theorem.*[4]

The role of the personal income tax rate τ_i in equation (3) merits particular attention. Holders of the "old" view often argue that the corporate tax is a tax on investment and the personal income tax one on savings, largely irrelevant for the "investment wedge" as measured by the difference between the pretax rate of return to capital and the market rate of interest. In their opinion, all the personal tax does is create a "savings wedge" between the market rate of interest and the net rate of return the saver receives, but it has no implications for the investment tax wedge. Under the "new" view this argument seems highly misleading because equation (3) shows that both taxes are equally important for the investment tax wedge, perfectly offsetting each other when the tax rates are equal. It is true under the "new" view that the corporate tax is a tax on real investment and that the personal income tax is a tax on savings. However, the personal income tax is also seen as a subsidy on real investment because it reduces the opportunity cost of funds retained in the firm—after all, equation (3) was derived from a *portfolio* consideration where the shareholders' personal investment in bonds was compared with their company's investment in real assets. The higher the personal tax rate, the smaller is the investment tax wedge and the larger the firm's optimal level of investment with any given market rate of interest.

---

[3] On the definition and origins of this tax see Goode (1977).

[4] See Sinn (1985, Ch. 5) for further details. The theorem also gives a precise definition of true economic depreciation. When depreciation for tax purposes is accelerated relative to true economic depreciation, the cost of capital falls short of the interest rate, and, with an immediate write off, the cost of capital equals the rate of return the saver receives, $i(1-\tau_i)$. By way of contrast, under the "old" view of corporate taxation, the cost of capital with immediate depreciation equals the interest rate, i.

Apart from the fact that it implies lower intertemporal and intersectoral distortions than suggested by the "old" view, this particular role of the personal income tax results in paradoxical changes in the allocation of the available aggregate capital stock. An increase in the personal income tax rate for owners of corporate shares induces a reallocation of the aggregate stock of capital from the noncorporate to the corporate sector regardless of whether it is matched by a tax increase for the owners of noncorporate firms. And, provided the OECD's residence rules for the taxation of international interest income flows are kept, a unilateral increase in one country's personal income tax rate will induce capital imports. The higher the personal income tax rate, the more profits will be retained by domestic companies for the purpose of internal investment and the less capital is available for reinvestment in the capital market. The shortage of funds boosts the domestic interest rate and attracts foreign capital. Via a revaluation of the domestic currency and the subsequent current account deficit, the foreign capital succeeds in entering the domestic economy and makes an increase in aggregate domestic investment possible (see Sinn, 1988a, 1989).

It is obvious from equation (3) that capital gains taxes are the counterpart of personal taxes on interest income. A cut in the capital gains tax rate brings about the same portfolio effect as an increase in the personal tax rate does. The "compensation" of a cut in the capital gains tax rate with an increase in the personal income tax rate that has recently been considered as a potential U.S. budget compromise between Republicans and Democrats would therefore be strongly nonneutral with regard to international capital movements. It would create domestic investment incentives, raise the U.S. interest rate, support the dollar, and increase the American current account deficit.

An important aspect of equation (3) is that no dividend taxes appear in it. Economists have often been misled by this aspect into believing that the equation refers to the case where the profits generated by the marginal investment project (π) are retained in order to avoid the high burden of dividend taxes. In fact, holders of the "old" view often assume that equation (3) is the appropriate formula for the case where all proceeds of an investment are retained; and they often use a weighted average of equations (1) and (3) where the weights are determined by the dividend–payout ratio.[5] Unfortunately, however, it

---

[5] Cf. Miller (1977, pp. 266–267), Gordon and Malkiel (1981, pp. 141–143), or, to refer to more recent examples, Bernheim and Shoven (1987, 1989). On p. 18 of their 1989 article, the latter argue that, in the King–Fullerton model, "net earnings flowing from an investment financed with retained earnings must be entirely retained," deplore this assumption as counterfactual, and then seek greater generality by allowing the use of profits to be

seems that the formula has never been consistently derived from an optimization approach that would justify such a use or interpretation and, in fact, Section V will raise doubts that it ever can be derived.[6] Under the "new" view, the true interpretation of equation (3) is not that the profits from the marginal investment project are retained but, on the contrary, that they are fully distributed in the form of dividends. The message of the new view is not that the dividend taxes are neutral when the firm avoids them, but that they are neutral when, and in an important sense even *because*, it pays them. This exemplifies the more general point that the cost of capital depends as critically on the use of profits as on the source of finance.

The very fact that the firm pays dividends and dividend taxes in the investment phase implies that the marginal investment project is subsidized at the rate $1-(1-\tau_d)(1-\tau_{dp})$, which is the same rate at which its returns are taxed. This symmetry explains why the dividend taxes drop out of the equation and why they are neutral. The personal and corporate taxes on retained earnings that do appear on the right-hand side of equation (3) are *not* the taxes on the profits generated by the marginal investment project, they are taxes on the funds invested. This aspect is

---

determined by an exogenous dividend–payout ratio. This ratio is used to calculate the weighted average expression mentioned. Admittedly, Fullerton and King's (1984, p. 23) derivation of equation (3) can indeed be misunderstood, because they begin their discussion of the retained earnings case with the marginal condition $\pi(1-\tau_c)(1-\tau_r) = i(1-\tau_i)$, which above was merely the last step in a chain of transformations. There can be no doubt, however, that only the interpretation given here reflects the literature summarized under the heading "new view" adequately—including the work of King and Fullerton. For formal proofs of equation (3) in the context of explicit optimization models of the firm that support this interpretation see Sinn (1985, Ch. 5, and 1989, appendix).

[6] Section VIIA will show, however, that equation (3) can also be derived in the case where the marginal profits are used for share repurchases and where new share issues are the source of finance. Note, moreover, that the equation is compatible with retentions where these are equivalent to dividend payments. The point that will be made in Section V is that equation (3) is inappropriate when retentions are *preferred* to dividend payments, because then the marginal value of equity, q, cannot be a constant [cf. equation (6) below].

To the best of my knowledge the consistently derived expression that comes closest to the weighted average of equations (1) and (3) is Poterba and Summers's (1985) equation (my notation)

$$\pi = \frac{\rho/(1-\tau)}{(1-\tau_{pd})\alpha + (1-\tau_c)(1-\alpha)}$$

where ρ is the shareholders' discount rate, $\tau = \tau_r = \tau_d$, and α is the dividend–payout ratio. Poterba and Summers's equation is not a weighted average of (1) and (3) since ρ is assumed to deviate from the net-of-tax interest rate $i(1-\tau_i)$ by an amount that is inversely related to the dividend–payout ratio α. Moreover, these authors do not assume that marginal profits are retained. They assume that marginal profits are paid out in the form of share repurchases and dividends.

often overlooked, but it is obvious from the arbitrage calculus presented and it is essential for the new view.

The deeper economic reason for the neutrality of the dividend taxes is that dividend taxes are cash flow taxes that make the government a silent partner in the business. From the viewpoint of a single shareholder the government is very similar to another shareholder who claims a constant fraction of the distributed profits but does not make effective use of his voting rights. It is true that, unlike other shareholders, the government may have received its partnership in an unfair manner by establishing the tax law, but for a dividend paying firm this is merely a part of its miserable history. It is not an aspect that gives the shareholders incentives to vote for a policy other than the one they would prefer if they could claim the tax-inclusive fraction of dividends.

The neutrality properties of taxes on corporate distributions were emphasized by Bradford (1981) and induced the Meade Committee (1978) to propose a dividend tax as the only tax on corporate profits. Many economists believe that such taxes are among the most neutral ones available.

Although holders of the "new" view may have different opinions about the introduction of a dividend tax, most of them would object to the abolition of existing dividend taxes. They would argue that this abolition would reduce tax revenue, would create unjustified windfall gains for those who currently happen to hold their wealth in corporate shares, and would not induce firms to deviate from the investment behavior described by equation (3). The case is not as hypothetical as it may seem. A major reason for Congress not following the Treasury Department's (1985) proposal to integrate the corporate and personal tax systems in the course of the 1986 reform was the fear that this integration would incur substantial revenue losses without promising significant efficiency gains.[7]

IV. FINANCIAL FLEXIBILITY AND REAL DISTORTIONS

The existence of at least three alternative cost-of-capital expressions poses severe problems for economic models designed to measure tax distortions, for the magnitude of the predicted distortions will obviously depend on the financial behavior assumed. Ideally, the financial behavior should be determined endogenously together with the firm's invest-

---

[7] This was communicated to the author by Charles McLure, the academic supervisor of the proposal.

ment behavior, and the cost of financial and real distortions should be aggregated to overall welfare measures. However, in the absence of sound theories of the firms' financial choices, this approach has rarely been taken in the literature and no simple solutions have been offered so far.[8]

Holders of the "old" view often solve the problem by neglecting it. Frequently, they simply run their models on the basis of equation (1), finding huge real distortions and writing alarming reports about the devastating effects of the tax system. The results are not overly surprising if one realizes that, with the classical system of corporate taxation, they are based on the implicit assumption that firms *maximize* their cost of finance.

A more promising approach may be that of Fullerton and King (1984). These authors provide a methodology for measuring tax distortions that is probably now the most frequently used by research institutes and tax authorities throughout the world. They assume that the cost of capital is a weighted average of the costs of debt, retained earnings, and new share issues where the weights are the fractions of debt, surplus capital, and original capital in a firm's assets. The King–Fullerton methodology has been criticized on the grounds that it equates average with marginal financial structures and imposes these structures exogenously on the firm.

Another possibility is Sinn's (1985) approach, which is based on the assumption that firms *minimize* their cost of finance subject to the constraint that a minimum marginal equity–asset ratio is required. The resulting cost of capital in this approach is a weighted average of the cost of debt finance and the lower of the cost of internal and external equity finance. Naturally, the economic distortions it predicts tend to be lower than those suggested by old-view models or models of the King–Fullerton variety. The approach includes an endogenous explanation of the equity–asset ratio along the lines suggested by DeAngelo and Masulis (1980). Among other things this explanation implies that the equity–asset ratio increases with the allowed acceleration of tax depreciation and with the firm's planned rate of growth.

The constrained cost-of-capital minimization approach rests on the assumption that the firm pays dividends and retains profits only to finance its investment in real assets. For a firm that does not pay dividends, the cost of capital may be determined according to different rules.

One reason for not paying dividends is the existence of a tax system

---

[8] Cf. Miller (1977), DeAngelo and Masulis (1980), and Gordon and Malkiel (1981).

that favors retentions over debt since $(1-\tau_c)(1-\tau_r) > 1-\tau_i$.[9] Stiglitz (1973) believed that such a system prevailed in the United States before the 1981 tax reform and he argued that it would induce firms to use the part of profits exceeding their real investment for financial investments in the capital market. A marginal decision to invest in real assets would under these circumstances require a reduction in the capital market investment and, as this would be equivalent to marginal debt finance, the cost of capital would equal the market rate of interest. Taxes on the returns from equity capital do not matter in this approach even though all real investment is equity financed.

Stiglitz's argument was recently used in the work of Howitt and Sinn (1989) who analyzed investment in the case of anticipated changes in dividend tax rates. These changes resulted in strong changes in the firm's financial behavior, but left its real investment unaffected. The cost of capital was invariant to tax rate changes.

The result emerging from this discussion is that the firms' financial flexibility is crucial for the amount of real distortions a tax system causes. Obviously, the financial decisions can serve as a cushion that protects the economy from the blows imposed by the tax system. The higher the degree of financial flexibility, the easier it is for firms to escape discriminatory taxation and the lower are the real distortions.[10] Models that are built on the assumptions of fixed financial structures, or even of maximizing the cost of finance, may miss an important economic self-protection device and are likely to overstate the economy's distortions.

V. DO FIRMS MAXIMIZE THEIR COST OF CAPITAL?

Although the old view's assumption that firms maximize their cost of capital may at first look awkward to say the least, this assumption has recently been defended by Hansson and Stuart (1985) with an interesting argument. The argument rests on the widespread view that, unlike equity finance, debt finance involves invisible costs that, in a financial optimum, just compensate for its tax advantages at the margin (see Gordon and Malkiel, 1981). The invisible costs are similar to the costs of rent seeking in public choice models and can, for example, be taken to represent the cost of avoiding bankruptcy or, more generally, the differ-

---

[9] Another reason is that the firm may not have enough profits. See Section VI for an analysis of this case.

[10] Fullerton and Mackie (1989) estimate the welfare implications of the 1986 U.S. tax reform alternatively under the "new" and "old" view. Although their formal specification of these views is not exactly compatible with the interpretation given in this paper, they find that the "old" view implies larger distortions than the "new" view.

ential transactions costs resulting from the use of debt in lieu of equity capital. According to Hansson and Stuart, the presence of these costs implies that, although firms actually *minimize* their cost of finance, they make their real investment decisions *as if they maximized* the cost of finance with regard to the visible costs and as if they used only equity at the margin.

If correct, this argument would help rehabilitate models that neglect the role of financial decisions and would constitute a strong criticism of all models that allow for financial flexibility or that assume the cost of capital to be a weighted average of the direct, visible costs of different sources of finance.

To check the argument, neglect the difference between external and internal equity finance and assume that the invisible cost of debt finance can be described by a function $\varphi(K,D)$ where K is the firm's stock of assets and D its debt.[11] Let e be the visible cost of equity finance as given in equation (1) or (3) and i the (visible) cost of debt financing as given in equation (2). Assume that the tax system favors debt over equity and that $i < e$. An interior solution of the debt–equity choice that captures the Hansson-Stuart view is presumably characterized by

$$e = i + \varphi_D \qquad (4)$$

where φ_D is the marginal invisible cost of debt finance. The equation expresses that the sum of the marginal visible and invisible costs of debt finance equals the visible cost of equity, as the authors maintained. However does this mean that the cost of capital is equal to the cost of equity capital e?

Probably not. The general condition for an optimal marginal investment is that its rate of return, π, be equal to the marginal visible cost of a source of finance plus the marginal invisible cost where, because of the interior solution, it does not matter which source is chosen. Consider the case where retained earnings constitute the marginal source. In this case the condition becomes[12]

$$\pi = e + \varphi_K \qquad (5)$$

with φ_K as the change in the invisible cost resulting from a marginal equity-financed increase in the cost of capital.

---

[11] For a more detailed analysis see Sinn (1987).

[12] In the case of debt financing the marginal investment condition is $\pi = i + \varphi_D + \varphi_K$, which, because of equation (4), is the same as equation (5).

According to equation (5), the Hansson–Stuart proposition that $\pi = e$ is correct if, and only if, $\varphi_K = 0$. This, however, is a problematic assumption. If the invisible costs reflect bankruptcy or agency costs, as the authors suggested, then it seems very plausible that an increase in the firm's stock of equity reduces these costs and that $\varphi_K < 0$. If it were indeed true that $\varphi_K = 0$ for all levels of D, then the cross derivatives φ_{KD} and φ_{DK} would both be zero and the stock of debt that satisfies equation (4) would be independent of the firm's stock of assets. The firm could grow indefinitely, but there would never be an incentive to use more debt. Obviously, the Hansson–Stuart argument rests on the implicit assumption that equity is the only marginal source of finance. It is not surprising then that the cost of finance is not a weighted average of the costs of debt and equity finance, but equals the latter.

If these implausible implications are removed by using the more realistic assumption $\varphi_K < 0$ (and $\varphi_{DK} < 0$), then, despite the interior debt equity choice, the cost of capital is between the costs of debt and equity, just as weighted average models predict. Even in a Hansson–Stuart world, firms do not behave as if they were maximizing their cost of finance, they behave as if the weighted average formulations were correct!

VI. THE ROLE OF IMMATURE FIRMS

It is certainly not reasonable to expect firms that have access to alternative sources of finance to behave as if they were maximizing their cost of finance, but neither is it true that the most attractive sources of finance are always available. This is obvious for debt financing, which is often subject to tight constraints imposed by the banking system. However, it is also true for retained earnings. Young and immature firms may not have enough profits to finance all available investment projects profitable enough to bear the cost of retentions given in equation (3).

This is a severe problem for the "new" view. Even in mature economies there are always inventors who try to found corporations to cash in on their ideas. Moreover, new investment opportunities that require more equity funds than the firm is able to generate by withholding its dividends show up regularly for existing firms. In all these cases the new view is not very helpful for predicting the firm's cost of capital, because its basic assumption that the firm can finance more investment by withholding more dividends is not satisfied.

At first glance this seems to rehabilitate the "old" view and its basic cost-of-capital expression, equation (1). After all, new share issues may be unavoidable when other sources of finance are not available. Unfortunately, however, there is no reason to be optimistic. In fact there hardly seem to be any circumstances where equation (1) can possibly be true for value maximizing neoclassical firms when dividends are taxed more heavily than retentions [$(1-\tau_d)(1-\tau_{dp}) < (1-\tau_r)(1-\tau_c)$].

The fundamental problem with equation (1) is that it is based on a conceptual mistake. The equation is derived from the assumption that marginal profits are paid out as dividends, but it implies that the firm prefers to retain them. To understand this inconsistency, suppose the firm followed equation (1) and stopped issuing shares at the point where the last dollar invested yielded a return equal to $i/(1-\tau_d)$. In this case there would be a set of unexploited investment opportunities with a rate of return above the cost of withheld dividends as given by equation (3). In the presence of such opportunities, dividend payments cannot be optimal. Instead, it is optimal for the firm to enter an extended period of purely internal growth where it retains its profits and does not pay dividends until all of the projects have been implemented.

To calculate the true cost of new share issues in the presence of a phase of purely internal growth is not an easy task, and a parametric cost of capital formula does not seem readily available. Nevertheless, it has been shown in Sinn (1988b, 1990) that the cost of new share issues, as well as the length of the period of internal growth, increases with an increase in the dividend tax rate and will, under extremely mild conditions, *exceed* the value given by the traditional formula (1).

The first of these results says that an increase in the dividend tax burden reduces a young firm's starting stock of capital and slows down its development to maturity. It is a potential explanation of Poterba and Summers's (1985) empirical finding that the frequent changes in the British dividend tax rate exhibited adverse effects on aggregate investment.[13]

The second result implies that even the "old" view underestimates the cost of capital for newly founded firms. These firms may be endowed with only a very small nucleus of original capital and may be forced to generate more capital through internal investment than a focus on equations (1) and (3) would suggest. The result is the net effect of two countervailing forces. On the one hand, the deferral of dividend payments reduces the present value of the firm's tax burden. This, in itself, would reduce the cost of capital if there were unlimited internal investment

---

[13] The authors' own explanation is a signaling argument. According to this argument, an increase in the dividend tax rate reduces the optimal volume of dividends which in turn increases the shareholders' discount rate (cf. also fn. 6). A third explanation could simply be that, for at least some of the periods considered, the overall tax burden on dividends fell short of that on retentions. In this case new issues of shares would be the cheapest source of equity finance and it would not be surprising that dividend taxes entered the cost of capital. This point was made in Sinn (1985, Ch. 7).

opportunities that the firm could use up to a predetermined point of time.[14] On the other hand, the possibility of generating "cheap" capital through profit retentions makes it wise to economize on new share issues and to start with only a nucleus of equity capital if the set of internal investment opportunities is limited and the time of dividend payments is endogenously determined. New share issues reduce the scope of profitable retentions, and this reduction is an opportunity cost that increases the cost of external equity funds beyond the value implied by the traditional equation (1). Table 1 reports this result in the box that is in the first row and third column.

The phase of internal growth, which should necessarily follow the issue of new shares, is a phase in which the firm neither issues new shares nor pays any dividends and in which retentions are both the only source of finance and the only use of profits. The careless holder of the *new view* who focuses simply on the firm's marginal source of funds might interpret this phase as one in which the firm's cost of capital is given by equation (3). Similarly, the careless holder of the *old view* might do the same because he focuses on the firm's use of profits and interprets equation (3) in the "old" way described in Section III (shortly after presenting the equation). However, they would both be wrong. As long as there is a strict preference for profit retentions, the firm's marginal investment projects will obviously have a rate of return above the value given by equation (3), and the economic distortions will be *larger* than this value suggests.

Formally, the phase of internal growth can be shown to result in a decline in q, the firm's marginal value of equity, from one to $(1-\tau_d)(1-\tau_{dp})/[(1-\tau_r)(1-\tau_c)]$, the value that the new view predicts for a dividend paying firm.[15] This decline is a capital loss that increases the cost of capital beyond the value given by equation (3). Let $\dot{q}$ measure the annual increment of q, $\dot{q}$ being negative in the phase of internal growth. A shareholder whose only

---

[14] This is the argument that those who argue that the mere possibility of a deferral of dividend payments reduces the cost of capital may have in mind. The argument covers only one side of the problem.

[15] The variable q is the increase in the firm's market value resulting from a one dollar gift to the firm. Its value equals one when the firm issues new shares because the gift would be able to substitute a one dollar equity injection by the shareholders. To understand that $q = (1-\tau_d)(1-\tau_{dp})/[(1-\tau_r)(1-\tau_c)]$ if the firm pays dividends recall the arbitrage calculus given in Section III. There it was shown that one dollar that the shareholders give up in the form of dividend reductions and capital gains tax increases translates into investable funds equal to $(1-\tau_c)(1-\tau_r)/[(1-\tau_{dp})(1-\tau_d)]$. The inverse of this expression is the cash shareholders would receive if the gift were distributed or, equivalently, the capital gain they could enjoy if the gift were retained. See Auerbach (1979) for an early analysis of q in the phase of dividend payments.

returns are capital gains would be indifferent between a policy of profit retentions and a personal capital market investment if the rate of capital gains on his shares equalled the net-of-tax interest rate, i.e., if $(1-\tau_c)[\pi(1-\tau_r) + \dot{q}/q] = (1-\tau_i)i$. Solving for π, the pretax rate of return to real capital, one obtains the following modified cost-of-capital expression:[16]

$$\pi = i \frac{1-\tau_i}{(1-\tau_c)(1-\tau_r)} - \frac{\dot{q}/q}{1-\tau_r} \qquad (6)$$

As $\dot{q}/q < 0$, this expression indicates a higher cost of capital and higher distortions than equation (3). Its entry in Table 1 is in the second row and third column.

The work reported in this section has implications for the empirical literature on the tax influence on the cost of capital. Among others, two conclusions emerge. The first is that "new view" approaches of the King–Fullerton variety tend to underestimate the true cost of capital. These approaches use weighted averages of expressions (1)–(3) but do not take account of the facts that, when firms are immature, the cost of new share issues is likely to exceed the value given in equation (1) and the cost of retained earnings is likely to exceed that given in equation (3).

The second conclusion refers to "old view" approaches of the Harberger variety. It is the tradition of these approaches to explain the magnitudes of real distortions with the measurable income tax burden or, what amount to the same thing, to assume the cost of capital to be a weighted average of equations (1) and (3) where the dividend–payout ratio is used to construct the weights. In view of the above analysis of immature firms this procedure stands truth on its head. A high measurable tax burden signals that many firms are mature and pay dividends. The cost of capital is low, because investment can be financed with dividend reductions. On the other hand, a low dividend–payout ratio and a low measurable tax burden signal a shortage of funds. It means that many firms face the high cost of retained earnings as given by equation (6) or even a cost of new share issues in excess of the traditional value given in equation (1). In short, when it comes to a comparison of mature and immature firms, the true cost of capital is inversely related to that measured by "old view" approaches.

---

[16] See Sinn (1990). As profit retentions follow new share issues, this equation also applies to the case of new share issues. However, in itself, it does not reveal that this cost is above the traditional value $i/(1-\tau_d)$. The proof that the cost of new share issues will, under mild conditions, exceed $i/(1-\tau_d)$ is given in Sinn (1988b, 1990). It is based on a comparison of the time paths of the "true" q and the q implied by equation (1).

VII. WHY SHARE REPURCHASES DO NOT REHABILITATE THE "OLD VIEW"

Share repurchases and acquisitions have long constituted an important aspect of U.S. corporate behavior. Scherer and Ravenscraft (1984) found that, from 1950 to 1975, at least 1800 independent firms were acquired by those 148 firms that persistently belonged to the set of the 200 largest U.S. firms. And Shoven (1986) reported that, in the years following 1983, corporate share repurchases, predominantly acquisitions, exceeded ordinary dividend payments.

As shown in Sinn (1985, Ch. 6) the excessive acquisition activity of U.S. firms can, in principle, be explained by the undervaluation of corporate shares resulting from the high burden of dividend taxes. Buying shares is a cheaper way of acquiring real assets than buying investment goods, is a method of distributing dividends that circumvents personal income tax, and, if debt financed, is a convenient way of enjoying the tax advantages of a higher degree of corporate leverage.[17]

Quite surprisingly, the observation of corporate share repurchases has recently led to a revival of the "old" view of corporate taxation among North-American economists. The puzzling aspect about this development in the history of economic thought is that although share repurchases are a way of avoiding the dividend taxes, they are nevertheless believed to reinstate the distortionary image of these taxes.

The "naive" interpretation of the empirical fact of share repurchases is that, if anything, they reduce the cost of capital because they constitute a less heavily taxed use for marginal profits than dividends. Consider two straightforward thought experiments to derive the implication of share repurchases for the cost of capital before the "puzzle" will be addressed.

A. Share Repurchases and the Cost of Equity Capital

In the first experiment, the shareholders inject funds into their company in exchange for newly issued shares and receive the returns by gradually selling shares back to this company. The issue of new shares increases the market value of all shares simply because it injects money into the firm and has no immediate tax consequences when it occurs at the market clearing price. However, when the firm uses its profits to repurchase shares there are tax consequences. Although they avoid the per-

---

[17] To establish "acquisition neutrality" a removal of the affiliaton privilege or the introduction of a special tax on corporate acquisitions was recommended that under the present U.S. tax rate would have to be 52% of the purchase volume. For further discussion of the acquisition problem in the context of tax incentives see Poterba (1987), Auerbach and Reishus (1988), and Bagwell and Shoven (1988).

sonal income tax that the shareholder household would have to pay on ordinary dividends, the share repurchases do not prevent the firm from having to pay corporate tax on retained earnings and they in addition create a personal capital gains tax liability because the remaining shares are gaining in "weight."

To derive the corresponding cost of capital expression, suppose shareholders inject one dollar into their firm by purchasing new shares and this dollar generates a permanent annual return of π before tax or $\pi(1-\tau_r)$ after the corporate tax on retained earnings. The total market value of outstanding shares will rise at the time of the equity injection, but it will not be affected thereafter if this net-of-tax return is used for distributions in the form of share repurchases.[18] Because of the profit distributions the investment does not generate perpetuated increments in the market value of outstanding shares as would have been the case had the profits been reinvested for the purpose of further internal investment. This does not mean, however, that there are no taxable capital gains. On the contrary, since a given overall market value is divided by a smaller number of outstanding shares, there are capital gains in every year after the investment. The capital gains compensate for the decline in the number of shares, and when the repurchases occur at the respective current market prices of shares, they will just equal the annual repurchase volume $\pi(1-\tau_r)$. The capital gains tax is therefore $\tau_c\pi(1-\tau_r)$ and the shareholders' net of-all-tax return is $\pi(1-\tau_c)(1-\tau_r)$. In the optimum, this return must equal the interest rate net of the personal income tax at which shareholders could invest in the capital market, $i(1-\tau_i)$. Solving for π gives the corresponding value for the cost of capital in the case in which new share issues are the source of finance and share repurchases the use of profits:

$$\pi = i\frac{1-\tau_i}{(1-\tau_c)(1-\tau_r)} \tag{7}$$

Table 1 reports this (surprisingly familiar) value in the box in the first row and fourth column.

In the second thought experiment, retained earnings in the sense of dividend reductions are the source of finance and share repurchases the use of profits. As explained in Section III, one dollar given up by the shareholders via dividend cuts translates into $(1-\tau_c)(1-\tau_r)/[(1-\tau_d)(1-\tau_{dp})]$ dollars of investment. However, as the profits from this investment are channelled to the shareholders via share repurchases the net return per

---

[18] The same would be true for any other channel of corporate distributions.

dollar invested is $\pi(1-\tau_c)(1-\tau_r)$, as was shown in the previous paragraph. Multiplying the net return per dollar of investment with the number of dollars available for investment results in a return of $\pi(1-\tau_c)^2(1-\tau_r)^2/[(1-\tau_d)(1-\tau_{dp})]$ for the dollar given up by the shareholder. Equating this again to $i(1-\tau_i)$ and solving for π gives

$$\pi = i \frac{(1-\tau_d)(1-\tau_{dp})(1-\tau_i)}{(1-\tau_c)^2(1-\tau_r)^2} \tag{8}$$

whereby, as mentioned in Section II, $\tau_{dp} = \tau_i$ in practically all OECD tax systems. Equation (8) shows the cost of capital in the case in which dividend cuts are the source of finance and share repurchases the use of profits. It is represented by the box in the fourth column and second row of Table 1.

Both equations (7) and (8) confirm the "naive" view that share repurchases reduce the cost of capital. The value given by (7) is exactly the same as that which follows from the new view for the case in which retained earnings are the source of finance and dividends the use for marginal profits. As argued above for the U.S. tax system ($\tau_d = \tau_r = 0.34$, $\tau_p = 0.28$, $\tau_c = 0.14$) it exceeds the interest rate by only 27% versus 52% as predicted by the "old" view formula (1).

A particularly low value of the cost of capital is implied by equation (8). With the same U.S. tax rates, it exceeds the interest rate by just 6%. In the pre-1986 U.S. tax system, the corporate tax rate was $\tau_d = 0.46$ and it may well have been possible that $(1-\tau_i)/[(1-\tau_c)(1-\tau_r)]$ approximated one. Under these circumstances, the cost of capital given by equation (8) would have been about 50% *below* the interest rate. The reason for this cost of capital being so low is the fact that, by reducing its dividends and repurchasing shares, the firm can twice take advantage of the preferential tax treatment of retained compared to distributed profits. It gains when it replaces dividends with retentions in the investment phase and it gains when it substitutes share repurchases for dividends in the return phase. Without preferential treatment of retained earnings, i.e., with $(1-\tau_c)(1-\tau_r) = (1-\tau_d)(1-\tau_{dp})$, equation (8) would coincide with both equation (1) and equation (3).

Note that in striking contrast to the "old" view, the possibility of share repurchases may even reverse the role of dividend taxation. According to equation (8), a cut in the corporate tax rate on dividends—say through the introduction of an imputation system—would actually *increase* the cost of capital if retained earnings were the source of finance and share repurchases the use of profits. The reason for this unusual result is that the tax cut reduces the tax saving in the investment phase but does not imply a countervailing tax relief in the phase of profit distributions. This asymmetry induces a rational firm to invest less and to react in the opposite way as the "old" view suggests.

B. Share Repurchases and Economic Model Building

What then is the explanation of the puzzle that holders of the "old" view defend their results with the allusion to share repurchases?

It is simply their assumption that dividends are a fixed fraction of profits while the remainder is used for net investment and share repurchases.[19] This seemingly innocuous assumption, which is currently spreading fast among new models with old views, implies that new share issues are the *only* marginal source of finance while dividends and share repurchases are the use of marginal profits. The cost of capital that the assumption generates is a weighted average of equations (1) and (7) where the dividend–payout ratio determines the weights.[20]

Although popular this approach is not, in this author's opinion, an ultimately convincing response to the important phenomenon of share repurchases. It may be a theoretical artifact with little economic meaning.

Holders of the new view could easily counter the trick by constructing models in which share repurchases are a fixed fraction of profits and the remainder is used for dividends and net investment. In these models, retained earnings in the sense of dividend reductions would be the *only* marginal source of finance and marginal profits would be used for share repurchases and dividends. The cost of capital would be a weighted average of equations (3) and (8) where the weights would again be derived from the dividend–payout ratio.[21] Obviously, the cost of capital

---

[19] See, e.g., Poterba and Summers (1985), Goulder and Summers (1989), or Jun (1989).

[20] Solving the problem with an explicit dynamic optimization approach shows that the weighted average takes the form

$$\pi = \frac{i}{\alpha(1-\tau_d) + (1-\alpha)\frac{(1-\tau_c)(1-\tau_r)}{1-\tau_i}}$$

where α is the dividend-pay-out ratio and $1-\alpha$ is the fraction of profits used for share repurchases and investment.

[21] The exact formula following from an explicit optimization approach is

$$\pi = i\frac{(1-\tau_d)(1-\tau_{dp})(1-\tau_i)}{(1-\tau_c)^2(1-\tau_r)} \cdot \frac{1}{\alpha\frac{(1-\tau_{dp})(1-\tau_d)}{1-\tau_c} + (1-\alpha)(1-\tau_r)}$$

where $1-\alpha$ is the fraction of profits used for share repurchases and α the fraction used for dividends and investment.

would be much lower than in the popular specification, and the perverted role of the dividend tax rate that equation (8) implies would still be present.

An equally arbitrary, but less biased, assumption would be fixing the volume of share repurchases relative to dividend payments where the sum of these quantities exhaust the part of profits not needed for real investment. This specification would imply that new share issues and retained earnings are the marginal sources of finance and that share repurchases and dividends are the uses for marginal profits. It would be indistinguishable from a reduction of the dividend tax rate under the "new" view and would be fully neutral since it would mean a reduced subsidy in the investment phase, which is compensated for by a reduced tax in the return phase. The cost of capital would be a weighted average of the identical equations (3) and (7). It would be exactly what the "new" view suggests.

These considerations show that the "naive" interpretation of share repurchases may, after all, not be all that wrong. However, from a theoretical viewpoint, there is no reason to believe that share repurchases revalidate the "old" view of corporate taxation. On the contrary, the possibility of share repurchases conflicts sharply with the "old" view and, if anything, it supports the "new" view of corporate taxation. It is true that formal models that offer the "new" view often exclude the possibility of share repurchases. It is also true that the dividend puzzle—the question why firms pay dividends after all—cannot really be resolved by these models.[22] However, as was shown, this does not mean that the cost-of-capital expression [equation (3)] that the "new" view offers is no longer correct. Although this expression does not necessarily follow from the joint observation of share repurchases and dividend payments it is perfectly compatible with this observation when the relative composition of corporate distributions stays constant.

VIII. THE POLITICAL MILLER EQUILIBRIUM

The previous analysis was concerned with the economy's reaction to the tax system; however, an equally important question is how the tax system reacts to the economy's behavior. All countries have their histories of tax reforms and certainly these reforms were largely introduced in response to unforeseen and unwanted economic developments caused by the preceding tax systems.

---

[22] The new view can explain why dividend taxes do not affect the timing of dividend payments but not why firms pay dividends instead of repurchasing shares. See Bradford (1981, 1989), Auerbach (1983, 1989), or Sinn (1985, Ch. 4).

One of the major issues in capital income tax reforms has always been the problem of financial distortions. Be it because financial reactions to tax reforms often come fast and strong, because politicians and lobbyists find it easier to understand financial rather than real distortions, or because differently leveraged firms called for "fair" comparative tax treatments, legislators have always paid particular attention to financial distortions and have sought to introduce tax reforms that are in harmony with the principle of financial neutrality. As a result of this type of behavior, many tax systems of OECD countries approximate what may be called a *political Miller equilibrium*.

The term Miller equilibrium usually refers to segmentation equilibria in which shareholders rather than legislators are the agents. However, for the economist the term does have the connotation of an adjustment process toward financial neutrality, and this is the sense in which it is used here.[23]

The political Miller equilibrium is a first, albeit crude, approximation to reality. Actual tax systems hover around the neutrality path deviating sufficiently from it to motivate papers like this one. However, there are forces that push the existing economies toward the Miller equilibrium and the deviation from this equilibrium may be less than what a focus on one country's tax system at one point in time would suggest.

Seen from an American perspective, it may seem obvious that the tax system discriminates heavily against corporate equity. After all, the returns to equity are taxed twice and the return to debt only once. However, as mentioned earlier, from a worldwide perspective the picture is not as clear as that. *Two of three OECD countries do not tax capital gains* realized after a holding period of more than 1 year, but *four of five countries tax dividends twice*. In most countries, there is only a double taxation of dividends, not a double taxation of corporate earnings in general.

It is true, of course, that the number of taxes imposed on the same base does not necessarily reveal the magnitude of the overall tax burden. Nevertheless, the rare occurrence of capital gains taxes is a fact and it shows that the tax discrimination against corporate equity capital may be more an Anglo-Saxon speciality than a phenomenon with worldwide significance. The double taxation of dividends *is* a worldwide phenomenon, but *it* merely discriminates against a particular way of generating equity capital, not against equity capital as such. For the vast majority of existing firms in mature economies, a balanced tax treatment of retained earnings and interest income is sufficient to ensure financial neutrality,

---

[23] See Miller (1977).

and the reality may often not be far away from that. The political forces operating toward a balanced treatment of retained earnings and interest income have always been strong. They explain why most countries do not have genuine capital gains taxes and why those that do offer substantial reliefs such as a less than full inclusion of the gains in the personal tax base or a taxation on realization rather than accrual.

By way of contrast, comparative forces demanding dividend tax cuts to facilitate the foundation of new firms and avoid the distortions described in Section VI do not seem to exist. The well-established lobbies of mature firms do not have an interest in pushing this particular path toward financial neutrality.

The United States, which has a long-standing tradition of double taxing retained earnings, is not free from the forces driving toward a political Miller equilibrium. In 1986, the capital gains tax base was increased from 40 to 100% of realized gains, but in 1990, after only 4 years, the government proposed reducing the tax burden again. At the same time, plans were being discussed for increasing the maximum average personal tax rate (and the marginal tax rate for very high incomes) from 28 to 33%. Both moves would have been steps toward a more balanced treatment of debt and retained profits, but the first one of them has been ruled out by a budget compromise. The issue is almost certain to come up again.

The 1981 U.S. tax reform can, in part, also be seen as a step toward financial neutrality. Before 1981, rich people's income tax rates exceeded the corporate tax rate sufficiently to create strong preferences for profit retentions. It was the time when doctors and baseball players incorporated to enjoy the privilege of accumulating their earnings under the rules of the corporate tax law. The 1981 reform reduced the maximum marginal personal tax rate to 50%, just four percentage points above the corporate tax rate, and largely abolished the preferences for retentions.

Anecdotal evidence that demonstrates the general dominance of financial over real distortions in political debates about tax reforms comes from the discussion preceding the German tax reform of 1977. The achievement of financial neutrality was the official goal of the reform and detailed numerical examples demonstrating the seeming nonneutrality of the previous laws were published in numerous reports and newspaper articles. Allocative arguments focusing on real rather than financial distortions had virtually no survival chances in debate.

To make a final point, note that many countries have recently reduced their capital income tax rates following the example of the United States. Typically, these reductions were not limited to one tax, but included both the personal *and* corporate tax rates. Surely this symmetry was predominantly motivated by the attempt to avoid substantial deviations from financial neutrality.

These reflections on the political Miller equilibrium do not imply that there is no point in studying distortions resulting from differences in the tax treatment of retained earnings, dividends, and interest income where such differences occur. However, they do suggest a stylized tax model that has the same overall tax rates on interest income and retained profits, but allows for a discriminatory taxation of dividends. This model may be a good first-order approximation to the tax laws of many countries and may serve well in many economic applications. It would imply that the cost of capital for mature firms equals the market rate of interest, and it would have various technical advantages. It would be simple and avoid the unsatisfactory task of modelling financial constraints when mature firms are considered. It would allow focusing on the distortion that the double taxation of dividends causes for immature firms. And it would pave the way for an analysis of provisions of the tax laws that may cause more severe distortions than mere tax differentials, examples being the ITC, accelerated depreciation allowances, accounting practices in the presence of inflation, or discriminatory treatments of border crossing interest and dividend flows.

IX. CONCLUSIONS

This paper discussed the influence of statutory capital income tax rates on the cost of capital, starting with a comparison of the "old" and "new" views of corporate taxation. It corrected a common misinterpretation of the "new" view, emphasized the cushioning effect of financial optimization, dismissed the view that firms behave as if they maximized their cost of finance, studied the role of immature firms, questioned the alleged support of the old view by the occurrence of share repurchases, and suggested the idea of a political Miller equilibrium. Various conclusions emerge from the discussion.

1. For mature firms, the distortionary effects of the corporate tax may not be very large, because they are mitigated by the firms' financial decisions and by compensatory tax reforms that aim at establishing conditions of financial neutrality. Seen from a worldwide perspective, these tax reforms have reduced or even abolished the double taxation of retained corporate profits and may have driven the allocation of resources close to that implied by an integrated corporate tax system (which, of course, is not free from distortionary effects either).
2. When mature and immature firms are considered, the double taxa-

tion of corporate dividends is a more severe problem than the "new" view suggests, but does not generate the distortions exactly where the "old" view suspects them. It is not true that firms that pay dividend taxes suffer from a high cost of capital. On the contrary, those that do not pay these taxes because they are immature and retain their profits suffer most. The dividend tax burden expected in the future makes it wise to economize on new share issues and to invest even less capital than the "old" view's cost of capital formula suggests. The possibility of a deferral of dividend taxes increases the cost of outside equity finance.
3. Share repurchases are a more severe problem for the "old" view than for the "new" view, for if they are the way through which companies channel their marginal profits to shareholders, the cost of capital will be equal to that implied by the "new" view or even below this value, depending on whether new share issues or dividend cuts are the marginal source of finance. The cost-of-capital expression resulting from the "new" view harmonizes perfectly with share repurchases when corporate distributions split in fixed proportions into share repurchases and ordinary dividend payments.
4. Under the "new" view, both an increase in the personal income tax rate and a decrease of the personal capital gains tax rate stimulate corporate investment demand with any given market rate of interest. In an open economy that taxes cross-border interest income flows according to the OECD's residence principle, the substitution of personal income taxes for capital gains taxes results in a domestic investment boom, higher domestic interest rates, a revaluation of the domestic currency, and a capital import.
5. The fact that an interior debt–equity choice implies marginal costs of debt and equity finance does not legitimate the assumption that firms invest as if they used only equity at the margin. Despite the interior solution, the firm's cost of capital remains between the costs of debt and equity finance if debt and equity participate in financing marginal investment projects.

Arguably, the first two of these results are the most important. They suggest that tax distortions are to be found not in established corporations that currently suffer most from the high burden of dividend taxes. They are to be found with young and immature firms and with firms that as yet do not exist. These firms do not currently suffer from a high tax burden, but the prospect that they will makes them overly timid in the present. Holders of the "old" and "new" views alike have concentrated on the behavior of firms that pay dividends and dividend taxes.

How the tax system affects the foundation and development of new firms is a question that merits equal professional attention.

REFERENCES

Auerbach, A. J. (1979). "Wealth Maximization and the Cost of Capital." *Quarterly Journal of Economics* 94, 433–436.

Auerbach, A. J. (1983). "Taxation, Corporate Financial Policy and the Cost of Capital." *Journal of Economic Literature* 21, 905–940.

Auerbach, A. J. (1989). "Tax Policy and Corporate Borrowing." In R. W. Kopcke and E. S. Rosengren, eds., *Are the Distinctions between Debt and Equity Disappearing?*, pp. 136–162. Federal Reserve Bank of Boston.

Auerbach, A., and D. Reishus. (1988). "The Effects of Taxation on the Merger Decision." In A. Auerbach, ed., *Corporate Takeovers: Causes and Consequences.* Chicago: University of Chicago Press.

Bagwell, L. S., and J. B. Shoven. (1989). "Cash Distributions to Shareholders." *Journal of Economic Perspectives* 3, 129–140.

Bernheim, B. D., and J. B. Shoven. (1987). "Taxation and the Cost of Capital: An International Comparison." In Ch. E. Walker and M. A. Bloomfiled, eds., *The Consumption Tax: A Better Alternative?*, pp. 61–86. Cambridge, MA: Ballinger.

Bernheim, B. D., and J. B. Shoven. (1989). "Comparison of the Cost of Capital in the U.S. and Japan: The Roles of Risk and Taxes." Center for Economic Policy Research, Stanford University, working paper No. 179.

Bradford, D. F. (1980). "The Economics of Tax Policy toward Savings." In G. M. von Fürstenberg, ed., *The Government and Capital Formation.* Cambridge, MA: Ballinger.

Bradford, D. F. (1981). "The Incidence and Allocation Effects of a Tax on Corporate Distributions." *Journal of Public Economics* 15, 1–22.

Bradford, D. F. (1989). "Tax Policy and Corporate Borrowing," Discussion of Auerbach (1989). In R. W. Kopcke and E. S. Rosengren, eds., *Are the Distinctions between Debt and Equity Disappearing?*, pp. 163–168. Federal Reserve Bank of Boston.

DeAngelo, H., and R. W. Masulis. (1980). "Optimal Capital Structure under Corporate and Personal Taxation." *Journal of Financial Economics* 8, 3–29.

Edwards, J. S. S., and M. J. Keen. (1984). "Wealth Maximization and the Cost of Capital: A Comment." *Quarterly Journal of Economics* 99, 211–214.

Fullerton, D., and M. King. (1984). *The Taxation of Income from Capital. A Comparative Study of the United States, the United Kingdom, Sweden and West Germany.* Chicago: University of Chicago Press.

Fullerton, D., and J. M. Mackie. (1989). "Economic Efficiency in Recent Tax Reform History: Policy Reversals or Consistent Improvements?" *National Tax Journal* 42, 1–13.

Gertler, M., and R. G. Hubbard. (1990). "Taxation, Corporate Capital Structure, and Financial Distress." *Tax Policy and the Economy* 4, 43–71.

Goode, R. (1977). "The Economic Definition of Income." In J. A. Pechman, ed., *Comprehensive Income Taxation.* Washington D.C.: Brookings Institution.

Gordon, R. H., and B. G. Malkiel. (1981). "Corporation Finance." In H. J. Aaron and J. A. Pechman, eds., *How Taxes Affect Economic Behavior*, pp. 131–198. Washington, D.C.: Brookings Institution.

Goulder, L. H., and L. H. Summers. (1989). "Tax Policy, Asset Prices, and Growth." *Journal of Public Economics* 38, 265–296.

Hamada, K. (1966). "Strategic Aspects of Taxation on Foreign Investment Income." *Quarterly Journal of Economics* 80, 361–375.

Hansson, I., and Ch. Stuart. (1985). "The Taxation of Income from Capital. A Comparative Study of the United States, the United Kingdom, Sweden, and West Germany." review article, *Journal of Political Economy* 93, 826–831.

Harberger, A. C. (1962). "The Incidence of the Corporation Income Tax." *Journal of Political Economy* 70, 215–240.

Harberger, A. C. (1966). "Efficiency Effects of Taxes on Income from Capital." In M. Krzyzaniak, ed., *Effects of Corporation Income Tax*. Detroit: Wayne State University Press.

Howitt, P., and H.-W. Sinn. (1989). "Gradual Reform of Capital Income Taxation." *American Economic Review* 79, 106–124.

Jun, J. (1989). "Tax Policy and International Direct Investment." National Bureau of Economic Research, working paper No. 3048.

Kemp, M. C. (1962). "Foreign Direct Investment and National Advantage." *Economic Record* 38, 56–62.

Kemp, M. C. (1964). *The Pure Theory of International Trade*. Englewood Cliffs, NJ: Prentice Hall.

King, M. A. (1974a). "Taxation and the Cost of Capital." *Review of Economic Studies* 41, 21–35.

King, M. A. (1974b). "Dividend Behaviour and the Theory of the Firm." *Economica* 41, 25–34.

King, M. A. (1977). *Public Policy and the Corporation*. London: Chapman and Hall; New York: Wiley.

MacDougall, G. D. A. (1960). "The Benefits and Costs of Private Investment from Abroad: A Theoretical Approach." *Oxford Bulletin of Economics and Statistics* 22, 189–211.

McLure, Ch. E. (1979). *Must Corporate Income Be Taxed Twice?* Washington D.C.: Brookings Institution.

Meade Committee (1978). *The Structure and Reform of Direct Taxation*. Report of a committee chaired by J. E. Meade, The Institute for Fiscal Studies, London: Allen & Unwin Ltd.

Miller, M. H. (1977). "Debt and Taxes." *Journal of Finance* 32, 261–275.

Oberhauser, A. (1963). *Finanzpolitik und private Vermögensbildung*. Köln: Westdeutscher Verlag.

Poterba, J. M. (1987). "Tax Policy and Corporate Saving." *Brookings Papers on Economic Activity*, 455–515.

Poterba, J. M., and L. H. Summers. (1985). "The Economic Effects of Dividend Taxation." In E. Altman and M. Subrahmanyam, eds., *Recent Advance in Corporate Finance*. Homewood, IL: Irwin.

Scherer, F. M., and D. Ravenscraft. (1984). "Growth by Diversification: Entrepreneurial Behavior in Large-scale United States Enterprises." *Zeitschrift für Nationalökonomie*, Supplement 4 (Schumpeter conference, Bonn 1983), 199–218.

Shoven, J. B. (1986). "New Developments in Corporate Finance and Tax Avoidance: Some Evidence." National Bureau of Economic Research, working paper No. 2091.

Sinn, H.-W. (1985). *Kapitaleinkommensbesteuerung*. Tübingen: Mohr. English edition: *Capital Income Taxation and Resource Allocation.* Amsterdam, New York: North Holland, 1987.

Sinn, H.-W. (1987). "Do Firms Maximize their Cost of Finance." University of Munich, discussion paper No. 87-14.

Sinn, H.-W. (1988a). "The 1986 U.S. Tax Reform and the World Capital Market." *European Economic Review* 32, 325–333.

Sinn, H.-W. (1988b). "The Vanishing Harberger Triangle." University of Munich, discussion paper No. 88-05, and National Bureau of Economic Research, working paper No. 3225, 1989. Forthcoming in *Journal of Public Economics.*

Sinn, H.-W. (1989). "The Policy of Tax-Cut-cum-Case-Broadening: Implications for International Capital Movements." In M. Neumann and K. Roskamp, eds., *Public Finance and Performance of Enterprises.* Proceedings of the 43rd Congress of the International Institute of Public Finance, Paris, 1987, Detroit: Wayne State University Press.

Sinn, H.-W. (1990). "Taxation and the Birth of Foreign Subsidiaries." University of Munich, discussion paper No. 90-30, and National Bureau of Economic Research, working paper No. 3519, 1990.

Stiglitz, J. E. (1973). "Taxation, Corporate Financial Policy, and the Cost of Capital." *Journal of Public Economics* 2, 1–34.

U.S. Department of the Treasury (1984). *Tax Reforms for Fairness, Simplicity, and Economic Growth.* Washington, D.C.: U.S. Government Printing Office.

GENERATIONAL ACCOUNTS: A MEANINGFUL ALTERNATIVE TO DEFICIT ACCOUNTING

Alan J. Auerbach
University of Pennsylvania and NBER

Jagadeesh Gokhale
The Federal Reserve Bank of Cleveland

Laurence J. Kotlikoff
Boston University and NBER

EXECUTIVE SUMMARY

This paper presents a set of generational accounts that can be used to assess the fiscal burden current generations are placing on future generations. The generational accounts indicate, in present value, the net amount that current and future generations are projected to pay to the government now and in the future. These accounts can be understood in terms of the government's intertemporal (long-run) budget constraint.

We thank Jinyong Cai, Ritu Nayyar, and Bash Hardeo for excellent research assistance and Albert Ando, David Bradford, Bill Gavin, and Mark Sniderman for very helpful comments. We are particularly grateful to Jane Gravelle for providing a variety of critical data and for numerous lengthy and extremely useful discussions. We thank The National Institute of Aging and The National Bureau of Economic Research for research support.

This constraint requires that the sum of generational accounts of all current and future generations plus existing government net wealth be sufficient to finance the present value of current and future government consumption.

The generational accounting system represents an alternative to using the federal budget deficit to gauge intergenerational policy. From a theoretical perspective, the measured deficit need bear no relationship to the underlying intergenerational stance of fiscal policy. Indeed, from a theoretical perspective the measured deficit simply reflects economically arbitrary labeling of government receipts and payments.

Within the range of reasonable growth and interest rate assumptions the difference between age zero and future generations in generational accounts ranges from 17 to 24%. This means that if the fiscal burden on current generations is not increased relative to that projected from current policy (ignoring the just enacted federal budget deal) and if future generations are treated equally (except for an adjustment for growth) the fiscal burden facing all future generations over their lifetimes will be 17 to 24% larger than that facing newborns in 1989. The just enacted budget will, if it sticks, significantly reduce the fiscal burden on future generations.

The calculations of generational accounts reported here are based solely on NIPA government receipts and expenditures, and reflect the age pattern of government receipts and payments as well as the projected substantial aging of the U.S. population.

I. INTRODUCTION

The federal deficit is widely viewed as the United States' number one economic problem. Yet there is no consensus as to how to measure the deficit. Some want to exclude the current social security surplus, others want to include the full value of the S&L bail out, and others are concerned about adjustments for unfunded government retirement liabilities, inflation, growth, and government acquisition and sale of assets. The debate has not been restricted to politicians. Economists have played a major role in lobbying for their favorite definitions of the deficit (e.g., Feldstein, 1974; Eisner and Pieper, 1984).

Of course, a lot is at stake in how one measures the deficit. Given current policy, leaving out social security surpluses means whopping deficits through the 1990s, while adjusting for inflation and growth almost turns the officially defined deficit into a surplus. As the underlying credo of fiscal policy is to cut spending or raise taxes to make the deficit zero, the attention given to how to define the deficit is not surprising.

The goal of setting the deficit to zero seems quite strange in light of our uncertainty about how the deficit should be measured. If we are not sure what the deficit is, how can we be sure it should be zero? Rather than continue debating the deficit's measurement, perhaps we should first ask what concept the deficit is supposed to measure and then determine a measure consistent with that concept.

The conceptual issue associated with the word "deficit" is the intergenerational distribution of welfare. Specifically, how much are different generations paying to finance government consumption and to subsidize each other? Unfortunately, from the perspective of economic theory, the deficit is an arbitrary accounting construct whose value has no necessary relation to the question of generational burdens. As demonstrated by Kotlikoff (1984, 1988, 1989) and Auerbach and Kotlikoff (1987), from a theoretical perspective the government can run any fiscal policy it chooses while simultaneously reporting any size deficit or surplus. It can do so simply through the choice of how it labels its receipts and payments. For example, the government can (and does) label workers' social security contributions "taxes" and retirees' social security benefits "transfers." Suppose, instead, the government labeled workers' contributions "loans" to the government and retirees' benefits "return of principal and interest" on these "loans" plus an additional "old age tax" equal to the difference between benefits and the "return of principal plus interest" on the "loans." In this case the reported deficit would be entirely different not only with respect to its level, but also with respect to its changes over time.[1] This is not an isolated example; every dollar the government takes in or pays out is labeled in a manner that is economically arbitrary.

If the deficit has no intrinsic relation to generational policy, what measure does? The answer according to economic theory is what we term generational accounts. These are accounts—one for each generation—that tally up, in present value, the amount of receipts less payments the government can expect to collect from each generation over its remaining life span. These generational accounts are comprehensive in that they consider all receipts and payments collected from or paid to all federal, state, and local governments. In contrast to the deficit, generational accounts are invariant to changes in accounting labels. This may be seen, for example, by considering the alternative labeling of social security just discussed. For each generation the present value of its social security "tax" contributions less its receipts of "transfers"

---

[1] *The Economic Report of the President 1982*—Appendix to Chapter 4 reports both the conventional deficit and the deficit that arises from defining social security contributions as "loans" to the government.

consisting of social security benefits is identically equal to the present value of its "old age tax."

The generational accounts are discussed in the context of the government's intertemporal budget constraint, which states that the government's current net wealth plus the present value of the government's net receipts from all current and future generations (the generational accounts) must be sufficient to pay for the present value of the government's current and future consumption. By comparing what the government is projected to take from current generations with the difference between its projected consumption expenditures and its current net wealth, one can estimate the amount that future generations will need to pay. Hence, the generational account approach indicates directly the burden on future generations imposed by increases in expenditures on existing generations, including existing elderly generations. This "zero sum" feature of the government's intertemporal budget constraint (some generation has to pay for any benefit to another generation) imposes a useful discipline on fiscal analysis. If the government were to adopt the accounting framework developed in this study, it would be required to specify the costs to be borne by future generations for programs that help existing generations, and vice versa.

The generational accounts can also be used to assess the effects on national saving of programs to redistribute more or less to current generations. For example, a decision to lower Medicare benefits means an increase in the expected present value of net payments to the government by the existing elderly. The change in the present value accounts of each elderly generation due to this policy represents the change in their lifetime resources. Using recent generation-specific estimates of the propensity to consume out of lifetime resources developed by Abel, Bernheim, and Kotlikoff (1991), one can consider the effect on national consumption and national saving of such policy changes.

The primary sources of data used in this study are the Bureau of the Census' Survey of Income and Program Participation (SIPP), the Social Security Administration's population projections, the Bureau of Labor Statistics Consumer Expenditure Surveys (from 1980 onward), and the National Income and Products Accounts reported in the July 1990 *Survey of Current Business*.

The findings of this paper suggest a larger fiscal burden—17 to 24% larger—on future generations than the burden to be imposed on 1989 newborns under current policy (ignoring the recently enacted federal budget deal). These figures are adjusted for growth, i.e., the increase is 17 to 24% *above* the increase in fiscal burden that would accompany trend growth. The assessment that future generations face 17 to 24% higher net taxes over the course of their lifetimes suggests a significant generational problem. The recently enacted federal budget deal will, if it is not subverted, substantially reduce, if not eliminate the additional burden that would otherwise be imposed on future generations.

The paper continues in Section II with a more precise description both of generational accounts and their relationship to the government's intertemporal budget constraint. Section III describes how one can use the generational accounts to assess the generational stance of fiscal policy. Section IV considers the relationship of each generation's account to its own lifetime budget constraint. Section V provides a detailed description of the data sources and methodology used in calculating the generational accounts. Section VI presents our findings, including our policy simulations. Our findings should be viewed as preliminary because there are a number of aspects of our calculations that can be improved with the additional data that we are in the process of procuring. We simulate (1) the President's proposed capital gains tax cut, (2) eliminating the 1983 social security benefit cuts scheduled to go into effect around the turn of this century, (3) growth in Medicare spending in excess of the economy-wide growth rate, (4) the impact of the $500 billion S&L bailout, (5) slower growth in government consumption spending, and (6) the budget deal just enacted by Congress and signed by the President. Finally, Section VII summarizes our findings and draws conclusions.

II. GENERATIONAL ACCOUNTS

The term "generations" refers in this paper to males and females by specific years of age. The term "net payments" refers to the difference between government tax receipts of all types (such as federal and state income taxes) and government transfer payments of all types (such as social security benefits, unemployment benefits, and food stamps). Finally, all present values reflect discounting at a pretax interest rate.

To make the generational accounts and their relationship to the government's budget constraint more precise, we write the government's intertemporal budget constraint for year t in equation (1):

$$\sum_{s=0}^{D} N_{t,t-s} + \sum_{s=1}^{\infty} N_{t,t+s} + W_t^g = \sum_{s=t}^{\infty} G_s \prod_{j=1}^{s} \frac{1}{(1+r_j)} \qquad (1)$$

The first term on the left hand side of (1) adds together the present value of the net payments of existing generations. The expression $N_{t,k}$ stands for the present value of net remaining lifetime payments to the government of the generation born in year k discounted to year t. The index s in this summation runs from age 0 to age D, the maximum length of life. Hence, the first element of this summation is $N_{t,t}$, which is the present value of net payments of the generation born in year t; the last term is $N_{t,t-D}$, the present value of remaining net payments of the oldest generation alive in year t, namely those born in year $t-D$. The second term on the left hand side of (1) adds together the present value of remaining net payments of future generations. The third term on the left-hand side, W_t^g, denotes the government's net wealth in year t. The right-hand side of (1) expresses the present value of government consumption. In the latter expression, G_s stands for government consumption expenditure in year s, and r_j stands for the pretax rate of return in year j.

Equation (1) indicates the zero sum nature of intergenerational fiscal policy. Holding the right-hand side of equation (1) fixed, increased (decreased) government payments to (receipts taken from) existing generations means a decrease in the first term on the left-hand side of (1) and requires an offsetting increase in the second term on the left-hand side of (1), i.e., it requires reduced payments to or increased payments from future generations.

The term $N_{t,k}$ is defined in equation (2):

$$N_{t,k} = \sum_{s=\max(t,k)}^{k+D} \tilde{T}_{s,k} P_{s,k} \prod_{j=t+1}^{s} \frac{1}{1+r_j} \qquad (2)$$

In expression (2) $\tilde{T}_{s,k}$ stands for the projected average net payment to the government made in year s by a member of the generation born in year k. By a generation's average net payment in year s we mean the average across all members of the generation alive in year s of payments made, such as income and FICA taxes, less all transfers received, such as social security, AFDC, and unemployment insurance. The term $P_{s,k}$ stands for the number of surviving members of the cohort in year s who were born in year k. For generations who are born prior to year t, the summation begins in year t. For generations who are born in year k, where $k>t$, the summation begins in year k. Regardless of the generation's year of birth, the discounting is always back to year t.

A set of generational accounts is simply a set of values of $N_{t,k}$, one for each existing and future generation, with the property that the combined total value adds up to the right-hand side of equation (1). In our calculation of the $N_{t,k}$s for existing generations (those whose $k \leq 1989$) we distinguish male from female cohorts, but, to ease notation, we do not append sex subscripts to the terms in (1) and (2).

III. ASSESSING THE INTERGENERATIONAL STANCE OF FISCAL POLICY

Once we have calculated the right-hand side of equation (1) and the first term on the left-hand side of equation (1), we determine, as a residual, the value of the second term on the right-hand side of equation (1), which is the present value of payments required of future generations. We further determine the amount that needs to be taken from each successive generation to balance the government's intertemporal budget, assuming that each successive generation's payment is the same up to an adjustment for real productivity growth.

This growth-adjusted constant amount is what must be taken from successive generations to maintain what Kotlikoff (1989) terms "fiscal balance"; one can compare this measure with the actual amount projected to be taken under current policy from existing generations, particularly the generation that has just been born. In other words, these data provide the answer to the question: Given the projected treatment of current generations as reflected in the values of their $N_{t,k}$s, do we need to take substantially more from future generations than we are planning (as reflected by current policy) to take from current generations? In particular, is $N_{t,t}$ substantially smaller than $N_{t,t+1}$ under the assumption that all values of $N_{t,s}$ for $s>t+1$ equal $N_{t,t+1}$ except for an adjustment for productivity growth?[2]

Note that our assumption that all values of $N_{t,s}$ for $s>t+1$ are equal, except for a growth adjustment, is just one of many assumptions one could make about the distribution across future generations of their collective net payment to the government. We could, for example, assume a phase-in of the additional fiscal burden (which could be negative) to be imposed on new young generations. Clearly, such a phase-in would mean that new young generations born after the phase-in period has elapsed would face a larger (possibly smaller) $N_{t,s}$ than we are calculating here. Our purpose in assuming (1) growth-adjusted equal treatment of future generations and (2) that the $N_{t,s}$s of current generations are those one would project under current policy is to illustrate the potential intergenerational imbalance in fiscal policy and the potential

---

[2] Our question is related to that posed in recent empirical studies (e.g., Hamilton and Flavin, 1986, and Wilcox, 1989), which asks whether government debt will explode given current policy. However, we address the question of intertemporal government budget balance in a different, and, in our view, more satisfactory manner.

need for adjusting current fiscal policy. It is not to claim that policy will necessarily deal with the intergenerational imbalance by treating all future generations equally or, indeed, by putting all the burden on future generations.

Understanding the size of the $N_{t,k}$s for current generations and their likely magnitude for future generations is not the end of the story with respect to assessing the intergenerational stance or incidence of fiscal policy. As studied in Auerbach and Kotlikoff (1987), intergenerational redistribution will alter the time path of factor prices and, thereby, the intergenerational distribution of welfare. Such changes in factor prices result from changes in the supply of capital relative to labor. But the changes in the supplies of capital and labor can, in turn, be traced back to changes in consumption and labor supply decisions, which are based on private lifetime budget constraints. As described in the next section, the $N_{t,k}$s enter private budget constraints. Hence, knowing how their values change is essential not only for understanding the direct effect of government policy on the intergenerational welfare distribution, but also for assessing the changes in factor prices that may result from the policy. In short, then, understanding fully the incidence of intergenerational fiscal policy requires knowledge of changes in the values of the $N_{t,k}$s arising from the policy.

Indeed, one of the future goals of this research is to consider how policies other than those examined here might affect the values of the $N_{t,k}$s for the elderly and other existing generations and to assess the impact of such policies on national saving. In a recent study Abel, Bernheim, and Kotlikoff (1990) used CES data to calculate average and marginal propensities to consume of U.S. households by the age of the household head. We intend to use these results to determine the U.S. consumption response to a range of potential intergenerational fiscal policies. A generation's consumption response to the hypothetical policies will simply be calculated as the change in the generation's $N_{t,k}$ multiplied by the corresponding marginal propensity to consume.

IV. HOW DO THE $N_{t,k}$s ENTER PRIVATE BUDGET CONSTRAINTS?

The lifetime budget constraint of each generation specifies that the present value of its consumption must equal its current net wealth, plus the present value of its human wealth, plus the present value of its net private intergenerational transfers, less the present value of its net payments to the government, its $N_{t,k}$. This section shows precisely how the

$N_{t,k}$s enter private budget constraints and how we can use our estimates on the $N_{t,k}$s and additional information to infer the extent of net private intergenerational transfers.

For the generation born in year k the year t remaining lifetime budget constraint is

$$\sum_{s=t}^{k+D} [\bar{C}_{s,k} + \bar{I}_{s,k}] P_{s,k} \prod_{j=t+1}^{s} \frac{1}{1+r_j} = W_{t,k}^p + \sum_{s=t}^{k+D} \bar{E}_{s,k} P_{s,k} \prod_{j=t+1}^{s} \frac{1}{1+r_j} - N_{t,k} \quad (3)$$

In (3) the terms $\bar{C}_{s,k}$, $\bar{I}_{s,k}$, and $\bar{E}_{s,k}$ stand, respectively, for the average values in year s of consumption, private net intergenerational transfers, and labor earnings of the generation born in year k. The term $W_{t,k}^p$ stands for the year t net wealth of the generation born in year k. This equation states that the present value of the cohort's projected consumption plus its net intergenerational transfers equals the present value of its resources. The present value of its resources equals, in turn, its net wealth, plus the present value of its labor earnings, less the present value of its net payments to the government, $N_{t,k}$. There are data available to estimate the present value of a cohort's consumption, the present value of its labor earnings, and its current net worth. Hence, in future work we intend to compare our estimates of $N_{t,k}$ with the projected present value of the cohort's remaining lifetime resources. We will also use these data and equation (3) to derive, as a residual, an estimate of the projected present value of the cohort's net private intergenerational transfers.

As mentioned, in our actual calculations we distinguish generations by sex as well as age in 1990. Our calculated age and sex-specific values for the present value of intergenerational transfers include, therefore, intragenerational transfers from males to females. Hence, in determining the magnitude of transfers that are truly intergenerational (across age groups) we add together the calculated private transfers of male and female generations of the same age. This provides us with a statement of the net present value of private transfers given by (received from) all members (both the males and the females) of a given generation to members of other generations.

In the previous section we discussed comparing the $N_{t,k}$s of future generations with $N_{t,t}$, which is the net lifetime payments of the generation that was born at time t. We also discussed comparing the $N_{t,k}$s of all existing generations under current policy with their respective values under a different policy. These comparisons, which involve differences (either across generations or across policies) in $N_{t,k}$s, are invariant to the accounting framework we are adopting, although the absolute values of the $N_{t,k}$s depend on our accounting framework.

To see this point, consider once again the labeling of social security receipts and payments. Although the U.S. government labels social security contributions as "taxes" and social security benefits as "transfers," from the perspective of economic theory one could equally well label social security contributions as "private saving" (invested in government bonds) and label social security benefits as the "return of principal plus interest" on that saving, less an "old age tax" that would be positive or negative depending on whether the social security system was less than or more than actuarially fair in present value. Under either choice of labels the right-hand side of the budget constraint (3) would retain the same value, but the division of the right-hand side between W_t^p and $N_{k,t}$ would change. It is in this sense that the absolute value of the $N_{k,t}$s depends on the accounting framework. However, regardless of which way one accounts for (labels) the social security system, the *change* in the value of $N_{t,k}$ from a policy change, such as a reduction in social security benefits, would be the same. Under the conventional labeling the change in the value of the $N_{t,k}$s would simply equal the reduction for generation k in the time t present value of their receipts from social security. Under the "private saving less an old age tax" labeling, the change in the value of the $N_{t,k}$s would simply equal the increase for generation k in the time t present value of their old age tax.

Although the change in the value of the $N_{t,k}$s associated with a policy change is invariant to the accounting convention (the choice of labels for government receipts and payments), the same is not true for the government's budget deficit. The same change in policy will lead to different changes in the reported budget deficit depending on one's choice of labels for government receipts and payments. For example, consider the impact of a equal reduction in social security contributions and benefit payments under the two labeling schemes for social security. In the case social security contributions are labeled "taxes" and social security benefits are labeled "transfers," this policy change will have no effect on the budget deficit, since the change in "taxes" equals the change in "transfer" spending. In contrast, if social security contributions are labeled "private saving" and social security benefits are labeled "return of principal plus interest" plus "an old age tax," an equal and simultaneous reduction in contributions and benefit payments will mean a larger "old age tax" for elderly recipients and imply a reduction in the budget deficit.

V. CALCULATING THE $N_{t,k}$s AND OTHER COMPONENTS OF THE GOVERNMENT AND EACH GENERATION'S INTERTEMPORAL BUDGET CONSTRAINTS

A. Data Sources for Calculating Net Payments

According to equation (2) estimating the values of the $N_{t,k}$s requires projections of net payments, the $\bar{T}_{s,k}$s for $D+k \geq s \geq k$, population projections, the $P_{s,k}$s for $D+k \geq s \geq k$, and the time path of interest rates. Projections of the population by age and sex are available from the Social Security Administration through 2050, and we have extrapolated these projections through the year 2100 in the course of a study of demographics and saving (Auerbach, Cai, and Kotlikoff, 1990).

We use SIPP data to calculate the average 1984 year values by age and sex of each of the different types of government receipts and payments covered in SIPP. The SIPP sample size is roughly 16,000 U.S. households. The SIPP is a panel survey that reinterviewed respondent households eight times (every 4 months) over the course of 2 years. The first wave of interviews began in July 1983 and ended in July 1985. Thus, for 1984, there is a complete calendar year of SIPP data. The government receipts and payments in the SIPP survey include federal and state income and FICA taxes, Food Stamps, AFDC and WIC benefits, Supplemental Security Income, general relief, unemployment compensation, Social Security retirement, survivor and disability benefits, other welfare, Foster Child Care, and other government transfers. Denton Vaughan (1989) provides a detailed analysis of the improvements in the measurement of government receipts and payments in the SIPP as compared with other surveys such as The Current Population Survey.

The major deficiency with respect to SIPP's coverage of government receipts and payments is with respect to Medicaid and Medicare health care payments. To determine the average amount of Medicare payments by age (the data are not available by sex) for Medicare payments we use Waldo, Sonnefeld, and McKusick's (1989) calculations of average Medicare expenditures by age.

Data on Medicaid expenditures by age and sex will ultimately be obtained from the National Center for Health Services Research's National Medical Care Expenditure Survey for 1987. These data are scheduled to be released later this year. At the moment, however, we assume that the distribution of Medicaid expenditures by age and sex is the same as that of general welfare payments.

B. Determining Net Payments

The average values of the receipts and payments by age and sex calculated from SIPP and the Medicare data are only used to determine the values of these receipts and payments by age and sex relative to that of a base age–sex category, which we take to be 40-year-old males. Given these age–sex relative profiles we determine our initial year (1990) average values of each type of payment and receipt by age and sex by benchmarking against aggregate totals reported in the National Income and Product Account's aggregate values of government receipts and transfers. We then assume that the age and sex-specific average values of these payments and receipts in future years equal those calculated for 1990 adjusted for an assumed growth rate.

To provide an example of this procedure in a simple two-period context where there are only young and old, suppose total receipts of a certain type at a given date equals $1000 and suppose we know that the average payment of old people equals twice the average for the young. Also suppose we know that there are 200 young and 150 old. Then the amount paid by each young person Z must satisfy: $1000 = Z \times 200 + Z \times 2 \times 150$. Solving this equation for Z and multiplying by 2 gives the amount paid on average by old people. If the growth rate is g, then the projected payment of the young (old) k periods from now is $Z \times (1+g)^k$ [$2 \times Z \times (1+g)^k$].

More generally, we denote by $R^m_{a,i}$ ($R^f_{a,i}$) average value of the ith payment or receipt made by (received by) an age a male (female) in 1984 divided by the average value of the type i payment (receipt) made by 40-year-old males in 1984. Let $H_{i,t}$ denote the aggregate revenues (expenditures) of type i received by (made by) the government in year t (1990). Finally, let $\bar{h}^m_{a,i,t}$ and $\bar{h}^f_{a,i,t}$ denote, respectively, the average values for males and females of payment (receipt) i in year t. Then we have

$$H_{it} = \bar{h}^m_{40,i,t} \sum_{j=0}^{D} [R^m_{j,i} P^m_{t,t-j} + R^f_{j,i} P^f_{t,t-j}] \tag{4}$$

Equation (4) states that total payments (receipts) of type i in year t equals the average value of these payments (receipts) for 40-year-old males times the cross-product of the age–sex profile for payment (receipt) i and the population by age and sex. We use equation (4) to solve for $\bar{h}^m_{40,i,t}$. The values of the $\bar{h}^m_{a,i,t}$s $a \neq 40$ and the $\bar{h}^f_{a,i,t}$s are obtained by multiplying $\bar{h}^m_{40,i,t}$ by $R^m_{a,i}$ and $R^f_{a,i}$, respectively. We assume that $\bar{h}^m_{a,i,s}$ and $\bar{h}^f_{a,i,s}$ for $s>t$ equal their respective year t values multiplied by an assumed growth factor.

The term $\bar{T}_{s,k}$ for males (for females) in equation (2) is determined by summing over i the values of $\bar{h}^m_{s-k,i,s}$ ($\bar{h}^f_{s-k,i,s}$).

Clearly for certain types of payments and receipts, such as Medicare benefits, the choice of the proper growth factor may be particularly difficult. But rather than choose one value, we present results for different growth rate assumptions. The same type of sensitivity analysis applies to the choice of the interest rate to be used in the discounting. Although the absolute magnitude of the terms in the government's intertemporal budget constraint are sensitive to these assumptions, the assessment of the burden being placed on future generations *relative* to that being placed on current generations happens not to be very sensitive to these assumptions.

C. The Treatment of Labor Income Taxes

We determine the relative profile of total labor income by age and sex from the SIPP data and apply this profile to aggregate labor income taxes. The aggregate value of labor income tax payments is calculated as 80.4% of total federal, state, and local income taxes, where 80.4 is labor's share of net national product. In calculating labor's share of net national product we assume that labor's share of proprietorship and partnership income as well as its share of indirect tax payments equals its share of net national product. The resulting figure for aggregate labor income taxes is $446.1 billion.

D. The Treatment of Contributions for Social Insurance

We used information on labor earnings in the SIPP to infer the amount of FICA taxes paid by each household member. From these data we then determined the relative profile of FICA tax payments by age and sex. This profile was benchmarked against aggregate social insurance contributions, including contributions by government workers to their pension funds. The 1989 value of aggregate contributions for social insurance is $476.8 billion.

E. The Treatment of Capital Income Taxes

Taxes on capital income require special treatment. There are two related reasons for this. First, unlike other taxes, taxes on capital income may be capitalized into the value of existing (old) assets. Second, the time pattern of income and tax payments may differ. As a result of these features of capital income taxes, such taxes must be attributed with care to ensure that they are assigned to the proper generation. If all forms of capital income were taxed at the same rate, there would be no such problem: all assets would yield the same rate of return before tax (adjusted for risk) and each individual would face a rate of return reduced by the full extent of the tax. However, if tax rates on the income from some assets, typically older ones, are higher than those facing income from new assets (e.g., because of investment incentives targeted toward new investment) a simple arbitrage argument (see, for example, Auerbach and Kotlikoff, 1987, Chapter 9) indicates that the extra tax burden on the old assets should be capitalized into these assets' values, reflecting their less favorable treatment. This suggests that the flow of capital income taxes overstates the burden on new investment. On the other hand, the presence of accelerated depreciation allowances works in the opposite direction, since initial tax payments from new investment understate the long-run tax burden on such investments. Although current tax payments overstate the tax burden on new capital by their inclusion of taxes that are already capitalized in the value of existing assets, the understatement of the burden on new investment works in the opposite direction.

We require a method that calculates the value of capitalized taxes and corrects the flow of taxes for these two measurement problems. The appendix provides such a method. To illustrate the nature of the correction, consider the case of cash-flow taxation in which assets are written off immediately. A well-known result is that the effective marginal capital income tax rate under cash-flow taxation is zero. However, taxes would be collected each year on existing capital assets, and such assets should therefore be valued at a discount. Assigning these taxes to the assets' initial owners, rather than members of future generations who may purchase the assets, is consistent with the fact that such future generations of individuals may freely invest in new assets and pay a zero rate of tax on the resulting income. Our correction to actual tax payments should, in this case, result in a zero tax burden on the income from new assets.

The principle underlying our treatment of intramarginal capital income taxes and the discounting of other payments and receipts at pretax rates of return is that one can express private intertemporal budget constraints in the presence of government behavior as (1) the budget constraint that would prevail in the absence of the government with (2) a single modification to the present value of resources that equals, $N_{t,k}$, the present value of the generation's net payment to the government, i.e., one can express private budgets in terms of pretax prices less net taxes valued at pretax prices. In the case of our adjustment for intramarginal capital income taxes we are simply valuing capital at its pretax price and treating the capitalized value of taxes as another payment required by the government from the owners of that capital.

In allocating capital income taxes we (1) correct our estimate of future capital income taxes to account for their inclusion of taxes on old capital and the generational timing of capital income taxes, (2) use equation (4) and the SIPP profile of private net wealth holdings by age and sex to allocate total 1989 taxes on new capital by age and sex, (3) project future capital income taxes by age and sex using the 1989 age- and sex-specific values adjusted for growth, and (4) allocate to 1989 owners of capital as a one time tax payment the 1989 capitalized value of the excess taxation of older capital. The allocation of this one time tax by age and sex is based on the SIPP profile of asset holdings by age and sex. Note that in the budget constraint of each existing generation we value their holdings of existing capital at market value plus the capitalized value of intramarginal taxes.

In these calculations we set aggregate capital income taxes equal to 19.6% (capital's share of net national product) of total federal, state, and local income taxes, plus federal, state, and local corporate taxes (excluding the profits of the U.S. Federal Reserve System), plus estate taxes. The resulting value of 1989 aggregate capital income taxes is $234.9 billion. Using the method described in the Appendix, we estimate that the 1989 flow of capital income taxes overstated the capital income tax burden on new investment by $6.09 billion and that the capitalized value of excess taxes on old capital equals $609 billion. These estimates are calculated in the following manner. We take the value of nonresidential equipment plus structures plus the value of nonowner occupied housing owned by taxable investors (both of which are reported in the Federal Reserve Flow of Funds for 1989), $5,488.8 trillion, and multiply this by 11.1%, our estimate of the tax-induced percentage difference between the market value and replacement cost of these assets. We allocate the $609 billion ($5,488.8 × .111) in capitalized taxes as a one time tax to those age- and sex-specific 1989 cohorts according to the SIPP profile of relative net wealth holdings by age and sex.

F. Including the Present Value of Government Seignorage in the $N_{t,k}$s

Another form of payment to the government is the seignorage it collects on private holdings of money balances. Net of the negligible costs of printing money, the government collects, in each year, resources equal to the real value of new money printed. In holding this money, households forego the nominal rate of return available on other assets.

Our strategy for attributing seignorage to different generations may be illustrated using the analogy of an excise tax on durable goods. Suppose the government levied such an excise tax. Households would then spend more to obtain durables, and would therefore face a higher imputed cost of using them until the durables had depreciated or were sold. If the durable good were sold (tax free) in the future, it would command a price in excess of its replacement cost, reflecting the arbitrage with respect to new durables facing the excise tax. A measure of the net fiscal burden imposed on the household by the excise tax is the tax payment made by the household on purchase less this recoupment of the tax upon sale, discounted to the present. In the same way, we attribute the burden of seignorage to households of particular generations by treating the entire acquisition of money balances as a payment to the government and the disposition of money balances as a transfer from the government. This has the effect of imputing a cost equal to the nominal interest rate on the holding of money balances, and also attributes to all current and future generations taken together a total fiscal burden equal to the present value of government receipts from printing money.

We add the present value of such seignorage payments to the present value of other net payments in forming the $N_{t,k}$s. Specifically, we project average money balances held by each age- and sex-specific generation through the remainder of its life and add each year's net acquisitions (positive or negative) of the monetary base to the $N_{t,k}$s. As with all our calculations, we have been careful to benchmark against national aggregates. In this case we have ensured that the sum of age- and sex-specific generation net acquisitions of the monetary base sums to the December 1988 to December 1989 change in aggregate base money, which equals $21.6 billion.

G. Including Excise Taxes in the $N_{t,k}$s

Excise tax payments are not included in the SIPP data. To determine the amount of excise taxes paid by the age- and sex-specific generations we use the CES data. We use these calculations as well to project each generation's annual flow and present value of excise taxes. Our benchmark value of aggregate 1989 excise taxes of $414.0 billion equals the 1989 NIPA value of total excise taxes, less total property taxes, plus business property taxes, i.e., we include in excise taxes only those property taxes assessed on business. We use the Department of Commerce's (1987) share of business property tax assessments in total (business plus residential) property tax assessments to divide total property taxes between business and residences. This share is 43.9%. In determining the 1989 NIPA value of total excise taxes we include those state and local property and excise taxes listed in the NIPA accounts as "Personal Tax and Nontax Receipts." We do not, however, include those nontax receipts that are included as part of "Personal Tax and Nontax Receipts" as excise taxes. Instead, we treat these items, which include tuition and hospital charges, as a return to government assets.

H. Including Residential Property Taxes in the $N_{t,k}s$

We treat residential property taxes as excise taxes on home ownership and allocate these taxes by age and sex using an age–sex profile of relative house values. This profile was obtained from the SIPP data for 1984. In this calculation house values for married couples were divided evenly between the spouses. As in the case of other taxes, we benchmark average property taxes by age and sex using the 1989 value of total residential property taxes, which equals $62.4 billion, and we project future average property tax payments using the 1989 age- and sex-specific averages with an adjustment for growth.

I. Treatment of Social Security and Other Government Transfers

We divide total government transfer payments excluding federal, state, and local civil service, railroad retirement, and veterans benefits into six categories: OASDI (including Federal Supplementary Security Income), HI (Medicare), AFDC, General Welfare (including Medicare), UI (unemployment insurance), and Food Stamps (including WIC). We use the SIPP data to determine relative profiles by age and sex of each of these categories of government transfers. To determine average 1989 values of these transfer payments by age and sex we benchmark the relative profiles against the NIPA aggregates using equation (4). The absolute average values of each type of transfer payment by age and sex in future years are assumed to equal their respective 1989 values adjusted for growth. The one exception to this procedure is with respect to future social security benefits. We make a rough adjustment for the impact for the 1983 Social Security amendments on future benefits of the baby boom and subsequent generations. These amendments reduced future social security benefits by (1) phasing in a 2-year delay in the receipt of normal retirement and (2) subjecting an increasing share of social security benefits to federal income taxation. Our adjustment involves reducing the average social security benefits of each new cohort that reaches age 65 in the year 2000 and beyond. The reduction in each year's post-age 65 benefits is 1% for cohorts who are age 65 in the year 2000. It is 2% for cohorts who are age 65 in 2001, 3% for cohorts who are age 65 in 2002, etc., with a maximum reduction of 15%, i.e., cohorts who reach age 65 in 2014 or later experience a 15% reduction in the average annual value of their post-age 64 social security benefits relative to the growth adjusted value of post-age 64 social security benefits prevailing in 1989.

J. Calculating the Present Value of Government Consumption

Our procedure for projecting the future path of total government consumption is to decompose total 1990 government consumption expenditure into (1) expenditures on those age 0–24, 25–64, and 65+ and (2) non-age-specific expenditures, such as defense.[3] We denote year t expenditures on those age 0 to 24 divided by the year t population age 0 to 64 as $\bar{g}_{y,t}$, where y stands for young. We denote $\bar{g}_{m,t}$ and $\bar{g}_{o,t}$ as the corresponding year t average government consumption expenditures on the middle age (those 25 to 64) and old (those 65 and older). Finally, we denote $\bar{g}_t$ as the year t level of non-age-specific government expenditure divided by the total year t population. We assume that the values of $\bar{g}_{y,s}$, $\bar{g}_{m,s}$, $\bar{g}_{o,s}$, and $\bar{g}_s$ for $s>t$ equal their respective year t values multiplied by a common growth factor. Total government consumption expenditure in year s is then determined as

$$G_s = \bar{g}_{y,s} P_{y,s} + \bar{g}_{m,s} P_{m,s} + \bar{g}_{o,s} P_{o,s} + \bar{g}_s P_s \tag{5}$$

where $P_{y,s}$, $P_{m,s}$, $P_{o,s}$, and P_s stand for the population of young, middle age, old, and the total population in year s. We use the OECD's 1986 division of total U.S. government consumption expenditures among the four expenditure categories plus our benchmark value of aggregate expenditures, G_s, to determine the values of $\bar{g}_{y,t}$, $\bar{g}_{m,t}$, $\bar{g}_{o,t}$, and $\bar{g}_t$. The OECD's division of U.S. government consumption expenditures was 29.1% on the young (age 0–24), 6.0% on the middle age (age 25–64), 7.1% on the old (65+), and the remaining 57.8% on the total population. Our measure of G_t is the 1989 NIPA value of total government consumption expenditures plus the value of civil service, military, and veterans retirement, medical, and disability benefits. We include these additional payments as part of government consumption rather than as transfer payments because they are part of government compensation

---

[3] The fact that components of government consumption expenditure are targeted toward specific age groups suggests including the present value of such expenditures in forming the $N_{t,k}$s and the $\tilde{C}_{s,k}$s in equation (3). In future work we intend to present the generational accounts both including and excluding the present value of age-specific government consumption spending in forming the $N_{t,k}$s and the $\tilde{C}_{s,k}$s. However, for the economic, as opposed to accounting questions, of how the $N_{t,k}$s of future generations compare with that of the current newborn generation and how changes in policy will change the values of the $N_{t,k}$s for existing generations, the inclusion or exclusion of age-specific government consumption spending on existing generations is irrelevant, i.e., the analysis of the differential incidence of redistributing the burden across generations of paying for the government's consumption can be conducted holding the generational pattern of government consumption expenditures constant.

to its employees. The resulting value for 1989 total government consumption expenditure is $1.154 trillion.

An important issue that arises in considering government as well as private consumption is the treatment of durables. The proper economic treatment involves imputing rent on private and government durables and including this rent (and excluding expenditures on durables) in private and government consumption, respectively. Except for housing, however, the National Income and Product Accounts treats expenditures on durables as current consumption. Although we follow the NIPA treatment of durables in this paper, our future analysis will adjust for the proper economic treatment of private and government durables expenditures.

K. Determining Government Net Wealth

Since we want our generational accounts and analysis of different generations' private budget constraints to be consistent with National Income and Product Account data, including the total (federal, state, and local) government deficit, we take as our measure of 1989 total government net wealth net government interest payments divided by the sum of (1) our assumed real interest rate and (2) an assumed 5% inflation rate.[4] Our measure of government net interest payments is $79.4 billion smaller than the NIPA figure of $131.8 billion because we categorize state and local nontax receipts as positive capital income earned on state and local assets. Assuming a 6% real interest rate the 1989 value of government net wealth is $-$571 billion.

L. Determining Private Sector Wealth

The 1984 SIPP data are used to determine the age- and sex-specific relative wealth profile. Specifically, we calculate the weighted average values of net wealth by age and sex for 1984 and normalize these values by the weighted average value of net wealth of 40-year-old males. This provides values of Q^m_a and Q^f_a, the relative age–sex wealth profile. Total private sector wealth in 1989 can then be written as

$$W^p_t = \overline{q}^m_{40,t} \sum_{j=0}^{D} [Q^m_j P^m_{t,t-j} + Q^f_j P^f_{t,t-j}], \qquad (6)$$

---

[4] In future work in which we will measure imputed rent on government durables we will also take account of government tangible assets using measurements reported by Eisner and Pieper (1984) and Boskin et al. (1987).

where $\bar{q}^m_{40,t}$ stands for the average wealth of a 40-year-old male in year t, and W^p_t is total 1989 private net wealth. Equation (6) may be used to solve for $\bar{q}^m_{40,t}$. The corresponding values of $\bar{q}^m_{a,t}$, $a \neq 40$, and $\bar{q}^f_{a,t}$ are determined by multiplying $\bar{q}^m_{40,t}$ by Q^m_j and Q^f_j, respectively.

In using the SIPP data we distribute household wealth to the owner of that wealth, where the ownership is indicated. In the case of married couples, we allocate half of the household's total wealth to each spouse. We set future values of net wealth by age and sex equal to the 1989 values adjusted for growth.

M. The Choice of Interest Rate

The government budget constraint given in (1) depends crucially on the choice of the interest rate r that is used in discounting future flows to and from the government sector. If all such flows were certain and riskless, it would clearly be appropriate to use the government's borrowing rate, essentially a risk-free rate, in our calculations. Given that these flows are only estimated however, which rate is appropriate to use?

The answer to this question depends on what we mean by fiscal balance in the presence of uncertainty. On the one hand, there is a straightforward argument that the government's actual borrowing rate is still appropriate. Suppose, for example, that a future receipt has an expected value of, say, x, but that the true value of the receipt may turn out to be higher or lower. If it is higher, the government will have to borrow a bit more; if it is less, less borrowing will be required. Assuming that the government's borrowing rate is not affected by these fluctuations, the discounted values will cancel in a calculation of expected discounted revenue, leaving the discounted value of the expected revenue x in the budget constraint. Thus, if we wish to consider the payments from future generations that we expect will be needed to provide fiscal balance, the procedure based on expected flows discounted with the government's borrowing rate is correct.

However, expected fiscal balance may not be the only valid measure, or even the most informative about fiscal incidence. After all, raising a future individual's fiscal burden by $100 in some cases and lowering it by $100 with the same probability in others need not be a matter of indifference to the individual if he is risk averse. If the increased burden is associated with other negative news (as will be true, for example, if government revenue needs rise during recessions), then these deviations from expected revenues will not cancel from the taxpayer's perspective. To reflect this, we might wish to discount future receipts with a higher discount rate that accounts for this risk. The effect will be to raise the level of receipts necessary for fiscal balance to be achieved, reflecting the fact that the burden of uncertain taxes exceeds their expected value. Likewise, the treatment of government spending and transfers should be adjusted for risk, although one should use the same discount rate only if the fluctuations in such spending have the same risk characteristics as taxes do.

In our simulations below, we make different interest rate assumptions in calculating fiscal balance. This will accommodate the alternative views just discussed. The first approach is to apply a low, risk-free rate to the projected flows, in keeping with the view of fiscal balance as expected balance. The second is to apply a market rate, adjusted for risk, in our discounting of all the flows in the government's budget constraint. This approach is consistent with fiscal balance being satisfied in risk-adjusted terms.

VI. FINDINGS

A. The Burden on Future Generations

Tables 1 and 2 contain the generational accounts for males and females for different combinations of growth rate and interest rate assumptions. Tables 1a–c and 2a–c contain the same information for alternative assumptions about population structure, the treatment of capital income taxation and the discount rate, which we will discuss after reviewing the results in the first two tables.

All of these tables show positive values for the accounts for young and middle age cohorts alive in 1989, indicating that these generations will, on balance, pay more in present value than they receive. For generations of males age 65 and older the net present value of payments is negative. This primarily reflects the fact that older generations, whose members are typically retired, can expect to pay relatively little in labor income taxes and payroll taxes over the rest of their lives, while receiving significant social security medicare and retirement benefits. For females, the generational accounts are negative for ages 55 and over. The younger age at which this occurs for women is attributable to the lower labor force participation rates of women and the fact that many women receive social security benefits as dependents of older spouses.

In Tables 1 and 2 the values of the accounts more than double between age zero and age 25. For example, in the case $g=.0075$ and $r=.06$ (which we take as our "base case") the age zero account for males is $73.7 thousand and the age 25 account is $193.0 thousand. This simply reflects the fact that 25 year olds are closer to their peak taxpaying years than are newborns. The accounts are most negative around age 75. For the base case, the age 75 account is $-$$41.5 thousand.

TABLE 1
Accounts for Age Zero and Future Male Generations (thousands of dollars)

Generation's age in 1989	g=0			g=.0075			g=.015		
	r=.05	r=.06	r=.07	r=.05	r=.06	r=.07	r=.05	r=.06	r=.07
0	78.9	57.6	42.8	102.0	73.7	54.1	132.5	94.9	69.0
5	98.8	75.3	58.3	123.4	93.2	71.4	154.9	116.0	88.0
10	122.8	97.5	78.5	148.3	116.8	93.2	180.0	140.7	111.3
15	151.4	125.2	104.8	176.9	145.3	120.7	207.7	169.4	139.6
20	174.8	150.0	130.0	198.3	169.1	145.6	225.8	191.4	163.7
25	198.4	174.8	155.2	220.1	193.0	170.5	244.9	213.8	188.0
30	198.9	179.2	162.2	216.7	194.5	175.5	236.4	211.6	190.3
35	189.5	173.9	160.2	203.0	186.0	171.0	217.6	199.2	182.7
40	178.7	167.1	156.4	188.5	176.2	164.8	198.7	185.8	173.7
45	156.9	149.8	142.8	162.6	155.4	148.3	168.1	161.1	153.9
50	114.6	112.2	109.5	116.1	114.1	111.7	117.1	115.7	113.7
55	69.4	70.7	71.4	67.8	69.7	70.9	65.6	68.3	70.0
60	18.1	21.7	24.7	14.8	18.9	22.4	10.9	15.8	19.7
65	-32.7	-28.8	-25.3	-36.2	-31.8	-28.0	-40.0	-35.2	-31.0
70	-43.4	-40.2	-37.4	-46.1	-42.7	-39.6	-49.1	-45.3	-42.0
75	-42.0	-39.7	-37.6	-43.9	-41.5	-39.3	-46.0	-43.4	-41.0
80	-35.9	-34.5	-33.1	-37.2	-35.6	-34.2	-38.4	-36.8	-35.3
85	-28.4	-27.6	-26.8	-29.0	-28.2	-27.4	-29.7	-28.8	-28.0
90	-1.5	-1.5	-1.5	-1.5	-1.5	-1.5	-1.5	-1.5	-1.5
Future generations	95.9	69.6	51.1	124.4	89.5	65.1	162.6	115.9	83.6

Generational Accounts 77

TABLE 1a
Accounts for Age Zero and Future Male Generations with Population Age Distribution Constant after 1989
(thousands of dollars)

Generation's age in 1989	g=0			g=.0075			g=.015		
	r=.05	r=.06	r=.07	r=.05	r=.06	r=.07	r=.05	r=.06	r=.07
0	70.0	51.8	39.0	89.5	65.6	48.9	114.9	83.5	61.6
5	91.5	70.7	55.4	113.0	86.6	67.2	140.3	106.6	82.0
10	121.4	97.7	79.6	144.9	115.8	93.7	173.9	137.9	110.7
15	159.1	133.5	113.3	183.7	153.2	129.0	213.1	176.5	147.7
20	169.2	147.4	129.5	189.7	164.3	143.5	213.5	183.7	159.6
25	167.7	150.2	135.5	183.7	163.8	147.0	201.9	179.1	160.0
30	155.4	142.0	130.5	167.4	152.4	139.5	180.7	163.9	149.5
35	148.6	137.9	128.4	158.0	146.2	135.8	168.2	155.3	143.9
40	141.9	133.5	125.8	149.2	140.1	131.8	156.9	147.1	138.3
45	136.7	130.3	124.3	141.9	135.3	129.0	147.3	140.5	134.0
50	114.7	111.5	108.2	117.1	114.0	110.8	119.3	116.4	113.3
55	77.5	77.8	77.6	76.9	77.6	77.8	75.9	77.1	77.7
60	24.7	27.2	29.2	22.5	25.3	27.6	19.8	23.1	25.8
65	−24.3	−21.4	−18.9	−26.8	−23.6	−20.9	−29.5	−26.0	−23.0
70	−34.8	−32.5	−30.4	−36.8	−34.3	−32.1	−39.0	−36.3	−33.8
75	−34.9	−33.2	−31.6	−36.4	−34.6	−32.9	−38.0	−36.0	−34.2
80	−31.1	−30.0	−28.9	−32.1	−30.9	−29.7	−33.1	−31.8	−30.6
85	−26.0	−25.3	−24.7	−26.6	−25.9	−25.2	−27.2	−26.4	−25.7
90	−1.5	−1.5	−1.5	−1.5	−1.5	−1.5	−1.5	−1.5	−1.5
Future generations	84.8	66.1	52.5	104.5	80.2	62.8	130.5	98.6	76.1

78 Auerbach, Gokhale & Kotlikoff

TABLE 1b
Accounts for Age Zero and Future Male Generations with No Intramarginal Capital Income Tax
(thousands of dollars)

Generation's age in 1989	g=0			g=.0075			g=.015		
	r=.05	r=.06	r=.07	r=.05	r=.06	r=.07	r=.05	r=.06	r=.07
0	79.2	57.8	42.9	102.4	74.0	54.3	133.1	95.3	69.2
5	99.2	75.6	58.4	123.9	93.5	71.6	155.6	116.4	88.3
10	123.2	97.8	78.7	148.9	117.2	93.5	180.8	141.2	111.7
15	151.9	125.7	105.1	177.6	145.8	121.1	208.6	170.0	140.1
20	175.3	150.4	130.3	199.0	169.6	146.0	226.8	192.1	164.2
25	198.5	174.8	155.0	220.4	193.1	170.5	245.4	214.1	188.0
30	198.1	178.1	161.1	216.0	193.6	174.4	235.9	210.9	189.4
35	187.2	171.6	157.7	200.9	183.8	168.6	215.7	197.0	180.4
40	175.0	163.2	152.4	184.9	172.4	160.9	195.3	182.1	169.9
45	151.6	144.3	137.3	157.4	150.1	142.9	163.1	155.8	148.6
50	107.9	105.4	102.5	109.5	107.4	104.8	110.6	109.1	106.9
55	61.6	62.9	63.5	60.1	62.0	63.1	58.0	60.6	62.3
60	10.0	13.5	16.4	6.7	10.8	14.1	2.9	7.6	11.5
65	−40.7	−36.8	−33.4	−44.1	−39.8	−36.1	−47.9	−43.1	−39.0
70	−50.6	−47.5	−44.7	−53.3	−49.9	−46.9	−56.3	−52.6	−49.3
75	−48.2	−45.9	−43.8	−50.1	−47.7	−45.4	−52.1	−49.5	−47.2
80	−41.1	−39.7	−38.3	−42.3	−40.8	−39.4	−43.6	−42.0	−40.5
85	−33.2	−32.4	−31.7	−33.9	−33.1	−32.3	−34.5	−33.7	−32.9
90	−6.4	−6.4	−6.4	−6.4	−6.4	−6.4	−6.4	−6.4	−6.4
Future generations	105.3	81.2	64.9	132.1	99.4	77.1	168.7	124.1	93.9

TABLE 1c
Accounts for Age Zero and Future Male Generations (thousands of dollars)

Generation's age in 1989	g=0			g=.0075			g=.015		
	r=.025	r=.03	r=.035	r=.025	r=.03	r=.035	r=.025	r=.03	r=.035
0	185.1	155.0	130.2	244.3	203.8	170.5	322.9	268.8	224.2
5	207.2	177.5	152.5	263.7	225.3	192.9	336.3	286.6	244.8
10	230.6	202.1	177.6	283.4	247.7	217.0	348.9	304.4	266.0
15	255.1	228.6	205.4	302.9	270.7	242.5	360.1	321.3	287.2
20	266.9	244.2	223.8	306.8	280.1	256.2	353.1	322.0	293.9
25	280.8	261.1	243.2	314.4	292.0	271.5	352.2	326.9	303.7
30	264.0	249.0	235.0	289.0	272.5	257.0	316.0	298.1	281.1
35	237.4	226.7	216.6	254.5	243.2	232.4	272.3	260.6	249.2
40	211.9	204.9	198.0	222.7	215.7	208.7	233.2	226.4	219.4
45	174.5	171.2	167.8	179.1	176.2	173.0	182.6	180.4	177.8
50	117.5	117.4	117.1	116.7	117.3	117.5	114.8	116.2	117.1
55	61.8	63.9	65.7	57.7	60.5	62.8	52.4	56.0	59.0
60	5.2	8.4	11.2	−0.2	3.4	6.7	−6.6	−2.3	1.5
65	−45.4	−42.5	−39.8	−50.4	−47.1	−44.1	−55.9	−52.2	−48.8
70	−53.1	−50.9	−48.9	−56.7	−54.3	−52.1	−60.6	−58.0	−55.6
75	−48.8	−47.3	−45.9	−51.2	−49.6	−48.1	−53.8	−52.1	−50.4
80	−40.1	−39.2	−38.4	−41.5	−40.6	−39.7	−43.0	−42.1	−41.1
85	−30.5	−30.1	−29.6	−31.2	−30.8	−30.3	−32.0	−31.5	−31.0
90	−1.5	−1.5	−1.5	−1.5	−1.5	−1.5	−1.5	−1.5	−1.5
Future generations	225.7	188.9	158.7	299.7	249.7	208.8	399.9	332.0	276.5

TABLE 2
Accounts for Age Zero and Future Female Generations (thousands of dollars)

Generation's age in 1989	g=0				g=.0075			g=.015		
	r=.05	r=.06	r=.07	r=.05	r=.06	r=.07	r=.05	r=.06	r=.07
0	38.9	28.7	21.4	49.5	36.4	27.0	63.0	46.3	34.2
5	49.1	38.1	29.8	60.2	46.5	36.2	73.7	56.9	44.1
10	63.2	51.2	41.8	74.8	60.4	49.1	88.5	71.4	57.8
15	73.3	61.9	52.6	83.9	70.7	59.8	96.0	80.9	68.2
20	87.9	76.9	67.5	97.9	85.5	74.8	108.7	95.0	83.1
25	93.1	83.5	75.1	101.4	91.0	81.7	110.0	99.1	89.0
30	92.5	84.8	77.7	98.8	90.9	83.3	105.0	97.1	89.3
35	88.1	82.6	77.2	92.2	86.9	81.5	95.8	91.1	85.8
40	78.8	75.8	72.4	80.6	78.2	75.1	81.6	80.2	77.6
45	62.9	62.7	61.7	62.1	62.9	62.6	60.3	62.4	62.9
50	40.3	43.0	44.6	37.2	41.0	43.4	32.8	38.1	41.6
55	10.5	15.6	19.5	5.4	11.7	16.5	−0.8	6.9	12.8
60	−23.9	−17.8	−12.7	−29.7	−22.5	−16.7	−36.3	−28.0	−21.2
65	−55.0	−49.1	−44.0	−60.3	−53.7	−48.0	−66.3	−58.8	−52.4
70	−61.2	−56.4	−52.0	−65.5	−60.2	−55.4	−70.2	−64.3	−59.1
75	−58.7	−55.1	−51.8	−61.8	−57.9	−54.4	−65.1	−60.9	−57.1
80	−51.3	−49.0	−46.8	−53.3	−50.8	−48.5	−55.3	−52.7	−50.3
85	−42.9	−41.7	−40.6	−43.9	−42.7	−41.5	−44.9	−43.6	−42.4
90	−7.4	−7.4	−7.4	−7.4	−7.4	−7.4	−7.4	−7.4	−7.4
Future generations	47.3	34.7	25.5	60.4	44.2	32.5	77.3	56.6	41.4

TABLE 2a
Accounts for Age Zero and Future Female Generations with Population Age Distribution Constant after 1989 (thousands of dollars)

Generation's age in 1989	g=0					g=.0075					g=.015		
	r=.05	r=.06	r=.07			r=.05	r=.06	r=.07			r=.05	r=.06	r=.07
0	35.5	26.4	19.8			45.0	33.3	24.9			57.2	42.1	31.3
5	46.8	36.6	28.9			57.2	44.4	34.8			70.0	54.1	42.2
10	64.4	52.6	43.4			76.0	61.7	50.6			89.7	72.6	59.1
15	79.5	67.7	58.1			90.6	76.8	65.6			103.4	87.3	74.2
20	87.3	77.0	68.3			96.6	84.9	75.1			107.1	93.9	82.7
25	79.7	72.1	65.6			86.4	78.0	70.7			93.7	84.5	76.4
30	72.8	67.1	62.1			77.6	71.5	66.0			82.6	76.2	70.3
35	69.3	65.0	61.0			72.7	68.3	64.1			76.1	71.8	67.4
40	62.8	60.1	57.3			64.8	62.3	59.5			66.5	64.3	61.7
45	55.7	54.7	53.4			56.0	55.5	54.5			55.7	55.9	55.3
50	42.9	44.3	45.0			41.0	43.3	44.5			38.4	41.6	43.6
55	16.9	20.8	23.8			13.0	17.8	21.5			8.3	14.2	18.7
60	-15.8	-11.2	-7.4			-20.0	-14.7	-10.3			-24.9	-18.8	-13.8
65	-44.1	-39.8	-36.1			-48.0	-43.2	-39.0			-52.2	-46.9	-42.3
70	-50.4	-46.8	-43.6			-53.6	-49.6	-46.1			-57.0	-52.7	-48.9
75	-49.3	-46.6	-44.1			-51.7	-48.7	-46.1			-54.1	-51.0	-48.2
80	-44.5	-42.6	-40.9			-46.0	-44.1	-42.2			-47.7	-45.6	-43.7
85	-39.3	-38.3	-37.3			-40.2	-39.1	-38.1			-41.1	-40.0	-38.9
90	-7.4	-7.4	-7.4			-7.4	-7.4	-7.4			-7.4	-7.4	-7.4
Future generations	43.0	33.7	26.7			52.6	40.7	32.0			65.0	49.7	38.6

TABLE 2b
Accounts for Age Zero and Future Female Generations with No Intramarginal Capital Income Tax
(thousands of dollars)

Generation's age in 1989	g=0			g=.0075			g=.015		
	r=.05	r=.06	r=.07	r=.05	r=.06	r=.07	r=.05	r=.06	r=.07
0	39.0	28.8	21.4	49.7	36.5	27.1	63.2	46.5	34.3
5	49.2	38.2	29.8	60.4	46.6	36.3	74.0	57.1	44.2
10	63.4	51.3	41.9	75.1	60.6	49.2	88.8	71.6	58.0
15	73.5	62.0	52.7	84.2	70.9	60.0	96.4	81.1	68.4
20	88.2	77.1	67.7	98.2	85.7	75.0	109.1	95.3	83.3
25	93.5	83.8	75.3	101.8	91.3	81.9	110.5	99.5	89.3
30	92.6	84.8	77.7	99.0	90.9	83.3	105.2	97.2	89.3
35	87.7	82.1	76.6	91.9	86.5	81.0	95.5	90.7	85.3
40	77.7	74.6	71.2	79.6	77.1	73.9	80.7	79.2	76.5
45	61.1	60.8	59.8	60.4	61.1	60.7	58.6	60.7	61.1
50	37.8	40.4	42.0	34.7	38.5	40.8	30.4	35.7	39.1
55	7.4	12.4	16.2	2.3	8.5	13.3	−3.9	3.8	9.6
60	−27.6	−21.4	−16.4	−33.3	−26.2	−20.3	−39.9	−31.6	−24.8
65	−58.8	−52.9	−47.9	−64.1	−57.5	−51.8	−70.1	−62.6	−56.3
70	−65.1	−60.2	−55.9	−69.3	−64.0	−59.3	−74.0	−68.1	−63.0
75	−62.3	−58.7	−55.4	−65.3	−61.5	−58.0	−68.6	−64.5	−60.7
80	−54.4	−52.0	−49.9	−56.3	−53.9	−51.6	−58.3	−55.8	−53.4
85	−44.9	−43.7	−42.6	−45.9	−44.7	−43.5	−46.9	−45.6	−44.4
90	−7.8	−7.8	−7.8	−7.8	−7.8	−7.8	−7.8	−7.8	−7.8
Future generations	51.9	40.4	32.4	64.1	49.1	38.4	80.2	60.5	46.5

TABLE 2c
Accounts for Age Zero and Future Female Generations (thousands of dollars)

Generation's age in 1989	g=0			g=.0075			g=.015		
	r=.025	r=.03	r=.035	r=.025	r=.03	r=.035	r=.025	r=.03	r=.035
0	84.6	72.5	62.0	106.5	91.8	78.8	131.5	114.8	99.4
5	94.5	83.0	72.7	114.5	101.2	89.1	136.2	121.8	108.1
10	108.5	97.5	87.5	126.8	114.7	103.3	145.4	133.2	121.0
15	112.9	103.7	95.2	127.4	117.9	108.6	141.1	132.2	122.9
20	123.0	115.4	107.9	134.4	127.1	119.5	144.1	138.1	131.0
25	120.7	115.1	109.5	128.3	123.5	118.2	133.5	130.5	126.1
30	111.7	108.3	104.6	115.5	113.3	110.2	116.4	116.2	114.6
35	98.8	97.5	95.6	99.2	99.2	98.3	96.5	98.7	99.3
40	81.0	81.6	81.6	78.3	80.4	81.4	72.7	76.8	79.4
45	55.9	58.6	60.4	50.0	54.1	57.2	41.2	47.4	52.1
50	25.2	29.6	33.1	16.8	22.5	27.3	5.7	13.3	19.6
55	-10.5	-5.1	-0.3	-20.5	-13.8	-7.9	-32.6	-24.4	-17.2
60	-46.1	-40.7	-35.8	-55.6	-49.2	-43.6	-66.6	-59.2	-52.5
65	-74.7	-70.1	-65.8	-82.6	-77.4	-72.6	-91.6	-85.6	-80.1
70	-76.7	-73.2	-69.9	-82.6	-78.7	-75.1	-89.1	-84.8	-80.8
75	-69.6	-67.2	-64.9	-73.6	-70.9	-68.5	-77.8	-75.0	-72.3
80	-58.0	-56.6	-55.2	-60.3	-58.8	-57.3	-62.8	-61.2	-59.6
85	-46.2	-45.5	-44.9	-47.3	-46.6	-45.9	-48.5	-47.7	-47.0
90	-7.4	-7.4	-7.4	-7.4	-7.4	-7.4	-7.4	-7.4	-7.4
Future generations	103.2	88.4	75.6	130.6	112.5	96.5	162.8	141.8	122.5

The bottom row of each table, labeled "Future Generations," indicates the present value of amounts that males and females born in 1990 will, on average, pay, assuming that subsequent generations pay this same amount except for an adjustment for growth. For the base case, this amount is $89.5 thousand for males. This means that males born in 1990 will be greeted with a bill from all levels of government of $89.5 thousand, which is 21.4% larger than the bill facing 1989 age zero males. Males born in 1991 will face a bill for $90.2 thousand, which equals $89.5 thousand multiplied by 1.0075 (1 plus the growth rate); males born in 1992 will pay $90.8 thousand ($89.5 times 1.0075 squared), and so forth. For females born in 1990, the bill will be $44.2 thousand, based on the assumption that future female and male "birth bills" have the same ratio as those of age zero males and females in 1989.

Tables 1a–c (males) and 2a–c (females) present the same calculations under different assumptions. Tables 1a and 2a show the results of assuming that no further demographic change will occur in the United States, i.e., that the population age distribution will be constant after 1990. These tables are helpful in understanding the fiscal impact of the continuing demographic transition to an older population. These tables indicate that, were the population structure to remain constant, younger generations, those that will bear the brunt of the demographic shift's fiscal burdens, would be better off. This is particularly true for males.

Tables 1b and 2b demonstrate the importance of our special treatment of capital income taxes. Treating all capital income taxes as marginal taxes on new capital income lowers the fiscal burden on older living generations, since these groups are no longer being assigned the reduction in capital values associated with the inframarginal taxation of old capital. Very young living generations would face a somewhat higher fiscal burden, since these groups hold little capital and will face many years of somewhat higher marginal tax rates. On balance, the reduced capital income taxes facing older living generations and the slightly increased capital income taxes facing younger living generations imply a considerably larger burden on future generations. For the base case parameters the percentage difference in the accounts between age zero generations and future generations is now 34.3 rather than 21.4%. Thus, failure to take account of the capitalization of some capital income taxes causes one to understate the viability of the current tax structure by ignoring the taxes that will be collected on the income from previously acquired capital.

As we indicated above, the choice of which discount rate to use in these tables depends on how one interprets the concept of fiscal balance in the context of uncertainty. The preceding tables have provided estimates for a range of estimates around 6%, corresponding to our "high" interest rate assumption. Tables 1c and 2c repeat the exercise of Tables 1 and 2, but for a lower range of interest rates centered around 3%, closer to the real government borrowing rate. The most significant effect of this change is to increase the measured burdens facing newborns, since these are based largely on discounted payments and receipts that will occur many years hence. However, the same conclusion reached above, that the burdens must rise for future generations, still holds here.

The robustness of this last result is amplified by Table 3, which presents for a wide range of growth/interest rate combinations the percentage difference in accounts of age zero and future generations. The table indicates that for a range of reasonable interest and growth rate assumptions future generations will face larger fiscal burdens than current age zero generations based on current policy. For the base case, the difference is 21.4%. For the low interest rate case with the same rate of productivity growth ($r=.03$, $g=.0075$), the percentage difference is larger, namely 22.5%. More optimistic growth rate assumptions do not materially affect the conclusion of a roughly 20% larger burden on future generations compared with current generations.

B. The Composition of Generational Accounts

Appendix Tables 1 and 2 provide for current male and female generations a breakdown of the accounts by different types of receipts and expenditures. The growth and interest rates used in the table are the base case values. All figures are present values. Take the case of 30-year-old males. On average, the 1989 cohort of 30-year-old males will pay $194.5 thousand dollars in present value to the government over the course of their remaining lives. The $194.5 thousand dollar figure reflects the difference between $222.8 in present value of payments to the government less $28.3 thousand in present value of receipts from the government. The largest source of present value payments is the $74.4 thousand in FICA and other payroll taxes, followed by $69.6 thousand in labor income taxes, $38.4 thousand in capital income taxes, and $34.2 thousand in excise taxes. The largest sources of present value receipts are $14.3 thousand in social security OASDI benefits, followed by $5.4 thousand in general welfare (which includes Medicaid), $4.6 thousand in Medicare, and $.9 thousand in food stamps.

Appendix Tables 3 and 4 further clarify the determinants of these present values. They detail for different 1989 male and female generations the annual flows of payments and receipts (measured in constant 1989 dollars) members of these generations are projected to pay, on average, in specific years in the future. For the 1989 cohort of 30-year-old males, total 1989 net payments average $11,271.7. Their average net pay-

TABLE 3
Percentage Difference in Accounts of Age Zero and Future Generations

Interest rate	$g=0$	$g=.0025$	$g=.005$	$g=.0075$	$g=.01$	$g=.0125$	$g=.015$	$g=.0175$	$g=.02$
0.03	21.93	22.09	22.30	22.54	22.83	23.16	23.53	23.94	24.39
0.04	21.88	21.99	22.15	22.34	22.57	22.83	23.12	23.44	23.78
0.05	21.61	21.71	21.85	22.03	22.24	22.48	22.74	23.03	23.34
0.06	20.89	21.02	21.19	21.39	21.62	21.88	22.16	22.45	22.77
0.07	19.45	19.66	19.91	20.18	20.48	20.80	21.14	21.49	21.86
0.08	16.89	17.27	17.68	18.09	18.53	18.97	19.43	19.89	20.36
0.09	12.74	13.40	14.06	14.73	15.38	16.04	16.69	17.34	17.98
0.10	6.36	7.45	8.52	9.55	10.56	11.55	12.50	13.44	14.34

ments 30 years later when they reach age 60 are projected to equal $25,809. The tables show clearly the age pattern of the government's various payments and receipts. For example, OASDI benefits for 1989 30-year-old males average only $84, but grow to $8168.1 at age 80.

C. *The Effect of Policy Changes on Generational Accounts*

Tables 4 and 4a explore the impact on generational accounts of a variety of alternative fiscal policies assuming 6 and 3% rates of interest respectively. Both tables assume the base case 0.0075 growth rate. The tables compare the generational accounts of newborn and future generations prior to and after the change in policy. Appendix Tables 5 and 6 indicate the impact on the generational accounts of older generations of the various policies assuming base case parameter values; Tables 5a and 6a repeat the analysis assuming a 3% interest rate.

Capital Gains Tax Cut The first policy considered is the Administration's 1989 capital gains tax cut proposal. In analyzing this proposal we used the Joint Committee on Taxation's (the JCT) revenue estimates; specifically, we raised or lowered projected cohort-specific future average capital income tax payments each year in the future by a factor that would leave total projected capital income tax payments in that year larger or smaller by the amount of revenue gain or loss projected by the JCT. The results of this experiment indicate the Administration's proposal would place an additional burden equal to $1300 ($700) in present value on each future generation of males (females). Appendix Tables 5 and 6 and 5a and 6a indicate that most of the benefits from the capital gains proposal would accrue to currently middle age generations. For example, assuming base case parameters, 45-year-old males are, on average, projected to receive roughly $600 in present value as a result of the capital gains proposal.

No Reduction in Social Security The next policy experiment involves a cancellation of the 1983 Social Security amendments. In this simulation we do not reduce future social security benefits of generations attaining age 65 in the year 2000 and beyond according to the procedure described in Section VI. The impact of reversing the Social Security amendments is particularly strong for middle age women. According to Appendix Table 6, for base case parameters, 35-year-old women would benefit by $1,800 in present value from such a reversal in policy.

Faster Medicare Growth The third policy we consider is faster growth in medicare expenditures. Rather than projecting current spending levels

TABLE 4
Absolute Values and Percentage Difference in Accounts of Age Zero and Future Male Generations under Alternative Policy Changes ($r=.06$, $g=.0075$)

	Current policy	Capital gains tax cut	No reduction in Social Security	Faster Medicare growth	$500 billion S&L bailout	Slower growth in government consumption	Current budget agreement[1]		
							A	B	C
Age Zero in 1989	73716	73598	73325	73166	73716	73716	75827	75827	73819
Future generations	89484	90754	94478	105252	98930	64812	49770	70180	83110
Percentage difference	21.4	23.3	28.8	43.9	34.2	−12.1	−34.4	−7.4	12.6

[1] A, all changes are permanent; B, government expenditure reductions are temporary; C, all changes are temporary.

TABLE 4a
Absolute Values and Percentage Difference in Accounts of Age Zero and Future Generations under Alternative Policy Changes ($r=.03$, $g=.0075$)

	Current policy	Capital gains tax cut	No reduction in Social Security	Faster Medicare growth	$500 billion S&L bailout	Slower growth in government consumption	Current budget agreement[1]		
							A	B	C
Age Zero in 1989	203798	203327	200606	199098	203798	203798	210295	210295	203914
Future generations	249744	250820	258961	272939	253944	217923	203568	233219	246504
Percentage difference	22.5	23.4	29.1	37.1	24.6	6.9	−3.2	10.9	20.9

[1] A, all changes are permanent; B, government expenditure reductions are temporary; C, all changes are temporary.

forward at the growth rate of other spending, we assume that medical costs will continue to rise more quickly than other government expenses. In particular we assume that the rate of growth of Medicare expenditures is two percentage points higher than the economy's growth rate for the 20-year period between 1990 and 2010. The experiment produces a sharp jump in the extra burden to be placed on future generations: with base case parameters newborns in 1990 will face an extra burden of $15,800 for males and $7,200 for females; these figures translate into a 41.6% larger burden on future generations than on current age zero generations. The simulated Medicare policy provides a sizable benefit to existing older generations. For example, 65-year-old males are estimated to receive an additional $5,100 in present value from this policy option.

Given the extraordinary growth in health care spending in recent years, one might well believe that this simulation represents a more realistic view of current policy than our "current policy" projection which assumes only trend growth in Medicare. Clearly, one is free to consider alternative views of what constitutes the expected near and longer term treatment of current generations. Ideally, one would have information on the public's expectation of the future treatment of current generations to guide the formation of the "current policy" projection. Certainly there is no reason in assessing current policy to restrict oneself to what is actually legislated. We offer our "current policy" projection as an initial benchmark from which to consider possibly more realistic assessments of the future treatment of current generations.

Savings and Loan Bailout   The recent savings and loan debacle and bailout illustrates the difficulties of measuring the deficit. The episode included debates about whether bailout financing should be "off-budget" and whether the funds raised should "count" toward the Gramm–Rudman–Hollings targets. Such discussions are really irrelevant if one is interested in determining who will bear the costs of this mammoth new government spending program. To model this, we assume that the government issues $500 billion dollars of new bonds in 1990 to make good the claims against the insolvent S&Ls, and raises taxes only on new generations. We treat the bailout essentially as the undoing of a casualty loss, in that the current generations are assumed to be kept whole by the bailout, i.e., the $500 billion simply offsets $500 billion in losses due to the insolvencies. Tables 4 and 4a indicate that this exercise will cost each 1990 newborn male $9,446 assuming a 6% interest rate and $4,200 assuming a 3% interest rate.

Slower Growth in Government Consumption One of the goals of those who seek to improve the fiscal situation is to "get spending under control." We model this by simulating the effects of zero growth in government consumption for a period of 10 years with the growth in government consumption after the 10-year period occurring at the assumed economy-wide growth rate. For base case parameters, the impact of this reduced spending is to lower the burden of future generations substantially, by $24,672 per male and $12,200 per female. The reason this policy has such a large impact can be understood by considering the size of its effect with reference to the terms entering the government's intertemporal budget constraint given in equation (1). Under our base case assumptions the present value of government consumption is $25.385 trillion, the present value of payments by existing generations is $20.998 trillion, government net wealth is minus $.516 trillion, and the present value of payments by future generations is $4.903 trillion. The simulated 10-year policy of zero growth in government consumption followed by trend growth means the level of government consumption in year 10 and beyond is lower than under the "current policy" simulation. The effect of this policy is to lower the present value of government consumption by $1.306 trillion, which is sizable compared to what would otherwise be the burden on future generations, namely $4.903 trillion.

The Government's New Budget Deal We examine three alternative views of the recent budget deal. The first alternative, labeled A, assumes that the changes made to taxes and spending will be permanent; the second, labeled B, assumes that only the reductions in government consumption spending will be permanent; and the third, labeled C, assumes that the provisions will last for only 5 years, after which taxes and government consumption spending will revert to the values they would have had without the budget deal.[5] The results indicate that the importance of the budget deal depends very much on its duration. If the deal is temporary, case C, future male generations will benefit by $6,374, while if it is permanent, case A, they will benefit by $39,714. The loss to current generations is also quite sensitive to the duration of the new policy. If it is kept in place it will, for example, mean a $4,300 present value loss to

---

[5] In these simulations we assume that total taxes are increased in 1991 by $21.7 billion, in 1992 by $32.3 billion, in 1993 by $30.4 billion, in 1994 by $35.1 billion, and in 1995 by $35.1 billion. The respective annual reductions in total transfer payments are $3.4, $5.9, $8.4, $11.4, and $13.4 billion. Finally, the respective annual reductions in total government consumption are $15.8, $32.2, $46.1, $62.7, and $73.5 billion. These aggregate figures as well as the composition of taxes and transfers across the different types of taxes and transfers were obtained from Congressional documents describing the budget deal.

current age 35-year-old males, while if it is temporary, the loss to current age 35-year-old males is only $900. Tables 5, 5a, 6, and 6a indicate that the current elderly will pay a considerable share of the total costs to current generations of the new legislation, although this share differs depending on the longevity of the policy.

In understanding the magnitude of the new budget deal, it may help to consider the effects of the budget deal on the components of the government's intertemporal budget constraint. In the simulation(s) in which the budget deal is permanent (temporary) the present value of government consumption falls by $1.262 trillion; in the case it is temporary it falls by $176 billion. In the permanent simulation the present value burden on existing generations rises by $825 billion; in the temporary simulation it rises by $159 billion.

VII. SUMMARY

The ongoing debate about how to define the federal budget deficit is symptomatic of the need for a proper conceptual framework for describing generational policy. Unfortunately, the budget deficit, no matter how it is defined, cannot provide a proper assessment of generational policy. As an alternative to economically arbitrary budget deficits, this paper has provided a set of generational accounts indicating the net present value of payments of existing generations to the government. We have used these accounts and additional data concerning the government's intertemporal budget constraint to assess the magnitude of the fiscal burden being placed on future generations by current generations and to consider the burden on future generations of a set of hypothetical fiscal policies. The findings suggest that unless policy toward existing generations, including those who have just been born, is substantially altered (for example, through a real adherence to the just enacted budget deal), future generations will face a roughly 20% larger net tax burden over the course of their lifetimes than current newborns.

REFERENCES

Abel, Andrew, Douglas Bernheim, and Laurence J. Kotlikoff. (1991). "Does the Propensity to Consume Increase with Age?" mimeo.
Auerbach, Alan J. (1983). "Corporate Taxation in the United States." *Brookings Papers on Economic Activity*.
Auerbach, Alan J. (1987). "The Tax Reform Act of 1986 and the Cost of Capital." *Journal of Economic Perspectives*.
Auerbach, Alan J., and James Hines. (1987). "Anticipated Tax Changes and the

Timing of Investment." In Martin S. Feldstein, ed., *The Effect of Taxation on Capital Accumulation*. Chicago, IL: Chicago University Press.

Auerbach, Alan J., and Laurence J. Kotlikoff. (1987). *Dynamic Fiscal Policy*. Cambridge: Cambridge University Press.

Auerbach, Alan J., Robert Hagemann, Laurence J. Kotlikoff, and Giuseppe Nicoletti. (1989). "The Economics of Aging Populations: The Case of Four OECD Economies." *OECD Staff Papers*.

Auerbach, Alan J., Jinyong Cai, and Laurence J. Kotlikoff. (1990). "U.S. Demographics and Saving: Predictions of Three Saving Models." *Carnegie-Rochester Conference Series on Public Policy*, in press.

Boskin, Michael J., Mark S. Robinson, and A. M. Huber. (1987). "Government Saving, Capital Formation, and Wealth in the United States, 1947–85." NBER working paper No. 2352, August.

The Economic Report of the President 1982. (1982). Washington, DC: U.S. Government Printing Office.

Eisner, Robert, and Paul J. Pieper. (1984). "A New View of the Federal Debt and Budget Deficits." *American Economic Review* 74(1), 11–29.

Feldstein, Martin S. (1974). "Social Security, Induced Retirement, and Aggregate Capital Accumulation," *Journal of Political Economy*, 82(5), 905–26.

Hamilton, James D., and Marjorie A. Flavin. (1986). "On the Limitations of Government Borrowing: A Framework for Empirical Testing." *American Economic Review* 76, 808–819.

Kotlikoff, Laurence J. (1984). "Taxation and Savings—A Neoclassical Perspective." *Journal of Economic Literature*, 1576–1629.

Kotlikoff, Laurence J. (1988). "The Deficit Is Not a Meaningful Measure of Fiscal Policy." *Science*, 791–794.

Kotlikoff, Laurence J. (1989). "From Deficit Delusion to the Fiscal Balance Rule—Looking for a Sensible Way to Measure Fiscal Policy." NBER working paper, March.

Vaughan, Denton R. (1989). "Reflections on the Income Estimates from the Initial Panel of the Survey of Income and Program Participation (SIPP)." Department of Health and Human Services, Social Security Administration Office of Policy Research and Statistics, September.

Waldo, Daniel R., Sally T. Sonnefeld, and David R. McKusick. (1989). "Health Expenditures by Age Group, 1977 and 1987." *Health Care Financing* 10(4).

Wilcox, David W. (1989). "The Sustainability of Government Deficits: Implications of the Present Value Borrowing Constraint." *Journal of Money, Credit and Banking* 21, 291–306.

U.S. Department of Commerce, Bureau of the Census. (1987). *1987 Census of Governments' Taxable Property Values*. Washington, DC: U.S. Government Printing Office.

APPENDIX: THE ALLOCATION OF CAPITAL INCOME TAXES

As mentioned in the text, there are two related problems with using capital income taxes as measured to determine the burden of capital income taxation. First, existing assets may have excess future taxes capitalized into their values; such taxes should not be assigned to new investors even if they occur in the future. On the other hand, the timing of payments of taxes from new investment may have a different pattern than would an income tax, meaning that the ratio of current annual tax payments to income may not provide an accurate measure of the effective marginal tax rate facing new investment.

In this appendix we derive the formula used to calculate the capitalized value of taxes on existing capital and the correction needed to transform total capital income tax payments into an estimate of capital income tax payments on new investment. Our formula is based on the user cost of capital approach (see, for example, Auerbach, 1983), which assumes that the marginal product of capital equals the user cost of capital, C, where

$$C = (r+\delta)(1-\tau z)/(1-\tau) \tag{A1}$$

where r is the investor's required after-tax return, δ is the investment's economic rate of depreciation, τ is the investor's marginal tax rate, and z is the present value of depreciation allowances. We wish to calculate two measures. The first, which we denote by Q, is the tax-based discount on old capital, which equals the difference between tax savings from depreciation allowances per unit of new capital and those available per unit of existing capital:

$$Q = \tau(z-z^o) \tag{A2}$$

where z^o is the present value of depreciation allowances per unit of old capital.

Measured capital income tax payments are not based on the effective rate of tax on new capital m, where

$$m = \frac{C - (r+\delta)}{C-\delta} \tag{A3}$$

Instead they are based on an average tax rate, α, where

$$\alpha = \frac{\tau(C-b)}{C-\delta} \tag{A4}$$

and b is the average current depreciation deduction per unit of total capital. Comparing (A3) and (A4) indicates that we must correct measured taxes per unit of capital by subtracting from $\alpha(C-\delta)$ the term Δ, where

$$\Delta = (\alpha - m)(C - \delta) \tag{A5}$$

To calculate the terms z^o in (A2) and b in (A4) we must consider past patterns of investment. Assume investment grows at rate n. Then at date 0 (the present) the nominal amount of capital purchased at date $-s$ was $I_0 e^{-(n+\pi)s}$, where π is the inflation rate. If this investment has been written off at the constant geometric rate ψ, the asset at date 0 has a basis of $I_0 e^{-(n+\pi)s} e^{-\psi s}$ and receives depreciation allowances of ψ times this basis. Thus total allowances on the existing capital stock K are

$$bK = \psi \int_0^\infty I_0 e^{-(n+\pi)s} e^{-\psi s} ds = \frac{\psi}{n+\pi+\psi} I_0 \tag{A6}$$

Since the capital stock equals the sum of depreciated net investment we have

$$K = \int_0^\infty I_0 e^{-ns} e^{-\delta s} ds = \frac{1}{n+\delta} I_0 \tag{A7}$$

Equations (A6) and (A7) imply

$$b = \frac{\psi(n+\delta)}{n+\pi+\psi} \tag{A8}$$

The present value of all depreciation allowances on old capital equals the basis of each vintage multiplied by the present value of remaining depreciation deductions on that vintage, or

$$z^o = \frac{1}{K} \int_0^\infty I_0 e^{-(n+\pi)s} e^{-\psi s} \int_0^\infty e^{-(r+\pi)v} \psi e^{-\psi v} dv \, ds \tag{A9}$$

$$= \frac{\psi}{r+\pi+\psi} \frac{I_0}{K(n+\pi+\psi)} = \frac{\psi}{r+\pi+\psi} \frac{n+\delta}{n+\pi+\psi} = \hat{z} \frac{n+\delta}{n+\pi+\psi}$$

where $\hat{z}$ is the present value of depreciation allowances per unit of depreciated basis.

Substituting (A3), (A4), and (A8) into (A5) yields

$$\Delta = (r+\delta)\tau z - \frac{(r+\pi+\psi)(n+\delta)}{n+\pi+\psi} \tau \hat{z} \tag{A10}$$

Substituting (A9) into (A2) implies

$$Q = \tau z - \tau \hat{z} \, \frac{n+\delta}{n+\pi+\psi} \qquad (A11)$$

Expressions (A10) and (A11) may be simplified if we make the realistic (under current tax law) assumption that $\hat{z} = z$, thus,

$$\Delta = (r+\delta)\tau z \left[1 - \frac{(r+\pi+\psi)(n+\delta)}{(n+\pi+\psi)(r+\delta)} \right] \qquad (A12)$$

and

$$Q = \tau z \left(1 - \frac{n+\delta}{n+\pi+\psi} \right) \qquad (A13)$$

We assume that $\delta=.08$ and $n=.03$. These values are roughly consistent with the average depreciation rates and past growth rates for equipment and structures (see Auerbach and Hines, 1987). We further assume for purposes of these calculations that $r=.04$. For these values and for an inflation rate of 4% depreciation allowances [the right-hand side of (A14)] provide roughly the same present value as true economic depreciation [the left-hand side of (A14)].

$$\frac{\delta}{r+\delta} = \frac{\psi}{r+\pi+\psi} = z \qquad (A14)$$

When $r=\pi=.04$ and $\delta=.08$, we have from (A14) that $\psi=.16$. For our calculation of the actual value of z based on this value of ψ we assume $\pi=.05$ to maintain consistency with our other calculations. (Using $\pi=.04$ rather than .05 has no important impact on the results.) In addition, we assume that the tax rate τ equals .32. This value is less than the statutory rate of .34 with the difference reflecting the small difference between corporate and personal statutory rates. These assumptions lead to the values $\Delta=.00111$ and $Q=.111$. This value of Q is consistent with earlier direct calculations based on tax provisions similar to those enacted in 1986 (Auerbach and Hines, 1987). These fractions are multiplied by $5,488.8 billion, the value of depreciable assets held by taxable investors in 1989 to arrive at the numbers cited in the text, viz., a $6.09 billion subtraction from current total capital income taxes and a $609 billion capitalized burden on old capital.

APPENDIX TABLE 1
The Composition of Male Generational Accounts ($r=.06$, $g=.0075$)

Present values of receipts and payments
(thousands of dollars)

Generation's age in 1989	Net payment	Payments						Receipts					
		Labor income taxes	FICA taxes	Excise taxes	Capital income taxes	Seignor- age	Property taxes	OASDI	HI	Welfare		UI	Food Stamps
										AFDC	General		
0	73.7	24.8	26.5	22.9	9.5	0.0	1.6	4.5	1.1	0.3	4.4	1.0	0.3
5	93.2	31.8	34.0	26.3	12.2	0.1	2.0	5.5	1.5	0.4	4.3	1.2	0.4
10	116.8	40.8	43.6	29.8	15.6	0.1	2.6	6.7	1.9	0.5	4.6	1.6	0.5
15	145.3	52.2	55.8	32.8	20.0	0.1	3.3	8.1	2.4	0.6	5.1	2.0	0.7
20	169.1	61.9	66.2	33.9	24.8	0.1	4.1	9.5	2.9	0.7	5.3	2.4	0.8
25	193.0	70.3	75.1	35.8	32.4	0.1	5.3	12.0	3.8	0.9	5.6	2.6	0.9
30	194.5	69.6	74.4	34.2	38.4	0.1	6.1	14.3	4.6	0.8	5.4	2.3	0.9
35	186.0	65.2	69.7	32.0	43.8	0.0	6.9	17.2	5.7	0.6	5.2	2.0	0.8
40	176.2	60.9	65.1	30.5	49.8	0.0	7.6	21.9	7.4	0.5	5.3	1.8	0.7
45	155.4	54.4	58.1	28.7	54.2	0.0	7.8	29.8	10.0	0.4	5.5	1.5	0.6
50	114.1	42.1	45.0	24.4	52.1	0.0	7.1	37.1	12.4	0.3	5.4	1.1	0.5
55	69.7	31.0	33.2	20.8	48.7	0.0	6.6	47.9	16.0	0.2	5.4	0.7	0.4
60	18.9	20.2	21.5	17.9	44.1	0.0	6.1	62.6	22.0	0.1	5.6	0.3	0.3
65	−31.8	9.1	9.7	14.7	37.0	0.0	5.4	71.2	30.7	0.0	5.6	0.0	0.2
70	−42.7	4.0	4.3	11.9	29.3	0.0	4.5	61.9	29.6	0.0	4.9	0.0	0.2
75	−41.5	1.8	2.0	9.5	22.5	0.0	3.7	48.9	27.9	0.0	4.1	0.0	0.1
80	−35.6	0.6	0.6	7.5	17.2	0.0	3.0	36.9	24.4	0.0	3.0	0.0	0.1
85	−28.2	0.0	0.0	6.1	14.3	0.0	2.4	28.2	20.9	0.0	1.8	0.0	0.1
90	−1.5	0.0	0.0	1.2	6.7	0.0	0.5	5.4	4.2	0.0	0.2	0.0	0.0
Future Generations	89.5												

APPENDIX TABLE 2
The Composition of Female Generational Accounts ($r=.06$, $g=.0075$)

Present values of receipts and payments
(thousands of dollars)

Generation's age in 1989	Net payment	Payments						Receipts					
		Labor income taxes	FICA taxes	Excise taxes	Capital income taxes	Seignorage	Property taxes	OASDI	HI	Welfare		UI	Food Stamps
										AFDC	General		
0	36.4	14.0	14.9	20.2	3.5	0.0	2.1	5.0	1.5	2.3	7.8	0.4	1.3
5	46.5	17.7	18.9	23.0	4.5	0.0	2.6	6.1	1.9	2.9	7.2	0.6	1.7
10	60.4	23.3	24.9	27.2	5.9	0.1	3.5	7.5	2.5	3.8	7.8	0.7	2.2
15	70.7	28.1	30.1	29.0	7.2	0.1	4.2	8.6	3.0	4.6	8.2	0.9	2.6
20	85.5	34.8	37.2	32.2	9.3	0.0	5.4	10.9	3.9	5.2	9.2	1.1	3.3
25	91.0	36.3	38.8	33.2	11.7	0.0	6.5	13.1	4.8	4.5	9.0	1.1	3.0
30	90.9	35.1	37.5	33.1	14.9	0.0	7.4	15.7	6.1	3.5	8.5	1.0	2.4
35	86.9	32.9	35.2	32.1	18.3	0.0	8.1	18.6	7.7	2.5	8.2	0.9	1.9
40	78.2	29.7	31.7	30.1	21.4	0.0	8.6	21.9	9.8	1.7	7.8	0.7	1.4
45	62.9	25.4	27.2	27.4	23.8	0.0	8.9	27.0	12.6	1.0	7.6	0.6	1.0
50	41.0	20.4	21.8	24.2	25.0	0.0	8.9	34.0	16.3	0.6	7.3	0.4	0.7
55	11.7	14.9	15.9	20.8	24.9	0.0	8.7	43.9	21.3	0.2	7.2	0.3	0.5
60	−22.5	9.3	9.9	17.4	23.4	0.0	8.2	55.1	27.8	0.0	7.2	0.2	0.4
65	−53.7	4.8	5.1	14.2	20.8	0.0	7.6	61.2	37.4	0.0	7.2	0.1	0.4
70	−60.2	2.0	2.2	11.5	17.3	0.0	6.9	56.5	36.8	0.0	6.5	0.0	0.3
75	−57.9	0.7	0.7	9.1	13.2	0.0	6.0	47.4	34.5	0.0	5.5	0.0	0.3
80	−50.8	0.0	0.0	7.2	8.8	0.0	5.1	37.4	29.9	0.0	4.5	0.0	0.2
85	−42.7	0.0	0.0	5.8	4.5	0.0	4.2	28.7	24.7	0.0	3.6	0.0	0.2
90	−7.4	0.0	0.0	1.0	0.4	0.0	0.7	4.7	4.2	0.0	0.6	0.0	0.0
Future generations	44.2												

APPENDIX TABLE 3
The Components of Male Generational Accounts ($r=.06$, $g=.0075$)

Average annual values of receipts and payments

Cohort that is age 0 in 1989			Payments								Receipts					
			Labor income taxes	FICA taxes	Excise taxes	Capital income taxes	Seignor- age	Property taxes				Welfare			Food Stamps
Age	Year	Net payment							OASDI	HI	AFDC	General	UI	
0	1989	225.9	0.0	0.0	501.4	0.0	0.0	0.0	32.2	0.0	0.0	243.3	0.0	0.0
10	1999	659.3	0.0	0.0	867.5	0.0	0.0	0.0	72.3	0.0	0.0	136.0	0.0	0.0
20	2009	4434.6	1467.3	1568.4	1600.2	183.0	14.5	4.3	84.5	0.0	9.1	224.7	68.3	16.6
30	2019	14104.0	4461.1	4768.4	2307.5	3214.9	6.6	130.8	105.5	0.0	75.3	337.5	202.5	64.4
40	2029	24218.5	6085.1	6504.3	2755.2	9246.0	4.1	493.2	162.3	0.0	69.5	358.7	198.4	80.4
50	2039	31345.6	6336.7	6773.2	2868.5	15876.5	2.1	688.8	488.7	0.0	52.1	394.9	192.4	72.1
60	2049	32294.1	5652.7	6042.1	2715.4	19621.5	1.7	806.5	1784.5	0.0	32.4	538.2	139.4	51.4
70	2059	7454.7	1370.5	1464.9	2466.9	18162.6	2.4	895.5	10976.4	4954.7	8.4	932.0	0.0	36.6
80	2069	−754.0	410.2	438.5	2324.4	13721.6	1.2	920.2	10220.5	7226.0	0.0	1088.3	0.0	35.3
90	2079	−1421.1	0.0	0.0	2404.6	13121.9	−6.3	916.3	9073.6	8279.8	0.0	469.3	0.0	34.9
Cohort that is age 10 in 1989															
10	1989	611.0	0.0	0.0	805.1	0.0	0.0	0.0	67.1	0.0	0.0	126.2	0.0	0.0
20	1999	4115.3	1361.7	1455.5	1485.0	169.8	13.5	4.0	78.4	0.0	8.5	208.5	63.4	15.4
30	2009	13088.5	4139.9	4425.1	2141.3	2983.4	6.1	121.4	97.9	0.0	69.9	313.2	187.9	59.8
40	2019	22474.9	5646.9	6036.0	2556.8	8580.4	3.8	457.7	150.6	0.0	64.5	332.9	184.1	74.6
50	2029	29088.8	5880.5	6285.6	2661.9	14733.5	2.0	639.2	453.5	0.0	48.4	366.5	178.6	66.9
60	2039	29969.0	5245.7	5607.1	2519.9	18208.8	1.6	748.4	1656.0	0.0	30.0	499.4	129.3	47.7
70	2049	6918.0	1271.9	1359.5	2289.3	16854.9	2.2	831.0	10186.1	4598.0	7.8	864.9	0.0	34.0
80	2059	−699.7	380.7	406.9	2157.0	12733.7	1.1	853.9	9484.7	6705.7	0.0	1009.9	0.0	32.8
90	2069	−1318.8	0.0	0.0	2231.5	12177.2	−5.9	850.3	8420.3	7683.7	0.0	435.5	0.0	32.4

APPENDIX TABLE 3
Continued

Average annual values of receipts and payments

Cohort that is age 20 in 1989

			Payments							Receipts					
												Welfare			
Age	Year	Net payment	Labor income taxes	FICA taxes	Excise taxes	Capital income taxes	Seignor-age	Property taxes	OASDI	HI	AFDC	General	UI	Food Stamps
20	1989	3819.0	1263.6	1350.7	1378.1	157.6	12.5	3.7	72.8	0.0	7.9	193.5	58.9	14.3
30	1999	12146.2	3841.8	4106.5	1987.2	2768.6	5.7	112.6	90.8	0.0	64.9	290.6	174.4	55.5
40	2009	20856.8	5240.4	5601.4	2372.7	7962.6	3.5	424.8	139.8	0.0	59.9	308.9	170.9	69.2
50	2019	26994.5	5457.1	5833.0	2470.3	13672.7	1.8	593.2	420.8	0.0	44.9	340.1	165.7	62.1
60	2029	27811.3	4868.0	5203.4	2338.5	16897.8	1.5	694.5	1536.8	0.0	27.9	463.5	120.0	44.2
70	2039	6419.9	1180.3	1261.4	2124.5	15641.4	2.0	771.2	9452.7	4267.0	7.2	802.6	0.0	31.5
80	2049	−649.4	353.3	377.6	2001.7	11816.9	1.1	792.5	8801.8	6222.9	0.0	937.2	0.0	30.4
90	2059	−1223.9	0.0	0.0	2070.9	11300.4	−5.4	789.1	7814.1	7130.5	0.0	404.2	0.0	30.1

Cohort that is age 30 in 1989

			Payments							Receipts					
												Welfare			
Age	Year	Net payment	Labor income taxes	FICA taxes	Excise taxes	Capital income taxes	Seignor-age	Property taxes	OASDI	HI	AFDC	General	UI	Food Stamps
30	1989	11271.7	3565.2	3810.9	1844.1	2569.3	5.3	104.5	84.3	0.0	60.2	269.7	161.9	51.5
40	1999	19355.1	4863.1	5198.1	2201.9	7389.3	3.3	394.2	129.7	0.0	55.6	286.7	158.6	64.2
50	2009	25051.0	5064.2	5413.1	2292.4	12688.3	1.7	550.5	390.5	0.0	41.6	315.6	153.8	57.6
60	2019	25809.0	4517.6	4828.8	2170.1	15681.2	1.4	644.5	1426.1	0.0	25.9	430.1	111.4	41.0
70	2029	5957.7	1095.3	1170.8	1971.5	14515.3	1.9	715.7	8772.2	3959.7	6.7	744.8	0.0	29.3
80	2039	−602.6	327.9	350.4	1857.6	10966.1	1.0	735.4	8168.1	5774.9	0.0	869.7	0.0	28.2
90	2049	−1135.7	0.0	0.0	1921.8	10486.9	−5.1	732.3	7251.5	6617.1	0.0	375.1	0.0	27.9

Cohort that is age 40 in 1989

Age	Year	Net payment	Labor income taxes	FICA taxes	Excise taxes	Capital income taxes	Seignor-age	Property taxes	OASDI	HI	Welfare AFDC	Welfare General	UI	Food Stamps
40	1989	17961.6	4513.0	4823.9	2043.4	6857.3	3.1	365.8	120.4	0.0	51.6	266.0	147.1	59.6
50	1999	23247.4	4699.6	5023.4	2127.4	11774.8	1.6	510.8	362.4	0.0	38.6	292.9	142.7	53.5
60	2009	23950.8	4192.3	4481.1	2013.9	14552.2	1.3	598.1	1323.5	0.0	24.0	399.1	103.4	38.1
70	2019	5528.8	1016.5	1086.5	1829.6	13470.2	1.7	664.2	8140.6	3674.7	6.2	691.2	0.0	27.2
80	2029	−559.2	304.3	325.2	1723.9	10176.6	0.9	682.5	7580.0	5359.1	0.0	807.1	0.0	26.2
90	2039	−1054.0	0.0	0.0	1783.4	9731.8	−4.7	679.6	6729.4	6140.7	0.0	348.1	0.0	25.9

Cohort that is age 50 in 1989

Age	Year	Net payment	Labor income taxes	FICA taxes	Excise taxes	Capital income taxes	Seignor-age	Property taxes	OASDI	HI	Welfare AFDC	Welfare General	UI	Food Stamps
50	1989	21573.6	4361.2	4661.7	1974.2	10927.1	1.5	474.0	336.3	0.0	33.9	271.8	132.4	49.6
60	1999	22226.5	3890.5	4158.5	1868.9	13504.5	1.2	555.1	1228.2	0.0	22.3	370.4	95.9	35.3
70	2009	4242.0	943.3	1008.3	1697.9	12500.4	1.6	616.3	8443.3	3410.1	5.8	641.5	0.0	25.2
80	2019	−1346.5	282.3	301.8	1599.7	9443.9	0.8	633.3	7861.9	4973.3	0.0	749.0	0.0	24.3
90	2029	−1712.8	0.0	0.0	1655.0	9031.2	−4.4	630.6	6979.6	5698.6	0.0	323.0	0.0	24.0

Cohort that is age 60 in 1989

Age	Year	Net payment	Labor income taxes	FICA taxes	Excise taxes	Capital income taxes	Seignor-age	Property taxes	OASDI	HI	Welfare AFDC	Welfare General	UI	Food Stamps
60	1989	20626.2	3610.4	3859.1	1734.3	12532.2	1.1	515.1	1139.8	0.0	20.7	343.7	89.0	32.8
70	1999	3524.2	875.4	935.7	1575.6	11600.4	1.5	572.0	8247.8	3164.6	5.4	595.3	0.0	23.4
80	2009	−1633.6	262.0	280.1	1484.6	8764.0	0.8	587.7	7679.8	4615.2	0.0	695.1	0.0	22.6
90	2019	−1930.4	0.0	0.0	1535.8	8381.0	−4.0	585.2	6818.0	5288.3	0.0	299.7	0.0	22.3

APPENDIX TABLE 3
Continued

Average annual values of receipts and payments

			Payments							Receipts				
												Welfare		
		Net payment	Labor income taxes	FICA taxes	Excise taxes	Capital income taxes	Seignor-age	Property taxes	OASDI	HI	AFDC	General	UI	Food Stamps

Cohort that is age 70 in 1989

Age	Year	Net payment	Labor income taxes	FICA taxes	Excise taxes	Capital income taxes	Seignor-age	Property taxes	OASDI	HI	AFDC	General	UI	Food Stamps
70	1989	3270.4	812.3	868.3	1462.2	10765.2	1.4	530.8	7654.0	2936.7	5.0	552.4	0.0	21.7
80	1999	−1516.0	243.2	259.9	1377.7	8133.0	0.7	545.4	7126.9	4283.0	0.0	645.0	0.0	20.9
90	2009	−1791.4	0.0	0.0	1425.3	7777.6	−3.7	543.1	6327.1	4907.6	0.0	278.2	0.0	20.7

Cohort that is age 80 in 1989

Age	Year	Net payment	Labor income taxes	FICA taxes	Excise taxes	Capital income taxes	Seignor-age	Property taxes	OASDI	HI	AFDC	General	UI	Food Stamps
80	1989	−1406.8	225.6	241.2	1278.5	7547.4	0.7	506.1	6613.8	3974.6	0.0	598.6	0.0	19.4
90	1999	−1662.4	0.0	0.0	1322.7	7217.6	−3.5	504.0	5871.6	4554.2	0.0	258.1	0.0	19.2

Cohort that is age 90 in 1989

Age	Year	Net payment	Labor income taxes	FICA taxes	Excise taxes	Capital income taxes	Seignor-age	Property taxes	OASDI	HI	AFDC	General	UI	Food Stamps
90	1989	−1542.7	0.0	0.0	1227.4	6697.9	−3.2	467.7	5448.9	4226.3	0.0	239.5	0.0	17.8

APPENDIX TABLE 4
The Components of Female Generational Accounts ($r=.06$, $g=.0075$)

Average annual values of receipts and payments

Cohort that is age 0 in 1989				Payments								Receipts				
			Labor income taxes	FICA taxes	Excise taxes	Capital income taxes	Seignor-age	Property taxes	OASDI	HI		Welfare			
Age	Year	Net payment									AFDC	General	UI	Food Stamps
0	1989	26.2	0.0	0.0	501.4	0.0	0.0	0.0	21.4	0.0	0.0	453.8	0.0	0.0
10	1999	319.9	0.0	0.0	655.0	0.0	0.0	0.0	81.5	0.0	0.0	253.6	0.0	0.0
20	2009	2527.8	1074.3	1148.3	1358.1	0.0	5.2	30.3	80.0	0.0	389.0	390.4	42.7	186.3
30	2019	6509.9	2512.9	2686.0	2123.5	598.3	3.3	250.4	258.3	0.0	445.4	599.1	87.3	274.4
40	2029	10579.5	2981.7	3187.1	2632.1	2985.7	0.8	479.7	490.2	0.0	303.5	598.0	84.3	211.6
50	2039	14430.3	3022.8	3231.1	2744.8	6230.2	0.2	703.1	574.5	0.0	152.1	595.6	72.2	107.5
60	2049	15001.3	2374.1	2537.7	2500.1	8921.5	2.3	882.6	1449.1	0.0	32.8	622.8	50.8	61.4
70	2059	885.6	822.3	879.0	2090.5	9683.5	5.9	1021.5	7596.0	4954.7	0.0	1009.0	6.2	51.1
80	2069	−5558.9	57.4	61.4	1811.8	7978.8	6.6	1202.0	8281.0	7226.0	0.0	1114.8	0.0	55.1
90	2079	−13169.7	0.0	0.0	1974.6	873.2	−2.6	1429.6	7900.8	8279.8	0.0	1204.6	0.0	59.4

Cohort that is age 10 in 1989				Payments								Receipts				
			Labor income taxes	FICA taxes	Excise taxes	Capital income taxes	Seignor-age	Property taxes	OASDI	HI		Welfare			
Age	Year	Net payment									AFDC	General	UI	Food Stamps
10	1989	296.9	0.0	0.0	607.8	0.0	0.0	0.0	75.6	0.0	0.0	235.3	0.0	0.0
20	1999	2345.8	996.9	1865.6	1260.3	0.0	4.8	28.2	74.2	0.0	361.0	362.3	39.6	172.9
30	2009	6041.2	2332.0	2492.6	1970.6	555.2	3.0	232.4	239.7	0.0	413.4	556.0	81.0	254.6
40	2019	9817.8	2767.0	2957.6	2442.6	2770.8	0.7	445.2	454.9	0.0	281.7	554.9	78.2	196.3
50	2029	13391.4	2805.2	2998.5	2547.2	5781.6	0.2	652.5	533.2	0.0	141.2	552.7	67.0	99.8
60	2039	13921.3	2203.2	2355.0	2320.1	8279.2	2.2	819.0	1344.8	0.0	30.4	578.0	47.1	57.0
70	2049	821.9	763.1	815.7	1940.0	8986.3	5.5	948.0	7049.1	4598.0	0.0	936.4	5.8	47.5
80	2059	−5158.7	53.3	57.0	1681.4	7404.4	6.1	1115.4	7684.8	6705.7	0.0	1034.5	0.0	51.1
90	2069	−12221.5	0.0	0.0	1832.4	810.3	−2.4	1326.7	7331.9	7683.7	0.0	1117.8	0.0	55.1

APPENDIX TABLE 4
Continued

Average annual values of receipts and payments

						Payments						Receipts				
														Welfare		
		Net payment	Labor income taxes	FICA taxes	Excise taxes	Capital income taxes	Seignor- age	Property taxes	OASDI	HI	AFDC	General	UI	Food Stamps
Cohort that is age 20 in 1989														
Age	Year													
20	1989	2176.9	925.2	988.9	1169.6	0.0	4.5	26.1	68.9	0.0	335.0	336.2	36.8	160.5
30	1999	5606.2	2164.1	2313.2	1828.7	515.3	2.8	215.7	222.5	0.0	383.6	515.9	75.2	236.3
40	2009	9110.9	2567.8	2744.7	2266.7	2571.3	0.7	413.1	422.2	0.0	261.4	515.0	72.6	182.2
50	2019	12427.2	2603.2	2782.6	2363.8	5365.4	0.1	605.5	494.8	0.0	131.0	512.9	62.1	92.6
60	2029	12919.0	2044.6	2185.4	2153.0	7683.1	2.0	760.1	1248.0	0.0	28.2	536.4	43.7	52.9
70	2039	762.7	708.2	757.0	1800.3	8339.3	5.1	879.7	6541.6	4267.0	0.0	868.9	5.3	44.0
80	2049	−4787.3	49.5	52.9	1560.3	6871.3	5.6	1035.1	7131.5	6222.9	0.0	960.0	0.0	47.5
90	2059	−11341.6	0.0	0.0	1700.5	752.0	−2.3	1231.2	6804.0	7130.5	0.0	1037.4	0.0	51.1
Cohort that is age 30 in 1989														
Age	Year													
30	1989	5202.6	2008.3	2146.6	1697.1	478.2	2.6	200.2	206.5	0.0	356.0	478.8	69.7	219.3
40	1999	8455.0	2382.9	2547.1	2103.5	2386.2	0.6	383.4	391.0	0.0	242.6	477.9	67.4	169.1
50	2009	11532.5	2415.8	2582.2	2193.6	4979.1	0.1	561.9	459.2	0.0	121.6	476.0	57.7	85.9
60	2019	11988.9	1897.4	2028.1	1998.0	7129.9	1.9	705.3	1158.1	0.0	26.2	497.7	40.6	49.1
70	2029	707.8	657.2	702.5	1670.7	7738.9	4.8	816.4	6070.6	3959.7	0.0	806.4	5.0	40.9
80	2039	−4442.6	45.9	49.1	1448.0	6376.6	5.2	960.6	6618.0	5774.9	0.0	890.9	0.0	44.0
90	2049	−10525.0	0.0	0.0	1578.1	697.9	−2.1	1142.5	6314.2	6617.1	0.0	962.7	0.0	47.5

Cohort that is age 40 in 1989

Age	Year	Net payment	Labor income taxes	FICA taxes	Excise taxes	Capital income taxes	Seignor-age	Property taxes	OASDI	HI	Welfare AFDC	Welfare General	UI	Food Stamps
40	1989	7846.2	2211.4	2363.7	1952.1	2214.4	0.6	355.8	363.6	0.0	225.1	443.5	62.5	156.9
50	1999	10702.2	2241.9	2396.3	2035.7	4620.6	0.1	521.5	426.1	0.0	112.8	441.7	53.5	79.7
60	2009	11125.7	1760.8	1882.1	1854.2	6616.6	1.7	654.6	1074.7	0.0	24.3	461.9	37.7	45.5
70	2019	656.8	609.9	651.9	1550.4	7181.8	4.4	757.6	5633.6	3674.7	0.0	748.3	4.6	37.9
80	2029	−4122.7	42.6	45.5	1343.7	5917.5	4.9	891.4	6141.6	5359.1	0.0	826.8	0.0	40.9
90	2039	−9767.3	0.0	0.0	1464.4	647.6	−1.9	1060.3	5859.6	6140.7	0.0	893.4	0.0	44.0

Cohort that is age 50 in 1989

Age	Year	Net payment	Labor income taxes	FICA taxes	Excise taxes	Capital income taxes	Seignor-age	Property taxes	OASDI	HI	Welfare AFDC	Welfare General	UI	Food Stamps
50	1989	9931.7	2080.5	2223.8	1889.1	4287.9	0.1	483.9	395.4	0.0	104.7	409.9	49.7	74.0
60	1999	10324.7	1634.0	1746.6	1720.7	6140.2	1.6	607.4	997.4	0.0	22.6	428.7	35.0	42.3
70	2009	−5.5	566.0	605.0	1438.8	6664.7	4.1	703.1	5843.0	3410.1	0.0	694.5	4.3	35.2
80	2019	−4496.4	39.5	42.3	1247.0	5491.4	4.5	827.3	6369.9	4973.3	0.0	767.3	0.0	37.9
90	2029	−9703.8	0.0	0.0	1359.0	601.0	−1.8	983.9	6077.4	5698.6	0.0	829.0	0.0	40.9

Cohort that is age 60 in 1989

Age	Year	Net payment	Labor income taxes	FICA taxes	Excise taxes	Capital income taxes	Seignor-age	Property taxes	OASDI	HI	Welfare AFDC	Welfare General	UI	Food Stamps
60	1989	9581.3	1516.4	1620.8	1596.8	5698.2	1.5	563.7	925.6	0.0	20.9	397.8	32.4	39.2
70	1999	−290.5	525.2	561.4	1335.2	6184.9	3.8	652.4	5707.7	3164.6	0.0	644.5	4.0	32.7
80	2009	−4483.8	36.7	39.2	1157.2	5096.1	4.2	767.7	6222.4	4615.2	0.0	712.0	0.0	35.2
90	2019	−9302.0	0.0	0.0	1261.2	557.7	−1.7	913.1	5936.7	5288.3	0.0	769.4	0.0	37.9

APPENDIX TABLE 4
Continued

Average annual values of receipts and payments

Cohort that is age 70 in 1989															
			Payments								Receipts				
													Welfare		
Age	Year	Net payment	Labor income taxes	FICA taxes	Excise taxes	Capital income taxes	Seignor-age	Property taxes	OASDI	HI		AFDC	General	UI	Food Stamps
70	1989	−269.6	487.4	521.0	1239.1	5739.6	3.5	605.5	5296.8	2936.7		0.0	598.1	3.7	30.3
80	1999	−4161.0	34.0	36.4	1073.9	4729.2	3.9	712.4	5774.4	4283.0		0.0	660.8	0.0	32.7
90	2009	−8632.3	0.0	0.0	1170.4	517.6	−1.6	847.4	5509.3	4907.6		0.0	714.0	0.0	35.2

Cohort that is age 80 in 1989															
													Welfare		
Age	Year	Net payment	Labor income taxes	FICA taxes	Excise taxes	Capital income taxes	Seignor-age	Property taxes	OASDI	HI		AFDC	General	UI	Food Stamps
80	1989	−3861.4	31.6	33.8	996.6	4388.7	3.6	661.1	5358.7	3974.6		0.0	613.2	0.0	30.3
90	1999	−8010.8	0.0	0.0	1086.1	480.3	−1.4	786.4	5112.6	4554.2		0.0	662.6	0.0	32.7

Cohort that is age 90 in 1989															
													Welfare		
Age	Year	Net payment	Labor income taxes	FICA taxes	Excise taxes	Capital income taxes	Seignor-age	Property taxes	OASDI	HI		AFDC	General	UI	Food Stamps
90	1989	−7434.0	0.0	0.0	1007.9	445.7	−1.3	729.7	4744.5	4226.3		0.0	614.9	0.0	30.3

APPENDIX TABLE 5
Accounts for Age Zero and Future Male Generations under Alternative Policy Changes ($r=.06$, $g=.0075$)
(thousands of dollars)

Generation's age in 1989	Current policy	Capital gains tax cut	No reduction in Social Security	Faster Medicare growth	$500 billion S&L bailout	Slower growth in government consumption	Current budget agreement[1]		
							A	B	C
0	73.7	73.6	73.3	73.2	73.7	73.7	75.8	75.8	73.8
5	93.2	93.0	92.7	92.5	93.2	93.2	95.7	95.7	93.3
10	116.8	116.6	116.2	115.9	116.8	116.8	119.9	119.9	117.0
15	145.3	145.0	144.5	144.1	145.3	145.3	148.9	148.9	145.6
20	169.1	168.7	168.1	167.7	169.1	169.1	173.0	173.0	169.7
25	193.0	192.6	191.7	191.2	193.0	193.0	197.4	197.4	193.8
30	194.5	194.0	192.9	192.3	194.5	194.5	198.9	198.9	195.4
35	186.0	185.5	184.1	183.3	186.0	186.0	190.3	190.3	186.9
40	176.2	175.6	173.6	172.6	176.2	176.2	180.5	180.5	177.1
45	155.4	154.8	153.1	150.6	155.4	155.6	159.8	159.8	156.4
50	114.1	113.6	112.7	108.7	114.1	114.1	118.3	118.3	115.1
55	69.7	69.3	69.7	63.8	69.7	69.7	73.9	73.9	70.7
60	18.9	18.6	18.9	13.0	18.9	18.9	23.1	23.1	20.2
65	−31.8	−32.1	−31.8	−36.9	−31.8	−31.8	−28.3	−28.3	−30.5
70	−42.7	−42.9	−42.7	−46.5	−42.7	−42.7	−40.1	−40.1	−41.6
75	−41.5	−41.6	−41.5	−44.1	−41.5	−41.5	−39.7	−39.7	−40.6
80	−35.6	−35.7	−35.6	−37.2	−35.6	−35.6	−34.4	−34.4	−34.9
85	−28.2	−28.3	−28.2	−29.0	−28.2	−28.2	−27.4	−27.4	−27.4
90	−1.5	−1.5	−1.5	−1.5	−1.5	−1.5	−1.5	−1.5	−1.5
Future generations	89.5	90.8	94.5	105.3	98.9	64.8	49.8	70.2	83.1

[1] A, all changes are permanent; B, government expenditure reductions are temporary; C, all changes are temporary.

APPENDIX TABLE 5a

Accounts for Age Zero and Future Male Generations under Alternative Policy Simulations ($r=.03$, $g=.0075$)
(thousands of dollars)

Generation's age in 1989	Current policy	Capital gains tax cut	No reduction in Social Security	Faster Medicare growth	$500 billion S&L bailout	Slower growth in government consumption	Current budget agreement[1]		
							A	B	C
0	203.8	203.3	200.6	199.1	203.8	203.8	210.3	210.3	203.9
5	225.3	224.7	221.7	220.0	225.3	225.3	232.3	232.3	225.4
10	247.7	247.1	243.8	241.9	247.7	247.7	255.3	255.3	247.9
15	270.7	270.0	266.4	264.3	270.7	270.7	278.9	278.9	271.1
20	280.1	279.3	275.5	273.3	280.1	280.1	288.3	288.3	280.8
25	292.0	291.1	286.9	284.4	292.0	292.0	300.5	300.5	292.9
30	272.5	271.6	267.0	264.5	272.5	272.5	280.5	280.5	273.5
35	243.2	242.3	237.4	234.7	243.2	243.2	250.8	250.8	244.3
40	215.7	214.7	209.1	206.0	215.7	215.7	222.9	222.9	216.8
45	176.2	175.3	171.1	165.1	176.2	176.2	183.4	183.4	177.4
50	117.3	116.6	114.6	106.2	117.3	117.3	123.9	123.9	118.4
55	60.5	59.8	60.5	49.7	60.5	60.5	66.7	66.7	61.5
60	3.4	2.9	3.4	-6.4	3.4	3.4	9.2	9.2	4.8
65	-47.1	-47.5	-47.1	-54.9	-47.1	-47.1	-42.5	-42.5	-45.6
70	-54.3	-54.6	-54.3	-59.8	-54.3	-54.3	-51.0	-51.0	-53.1
75	-49.6	-49.8	-49.6	-53.1	-49.6	-49.6	-47.3	-47.3	-48.6
80	-40.6	-40.7	-40.6	-42.6	-40.6	-40.6	-39.1	-39.1	-39.8
85	-30.8	-30.8	-30.8	-31.6	-30.8	-30.8	-29.9	-29.9	-29.9
90	-1.5	-1.5	-1.5	-1.5	-1.5	-1.5	-1.5	-1.5	-1.5
Future generations	249.7	250.8	259.0	272.9	253.9	217.9	203.6	233.2	246.5

[1] A, all changes are permanent; B, government expenditure reductions are temporary; C, all changes are temporary.

APPENDIX TABLE 6

Accounts for Age Zero and Future Female Generations under Alternative Policy Changes ($r=.06$, $g=.0075$)
(thousands of dollars)

Generation's age in 1989	Current policy	Capital gains tax cut	No reduction in Social Security	Faster Medicare growth	$500 billion S&L bailout	Slower growth in government consumption	Current budget agreement[1]		
							A	B	C
0	36.4	36.4	36.1	35.7	36.4	36.4	38.1	38.1	36.5
5	46.5	46.4	46.0	45.6	46.5	46.5	48.4	48.4	46.6
10	60.4	60.3	59.8	59.2	60.4	60.4	62.8	62.8	60.6
15	70.7	70.6	70.0	69.3	70.7	70.7	73.3	73.3	71.0
20	85.5	85.3	84.5	83.6	85.5	85.5	88.5	88.5	85.9
25	91.0	90.8	89.8	88.7	91.0	91.0	94.2	94.2	91.6
30	90.9	90.7	89.4	87.9	90.9	90.9	94.1	94.1	91.5
35	86.9	86.7	85.1	83.2	86.9	86.9	90.2	90.2	87.6
40	78.2	77.9	75.8	73.5	78.2	78.2	81.4	81.4	78.9
45	62.9	62.6	60.9	56.9	62.9	62.9	66.2	66.2	63.6
50	41.0	40.7	39.7	33.7	41.0	41.0	44.3	44.3	41.6
55	11.7	11.5	11.7	3.5	11.7	11.7	15.2	15.2	12.3
60	−22.5	−22.7	−22.5	−30.8	−22.5	−22.5	−19.0	−19.0	−21.6
65	−53.7	−53.8	−53.7	−61.0	−53.7	−53.7	−50.5	−50.5	−52.7
70	−60.2	−60.3	−60.2	−66.0	−60.2	−60.2	−57.6	−57.6	−59.3
75	−57.9	−58.0	−57.9	−61.9	−57.9	−57.9	−56.0	−56.0	−57.1
80	−50.8	−50.8	−50.8	−53.2	−50.8	−50.8	−49.5	−49.5	−50.2
85	−42.7	−42.7	−42.7	−43.7	−42.7	−42.7	−41.8	−41.8	−41.8
90	−7.4	−7.4	−7.4	−7.4	−7.4	−7.4	−7.4	−7.4	−7.4
Future generations	44.2	44.9	46.5	51.4	48.9	32.0	25.0	35.2	41.1

[1] A, all changes are permanent; B, government expenditure reductions are temporary; C, all changes are temporary.

APPENDIX TABLE 6a
Accounts for Age Zero and Future Female Generations under Alternative Policy Simulations ($r=.03$, $g=.0075$) (thousands of dollars)

Generation's age in 1989	Current policy	Capital gains tax cut	No reduction in Social Security	Faster Medicare growth	$500 billion S&L bailout	Slower growth in government consumption	Current budget agreement[1]		
							A	B	C
0	91.8	91.6	88.7	85.4	91.8	91.8	96.9	96.9	91.9
5	101.2	101.0	97.8	94.2	101.2	101.2	106.6	106.6	101.3
10	114.7	114.4	110.8	106.7	114.7	114.7	120.7	120.7	114.9
15	117.9	117.6	113.8	109.5	117.9	117.9	124.0	124.0	118.2
20	127.1	126.7	122.5	117.7	127.1	127.1	133.5	133.5	127.6
25	123.5	123.1	118.6	113.4	123.5	123.5	129.9	129.9	124.1
30	113.3	112.9	107.9	102.2	113.3	113.3	119.5	119.5	114.0
35	99.2	98.8	93.3	87.1	99.2	99.2	105.3	105.3	99.9
40	80.4	79.9	73.9	67.1	80.4	80.4	86.2	86.2	81.1
45	54.1	53.7	49.3	39.5	54.1	54.1	59.8	59.8	54.9
50	22.5	22.1	19.8	6.9	22.5	22.5	28.1	28.1	23.2
55	−13.8	−14.1	−13.8	−29.5	−13.8	−13.8	−8.3	−8.3	−13.1
60	−49.2	−49.5	−49.2	−63.6	−49.2	−49.2	−44.1	−44.1	−48.2
65	−77.4	−77.6	−77.4	−89.2	−77.4	−77.4	−73.1	−73.1	−76.3
70	−78.7	−78.9	−78.7	−87.4	−78.7	−78.7	−75.3	−75.3	−77.7
75	−70.9	−71.0	−70.9	−76.4	−70.9	−70.9	−75.3	−68.5	−77.7
80	−58.8	−58.8	−58.8	−61.8	−58.8	−58.8	−57.2	−57.2	−58.1
85	−46.6	−46.6	−46.6	−47.8	−46.6	−46.6	−45.7	−45.7	−45.7
90	−7.4	−7.4	−7.4	−7.4	−7.4	−7.4	−7.4	−7.4	−7.4
Future generations	112.5	113.0	114.5	117.1	114.4	98.2	93.8	107.5	111.1

[1] A, all changes are permanent; B, government expenditure reductions are temporary; C, all changes are temporary.

THE INCIDENCE OF MANDATED EMPLOYER-PROVIDED INSURANCE: LESSONS FROM WORKERS' COMPENSATION INSURANCE

Jonathan Gruber
Harvard University

Alan B. Krueger
Princeton University and NBER

EXECUTIVE SUMMARY

Workers' compensation insurance provides cash payments and medical benefits to workers who incur a work-related injury or illness. Many features of the workers' compensation program parallel features of proposed mandated employer-paid health insurance plans. This paper empirically examines the incidence of the workers' compensation program

We are grateful to David Bradford, Dan Feenberg, Jim Hines, Larry Katz, Nancy Rose, Larry Summers, and seminar participants at the NBER and Harvard University for helpful comments, to John F. Burton, Jr. for providing unpublished data on workers' compensation insurance rates, and to Doug Hendrickson for assistance with data entry. J. Gruber acknowledges a Sloan Doctoral Dissertation Fellowship, and A. B. Krueger acknowledges financial support from an NBER Olin Fellowship. The data and computer programs used in the preparation of this paper are available on request to the authors.

to infer the likely consequences of mandated health insurance proposals. In certain industries, such as trucking and carpentry, workers' compensation insurance costs are quite large, and vary tremendously within states over time, and across states at a moment in time. This variation is used to identify the incidence of the program. Empirical analysis of two data sets suggests that changes in employers' costs of workers' compensation insurance are largely shifted to employees in the form of lower wages. In addition, higher insurance costs are found to have a negative but statistically insignificant effect on employment. The implied elasticity of labor demand from our results is about $-.50$.

There are two primary methods that a government can use to provide universal access to a good or service: it can provide the good or service directly, as in the case of public education and national parks, or it can mandate that employers arrange for provision of the good or service for their workers and dependents, as in the case of workers' compensation insurance and certain pension safeguards. These two approaches may have different implications for the efficiency and equity of a public program. Interest in understanding the economic impact of employer mandates has risen in recent years as several mandated employer-provided health insurance proposals have gained support.

An estimated 15.2% of Americans under age 65 (some 33 million people) lack health insurance coverage.[1] Bills that would require employers to provide the uninsured with a minimum level of medical insurance are currently pending before the Congress and many state legislatures, and such legislation has already been enacted in Hawaii and Massachusetts. These bills are markedly different from national health insurance plans in most European countries, which are funded by general revenues and administered directly by the state.

Several factors explain the current political popularity of mandated health insurance proposals. More than two-thirds of the uninsured are full-time, full-year workers or are in families that are headed by a full-time, full-year worker. Moreover, nearly 80% of those with medical insurance already obtain their insurance from an employer-sponsored plan.[2] Consequently, employer mandates have the potential to extend health insurance coverage to a large number of uninsured individuals without radically restructuring the insurance industry. Furthermore, mandating that employers provide health insurance for their workers is

---

[1] This estimate was calculated by the authors from the March 1989 Current Population Survey, and pertains to calendar year 1988.

[2] These statistics are from Chollet (1987).

a way for the government to expand health insurance coverage without raising taxes. This feature of mandated benefits takes on added significance in an era of tight budget constraints.

Although the government may be able to shed responsibility for the cost of providing health insurance in a mandated program, there may nevertheless be substantial societal costs to such a program. In particular, requiring employers to pay health insurance premiums may increase the cost of hiring workers and result in lower employment. Indeed, Dr. Lewis Sullivan, Secretary of Health and Human Services, recently based his opposition to mandated health benefits on the presumption that: "By adding overly burdensome mandates on business, we could retard economic growth and constrict employment opportunities."[3]

But will mandated health insurance dramatically reduce employment? Traditional payroll tax incidence models suggest that some portion of the rise in employer costs may be shifted to wages, mitigating the fall in employment. And perhaps more importantly, if employees value health insurance, the theory of compensating wage differentials suggests that wages will fall even further than in the case of a pure payroll tax, further reducing the employment decline. In equilibrium, if the value employees place on health insurance is equivalent to the employers' costs of providing insurance, wages will be reduced by the full cost of the benefit and employment will be unchanged.

Although economic models provide a clear framework for analyzing the impact of compulsory insurance, the available empirical evidence on the trade-off between fringe benefits and wages provides little evidence of wage offsets. In fact, an impressive number of published papers report the "wrong" signed coefficient in analyses of the wage–fringe benefit relationship.[4] More generally, the labor economics literature has been largely unsuccessful in documenting consistent evidence of compensating wage differentials for a variety of nonpecuniary factors, such as the risk of unemployment and workplace hazards.[5] The findings of this literature challenge the view that the costs of mandated employer-provided health insurance will be shifted to employees in the form of lower pay.

Nevertheless, there are several reasons why the empirical evidence may fail to find evidence of a trade-off between fringe benefits and wages even if such a trade-off exists. First, available data sets do not permit researchers to control for all aspects of worker productivity. This

---

[3] Quoted from *The New York Times*, July 24, 1990, p. A10.

[4] A good example of this literature is Smith and Ehrenberg (1983). Additional references are given in Section II.

[5] See Brown (1980) and Abowd and Ashenfelter (1981) for examples.

is a problem because more productive employees may prefer to take their compensation in the form of both higher wages and higher fringe benefits. Second, most of the literature has examined fringe benefits that are voluntarily chosen by employers and employees. With voluntary fringes, it is difficult to identify exogenous variation in benefits that should induce wage offsets. Finally, the studies that have examined the effect on wages of mandated benefits (e.g., unemployment insurance) are identified by relatively small differences in program costs across states and over time. As a result, any trade-off between fringes and wages could easily be swamped by greater variation in omitted, state-level factors, such as union power.

This paper presents new evidence on the incidence of mandated employer-provided insurance by examining the experience of the workers' compensation insurance program. Workers' compensation laws require employers to secure insurance to provide a minimum level of cash payments and medical benefits in the event of work-related injuries and illnesses. The laws are exclusively administered by the states, which leads to wide variation in the generosity of the program across the states at a point in time, and within states over time. For example, the insurance rate in the trucking industry in 1987 ranged from 3% of payroll in Indiana to 25% of payroll in Montana. We use two data sets to estimate the effect of increases in workers' compensation costs on wages and employment. Throughout much of the analysis we focus on five high-risk industries (truck drivers, carpenters, plumbers, gasoline station employees, and nonprofessional hospital employees) that have great cost variability.

The structure of the workers' compensation program enables us to overcome at least some of the limitations of the past literature. First, workers' compensation benefits are not voluntary fringe benefits. Second, we test for insurance shifting in narrowly defined industries and occupations, so bias due to omitted worker and job characteristics poses less of a problem. Third, most of the analysis uses the wide variation in the growth of insurance rates in states over a 10-year period to identify the extent of insurance rate shifting. We are aware of no other payroll "tax" that varies as much across states or over time as workers' compensation insurance rates.

Finally, we note that the workers' compensation insurance program has much in common with proposed mandated health insurance schemes. In both programs, employers are required to secure a minimum level of insurance for their workers, and employers directly pay the insurance premiums. Furthermore, a substantial component (over 35% of costs) of the workers' compensation program is medical insurance for workplace injuries and illnesses. Consequently, inferences drawn from the workers' compensation program may be relevant for mandated health insurance.

I. CONCEPTUAL FRAMEWORK AND INSTITUTIONAL ANALYSIS

Summers (1989) argues that, because of wage offsets, the incidence and welfare costs of employer mandated benefits are different from that of a pure payroll tax, which is used to finance public provision of benefits.[6] The basic point of his argument is illustrated in Figure 1.[7] The imposition of an employer mandate will shift the labor demand curve downward (from DD to $D'D'$) and, with a fixed labor supply schedule, employment would fall from E_0 to E_1 and wages from W_0 to W_1. However, if workers value the benefit that they are receiving, labor supply will shift outward, and employment will fall by a lesser amount (to E_2 in Figure 1), whereas wages will fall by an even greater amount (to W_2). Thus, wage offsets in response to mandated benefits have the potential to reduce the labor cost increases created by mandated benefits.[8]

Formally, suppose that labor demand (L_d) is given by

$$L_d = f_d(W + C) \tag{1}$$

and further suppose that labor supply (L_s) is given by

$$L_s = f_s(W + \alpha C) \tag{2}$$

where C is the cost of mandated health insurance, αC is the monetary value that employees place on health insurance, and W is the wage rate. Using this notation it can easily be shown that

$$\frac{dW}{dC} = -\frac{\eta^d - \alpha\eta^s}{\eta^d - \eta^s} \tag{3}$$

---

[6] Danzon (1989) provides a related analysis, which also models the impact of heterogeneous workers and considers the general equilibrium implications.

[7] We have drawn the labor supply curve assuming the substitution effect dominates the income effect in the relevant range.

[8] As Summers notes, this analysis must be construed differently for health care benefits, which are fixed with respect to hours of (full-time) work, and for other types of benefits. This does not affect the analysis as long as one assumes that employment, rather than hours, are represented on the horizontal axis.

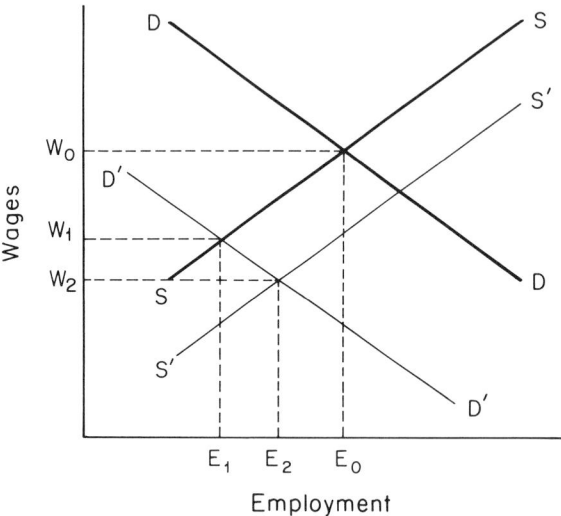

FIGURE 1. *The Labor Market Impact of Mandated Benefits*

where η^d and η^s are the elasticities of demand for and supply of labor, respectively. From equation (3) it is clear that if α equals one, wages would fall by the full cost of the mandated benefit. In this situation, the employer's cost of providing the mandated benefit would be fully shifted to employees. On the other hand, if employees place no value on mandated health insurance, which is the case if $\alpha = 0$, the incidence of mandated health insurance is exactly analogous to that of a payroll tax.

As explained below, we rely on interstate differences in workers' compensation costs across industrial groups over a 10-year time period in our empirical work. If, as seems likely, workers are mobile across states and/or industries over this time horizon, η^s will be quite large. In the limit, as η^s approaches infinity the proportion of costs that are shifted to wages tends to α.

The effect of mandating benefits on employment is

$$\frac{dL}{L} = \frac{W_0 - W_2 - C}{W_0} \eta^d \tag{4}$$

which indicates that the amount of employment sacrificed because of mandated health insurance is inversely related to the wage offset caused by the provision of health insurance. Thus, we can summarize the labor market effects of mandated benefits in terms of the elasticities of supply and demand for labor, the cost of the benefit, and the fraction of that cost that is valued by employees.

A. Previous Evidence

What is the evidence for the shifting of employer benefit costs? A large empirical literature addresses this question by estimating hedonic labor market relationships (see Rosen, 1987 for a survey). However, past efforts to find the expected negative coefficient on fringe benefits in wage equations have been largely unsuccessful, as is discussed by Triplett (1983), Smith and Ehrenberg (1983), Leibowitz (1983), and Monheit, Hagan, Berk, and Farley (1985). Perhaps the failure to find a trade-off between fringe benefits and wages should not be surprising in view of the difficulty establishing compensating wage differentials for a variety of other nonwage aspects of work, including the risk of layoff. In fact, with the notable exception of work fatalities, the labor economics literature has not found consistent evidence of compensating wage differentials for work disamenities (Brown, 1980, Smith, 1979).

One of the difficulties in interpreting this literature, however, is that most studies of compensating differentials compare wages and working conditions among workers in different occupations and industries. There is nothing in the theory of compensating differentials to suggest that lawyers should receive less generous fringe benefits than manual laborers because of their higher wage. Indeed, if fringe benefits are a normal good, one would expect higher-paid workers to take some of their compensation in the form of better working conditions and fringe benefits. Nevertheless, the past literature on compensating differentials should challenge researchers to search for additional evidence before assuming that employee valuation of fringe benefits will be reflected in the incidence of those benefits.

Finally, we note that a related empirical literature has developed within public finance attempting to measure the incidence of payroll taxes. Unlike research on compensating differentials, most of this research is based on time-series or cross-country data. In an early cross-country study, Brittain (1972) reports evidence that he interprets as showing payroll taxes are fully offset by lower wages.[9] In an analysis of an unusual natural social experiment, Holmlund (1983) uses time-series data on payroll taxes in Sweden to examine wage growth in a period when the payroll tax increased from 14 to 40%. He estimates that

---

[9] More specifically, Brittain finds that capital's share does not decline with the imposition of a payroll tax. See Feldstein (1972) for a detailed critique of Brittain's work, in which he points out that Brittain's test can be viewed simply as evidence that the gross wage equals the marginal product of labor.

roughly 50% of the employer payroll tax is shifted to wages in the short run. Finally, Hamermesh (1979) uses the variation in payroll tax rates due to the social security payroll tax limit to estimate wage offsets; his estimates indicate that from 0 to 35% of the social security tax is shifted to wages.[10]

Although it would be desirable to have estimates of all of the parameters in equation (3) to forecast the incidence of mandated insurance benefits, in view of the past literature we have a more modest goal: We simply would like to examine the empirical plausibility of wage offsets in response to changes in the employers' cost of providing mandated benefits in the workers' compensation insurance program. If the evidence suggests that the employers' cost of providing workers' compensation insurance are offset by lower wages, then the expectation that mandated health insurance costs would be shifted to wages will be strengthened.

B. Description of Health Insurance Proposals

The potential importance of cost shifting of mandated health benefits is highlighted in Table 1, which summarizes several recent Federal and state proposals to compel employers to provide health care benefits. The Federal proposal (The Basic Health Benefits for All Americans Act) would mandate that all full-time workers have health insurance, with firms paying at least 80% of the premiums.[11] Similarly, the state proposals include some employer costs, either through a strict provision mandate, through a payroll tax, or through a "pay-or-play" plan, in which firms that do not provide a certain minimum level of health care must pay the difference in the form of a payroll tax. For example, in Massachusetts, any firm that does not spend an average of 12% of the Medical Security Wage Base on employee health benefits must pay the difference into a fund from which the state will purchase insurance for the uninsured.[12]

Table 1 indicates that employers will nominally bear the cost of providing health insurance for their employees according to the proposed legislation in each state. In addition, many of the proposed laws would use tax revenue generated by employer mandates to fund a larger universal insurance system, which would extend coverage to uninsured individu-

---

[10] Hamermesh's range of tax rates is from 0 to 5.85%. By contrast, the range in workers' compensation insurance rates across states in the industries we examine is from 3 to 26% of payroll.

[11] This bill passed the Senate Labor and Human Resources Committee, and is currently being discussed, along with alternative proposals, by a bipartisan Senate working group.

[12] This base is currently $14,000, and is indexed for medical inflation.

als who do not work. If the insurance provided to nonemployed individuals is commensurate with that provided through employment, the labor supply curve depicted in Figure 1 would not shift. More generally, the extent the labor supply curve shifts is inversely related to the quality of health insurance provided to nonworkers.[13]

The ultimate incidence of mandated employer-provided health insurance plans is difficult to predict because of the modest experience with such plans in the United States. However, the structure of workers' compensation insurance, which in many respects is similar to proposed health insurance plans, provides an opportunity to estimate the actual incidence of mandated employer-provided insurance.

II. WORKERS' COMPENSATION INSURANCE

Workers' compensation insurance is the oldest and largest mandated employer benefit program in the United States. In 1987 (the latest year with available data) workers' compensation benefits totaled $27.4 billion, and employer insurance costs equalled $38 billion.[14] The structure of the program allows for a test of the incidence of mandated benefits. Employers are required to purchase insurance or self-insure to provide a minimum level of cash benefits and medical care for workers who suffer a work-related injury or illness. Employees are covered by workers' compensation immediately on being hired.

The level of benefits that employers are required to provide varies tremendously across states, and has increased substantially in many states since the mid-1970s.[15] Table 2 documents the variability in workers' compensation benefits for a sample of 10 states. In Indiana, for example, an employee whose arm is permanently disabled in a work-related accident is entitled to a maximum indemnity benefit of $27,450. The same injury in Illinois qualifies for a maximum benefit that is more than five times as generous ($142,112). Similarly, benefits for the other types of injuries exhibit tremendous variability across states.

In addition, although it is difficult to quantify, it is widely believed

---

[13] Notice also that as the quality of health insurance provided to nonworkers improves, the relative efficiency gains of mandated benefits vis-à-vis public provision, which Summers (1989) emphasizes, declines.

[14] These statistics are from Nelson (1990), Tables 1 and 7.

[15] In large part, several states increased their workers' compensation benefits in the 1970s to conform with the recommendations of the National Commission on Workmen's Compensation Laws.

TABLE 1
Selected State and Federal Health Insurance Proposals

State	Coverage	Funding	Other features
U.S. Sen. Bill 768	Full time workers; may be extended to all workers above 185% of poverty line	Firms pay 80% of premiums, but pay 100% if worker earns less than 125% of minimum wage; comprehensive coverage	Federal subsidies for small firms; new small firms may offer less protection
CA Ass. Bill 3032 (1)	All employees, except new hires and those covered by workers' comp	Employers pay 75% of individual premiums, and 50% of family premiums; part-time workers are prorated	Tax credit of 25% of cost for small firms; insurers must accept small groups and must set "comparable" rates across groups
(2) "Cal-Care"	Low profit firms; low income/uncovered workers	Redirected employer tax credits and other state funds—reduced benefits	Firms with low profits are subsidized; low-wage workers are subsidized
CT Sen. Bill 342	Small firms	Employers pay 100% for small firms; waive premium tax	Limited loss ratios

The Incidence of Mandated Employer-Provided Insurance

Act	Coverage	Financing	Small firm provisions
HI Prepd. Health Care Act	Employees >20 hours/week and above 0.867 × minimum wage	Employers pay 50% of premiums, but a limit on worker expense of 1.5% of wages	
MA Health Security Act	Universal	12% payroll tax capped at Medical Social Security wage base, minus firm's current medical benefits	Tax credit for small firms (under 50 employees)
MI Sen. Bill 97	Minimum wage employees and low-wage workers who work more than 17.5 hours/week	3% tax on workers not covered and firms not covering (if more than 10 employees)—state contributes 3% also	
NJ Ass. 3382	All full time workers at firms with at least 6 employees	12% payroll tax up to Medical Social Security wage base (currently $14,000)	Study measures to help small firms
OR Health Partnership Act	Firms with less than 25 workers	Firm pays 75% of worker premium and 50% of dependent premium	Tax credit of 50% of cost for small firms could expand coverage to all workers

TABLE 2
Maximum Indemnity Benefits Paid to Selected Types of Work Injuries: 12 States in 1990

State	Type of permanent impairment					Temporary injury (10 weeks)
	Arm	Hand	Finger[1]	Leg	Foot	
California	$58,975	$43,450	$3,360	$64,575	$33,740	$2,660
Georgia	39,375	28,000	7,000	39,375	23,625	1,750
Illinois	142,112	114,899	24,189	120,946	93,733	6,047
Indiana	27,450	21,960	4,392	24,705	19,215	2,741
Hawaii	119,496	93,452	17,618	110,304	78,515	3,830
Massachusetts	20,402	16,132	NA	18,504	13,760	4,745
Michigan	114,863	91,805	16,226	91,805	69,174	4,270
Mississippi	42,516	31,887	7,440	37,202	26,573	2,126
Missouri	40,333	30,424	7,823	35,987	26,947	2,898
New Jersey	89,539	54,390	4,933	85,469	45,386	3,700
New York	93,600	73,200	13,800	86,400	61,500	3,000
Texas	47,600	35,700	10,710	47,600	29,750	2,380

[1] Benefit is for loss of use of index finger.

Source: Derived from *1990 Analysis of Workers' Compensation Laws.* Washington, DC: U.S. Chamber of Commerce, 1990, Chart 6 and 7.

that some states are more restrictive than others in permitting certain kinds of claims. This is especially likely to be the case for back injuries, which are difficult to diagnose objectively, and costly to treat.[16] Finally, some states require more generous medical benefits than others. For example, states vary in the extent of choice they allow employees over their treating physician.[17]

In most states workers' compensation insurance rates are established by a rating bureau. In principle, these rates are based on the actuarial cost of workers' compensation insurance, which is the expected benefit paid to each injury times the probability that a worker will incur each type of injury. A different rate is established for several hundred detailed industrial/occupational groups, known as activities. In 36 states, a national rate-making organization known as the National Council on Compensation Insurance (NCCI) pools information on risks and proposes rates for each activity. Several other states follow procedures that

---

[16] We also note that there is variability across states in the waiting period required before benefit payments commence, and in the retroactive period on which benefits are paid retroactively to compensate for the waiting period.

[17] See Boden and Fleishman (1989) for an analysis of interstate differences in medical costs in workers' compensation insurance.

are similar to the NCCI. The rates adopted by the states are known as "manual" rates.

Manual rates are the initial rate posted to firms, but they are not the actual, bottom line cost of insurance in many cases. For many employers, manual rates are adjusted in response to the specific firm's loss experience (e.g., experience rating), dividends are paid by insurance companies, and large firms may be retrospectively rated.[18] Because manual rates and the bottom line insurance costs are highly correlated, manual rates provide a reasonable approximation of the actuarial cost of benefits for each activity.[19] Furthermore, unlike in unemployment insurance, there is no cross-industry subsidization in workers' compensation rates.

Table 3 summarizes the interstate variability in workers' compensation rates for 47 states with comparable rating systems in 1987.[20] The table focuses on five activities that are the focus of our empirical analysis on premium shifting (carpenters, gasoline station workers, nonprofessional hospital employees, plumbers, and truck drivers).[21] These activities were selected because they comprise a large sample of workers in most states, and because they concord well with the occupational and industry definitions used by the Census Bureau. Furthermore, we selected these activities because work-injury rates are high in these jobs. For example, Table 3 shows that 1 in 20 truck drivers receives workers' compensation in a year, as opposed to less than 1 in 50 workers in all jobs. Because work injuries are a prominent feature of employment in these jobs, it is more likely that workers will be aware of their benefits under workers' compensation insurance and that the cost of providing these benefits will be shifted onto wages.

Table 4 further illustrates the variability in insurance costs by listing the manual rates for truck drivers in each state in 1978 and 1987. The spread in insurance rates for truck drivers across the states is enormous. For example, in 1987 the rate for truck drivers in Minnesota was 21% of

---

[18] The rate-making process is described in detail in Burton, Hunt, and Krueger (1985). Although on net experience rating hardly changes the average cost of workers' compensation insurance in a state, the other rating devices tend to reduce employers' costs, on average.

[19] For example, the correlation between the average manual rate in a state and the average manual rates adjusted to reflect dividends, experience rating, premium discounts, and rate deviations is 0.85. (*Source:* authors' estimates based on Table 4 and Table 22 of Burton, Hunt, and Krueger, 1985.)

[20] The insurance rates are described in more detail in the Data Appendix.

[21] The rates for carpenters are a weighted average of two carpentry classes (NCCI class 5403 and 5645), where the weights are the payroll attributed to each class nationally.

TABLE 3
Characteristics of State Workers' Compensation Insurance Rates[1]: Selected Activities, 1987

Activity	(1) Mean[2] rate	(2) SD[2]	(3) Minimum	(4) Maximum	(5) Incidence rate[3]
1. Carpenters	11.32	4.86	3.35	26.25	3.28
2. Gasoline stations	5.18	1.85	1.73	11.09	2.16
3. Plumbers	6.02	2.45	1.74	15.05	3.34
4. Truck drivers	10.76	4.69	3.01	25.40	5.64
5. Nonprofessional hospital workers	4.43	2.32	1.42	13.00	2.93
6. All activities[4]	2.12	NA	NA	NA	1.72

[1] The insurance rates described in the first four columns refer to the "manual" rate for each state. No adjustments have been made for premium discounts, experience rating, dividends, and other competitive devices.

[2] Means and standard deviations (SD) are weighted by each industry's employment in the state. The sample consists of 46 states and the District of Columbia.

[3] The incidence rate measures the percent of private, non-self-employed workers who received income from workers' compensation insurance in calender years 1986 and 1987. These estimates were derived from the March 1987 and 1988 Current Population Survey tapes by the authors.

[4] The average manual rate for all activities is a payroll-weighted average of 44 activities, which account for 61% of payroll covered by workers' compensation insurance. This estimate is taken from Burton and Schmidle (1989, Table 1).

TABLE 4
Workers' Compensation Rates as a Percent of Payroll in the Trucking Industry (Class 7219)

State	1978	1987	Change 1987–1978
Alabama	4.49	10.07	5.58
Alaska	10.55	17.41	6.86
Arkansas	15.94	10.86	−5.08
Arizona	11.68	11.22	−0.46
California	10.04	17.26	7.22
Colorado	5.88	11.91	6.03
Connecticut	6.78	12.91	6.13
Delaware	10.45	9.79	−0.66
D.C.	15.04	16.04	1.00
Florida	17.71	15.12	−2.59
Georgia	4.70	7.73	3.03
Hawaii	9.71	20.29	10.58
Idaho	6.39	15.50	9.11
Illinois	6.01	11.45	5.44
Indiana	2.39	3.01	0.62

Iowa	5.89	8.77	2.88
Kansas	4.59	6.85	2.26
Kentucky	7.04	8.05	1.01
Louisiana	10.66	10.65	−0.01
Maine	7.05	9.16	2.11
Maryland	5.85	11.09	5.24
Massachusetts	5.50	8.48	2.98
Michigan	9.24	15.05	5.81
Minnesota	11.5	20.93	9.43
Mississippi	6.27	7.98	1.71
Missouri	NA	5.16	NA
Montana	8.27	25.40	17.13
Nebraska	5.04	6.47	1.43
New Hampshire	4.16	12.55	8.39
New Jersey	7.36	7.89	0.53
New Mexico	8.6	12.23	3.63
New York	9.62	5.97	−3.65
North Carolina	2.42	5.16	2.74
Ohio	5.32	12.20	6.88
Oklahoma	7.81	11.55	3.74
Oregon	14.68	23.46	8.78
Pennsylvania	NA	15.97	NA
Rhode Island	5.15	7.27	2.12
South Carolina	3.68	8.12	4.44
South Dakota	5.87	8.22	2.35
Tennessee	2.88	4.37	1.49
Texas	6.83	9.98	3.15
Utah	4.92	9.23	4.31
Vermont	3.11	6.53	3.42
Virginia	4.28	6.51	2.23
West Virginia	NA	5.67	NA
Wisconsin	3.41	8.86	5.45

payroll, while the rate for the same category of workers in Indiana was only 3% of payroll.[22] Furthermore, there is great diversity among the states in the growth in these insurance rates over the last 10 years. For example, rates soared from 9.7 to 20.3% of payroll in Hawaii between 1978 and 1987, while they fell by nearly 4 points in New York over the same time period. An important source of variation for within-state changes in workers' compensation costs over time is changes in benefit generosity (see Krueger and Burton, 1990; Butler and Worrall, 1990).

We are aware of only one study that uses interstate variation in work-

---

[22] Insurance rates for truck drivers are especially high because they have a high injury rate, and because their injuries tend to be relatively costly. Interestingly, data for Minnesota indicate that only 14% of truck drivers' injuries are from highway accidents, while almost half are from falls or strains and sprains (see Lewis, Meyers, and Senese, 1988).

ers' compensation costs to estimate the extent of shifting of mandated benefits.[23] Dorsey and Walzer (1983) use the May 1978 Current Population Survey to estimate the trade-off between employer liability for injuries as measured by workers' compensation costs and earnings. They find a large, negative effect of workers' compensation costs on wages in the nonunion sector, and a large, positive effect of workers' compensation costs in the union sector. Our analysis has several different features than Dorsey and Walzer's. Most importantly, we estimate the extent of cost shifting for narrowly defined activities that have wide interstate variability in costs, and we incorporate permanent state effects in the analysis. In addition, we provide estimates of the effect of workers' compensation insurance costs on employment.

III. ESTIMATES OF THE INCIDENCE OF WORKERS' COMPENSATION INSURANCE

We base our initial analysis of insurance cost shifting on microdata from the merged outgoing rotation group (OGRG) samples of the Current Population Survey (CPS). The CPS is a monthly survey of a rotating sample of over 55,000 households containing approximately 110,000 individuals. The Outgoing Rotation Group files consist of all individuals who are in their last survey month. The extracts of the CPS that we use are described in detail in the Data Appendix. Briefly, our sample contains privately employed carpenters, truck drivers, nonprofessional hospital employees, gasoline station employees, and plumbers. Self-employed workers are excluded from the sample. The data are taken from the 1979, 1980, 1981, 1987, and 1988 CPS files. For each worker in the sample we merge on the corresponding workers' compensation manual rate in the worker's state and industry/occupation group (activity).[24] A worker is observed in only one year, but we can control for permanent *state* effects because each year we have a sample of individuals from a constant set of states.

The CPS data have several advantages over other microdata sets for

---

[23] Moore and Viscusi (1990, Chapter 2) review several studies that estimate the relationship between wages and workers' compensation benefit levels. Most of these studies find a negative relationship.

[24] To be precise, we assign the 1978 workers' compensation rates to individuals in the 1979–1981 CPSs, and the 1987 rates to individuals in the 1987–1988 CPS. Data on workers' compensation rates for most states were provided to us by John F. Burton, Jr., from his ongoing research on measuring workers' compensation costs. Tracking down rates for all the intervening years would be a difficult task, and we suspect that using rates for 1978 and 1987 does not greatly affect the results.

this analysis. Most importantly, the large samples provided by the CPS enable us to focus on a narrow set of activities. Furthermore, the CPS contains information on several employee characteristics, including education, potential experience, marital status, and apprenticeship status.[25]

Using the pooled time-series/cross section of CPS data, we estimate a wage equation of the following form separately for each industry/occupation group:

$$\ln W_{ijt} = \beta_0 + \beta_1 C_{jt} + \beta_2 X_{ijt} + \alpha_t + \mu_j + \epsilon_{ijt} \qquad (5)$$

where $\ln W_{ijt}$ is the natural log of the usual hourly wage rate, C_{jt} is the appropriate workers' compensation rate, X_{ijt} is a vector of covariates, α_t represents a set of year dummy variables ($t=1980,1981,1987,1988$), μ_j represents a set of state dummy variables, and ϵ_{ijt} is a stochastic error term. The subscript i indicates individuals, j indicates states, and t indicates years. Coefficient estimates are denoted by βs.

In contrast to past studies of compensating differentials that pool individuals from different occupations and industries and then control for average injury rates at the three-digit occupation or industry level, we estimate the wage–cost trade-off relationship within each three-digit industry/occupation group. Furthermore, since state and year dummy variables are included in equation (5), the incidence of workers' compensation costs is identified by varying patterns in workers' compensation rates within states over time. An estimate -1 for β_1 would indicate that increases in workers' compensation costs are fully offset by lower wages, while a coefficient of 0 would imply no wage offsets.

Workers' compensation benefits are not subject to federal income tax. Therefore, one might expect that the appropriate specification of equation (5) would utilize the after-tax wage as the dependent variable. However, if the tax rate for individuals in these activities is proportional to wages, then because the dependent variable is specified in log form the tax rate will be absorbed by the intercept term. Furthermore, the assumption of proportional taxes is likely to be approximately correct in this sample because most workers in these activities are below the earnings ceiling for the OASDHI payroll tax, and because workers in these activities are likely to be in a common tax bracket for the federal income tax.

Estimates of equation (5) are reported for each activity in the first five columns of Table 5. In four of the five activities we find a negative relationship between workers' compensation insurance rates and wages, but the relationship is statistically significant only for truck drivers. Also, the

---

[25] One shortcoming of the OGRG CPS files is that union status is not available before 1983.

TABLE 5
OLS Regression Estimates of Wage Equations[1]

	Occupation/industry group						
Variable	Carpenters (1)	Gasoline stations (2)	Hospital workers (3)	Plumbers (4)	Truck drivers (5)	All Activities (6)	(7)
1. Workers Compensation insurance rate	−.517 (.327)	−.651 (.839)	−.119 (.577)	1.729 (1.050)	−.966 (.331)	−.187 (.136)	−.865 (.184)
2. Male (1=yes)	.021 (.065)	.096 (.020)	.029 (.016)	.191 (.355)	.078 (.059)	.049 (.014)	.050 (.014)
3. Black (1=yes)	−.108 (.027)	−.098 (.027)	−.005 (.014)	−.197 (.041)	−.082 (.022)	−.067 (.011)	−.078 (.011)
4. Other nonwhite (1=yes)	−.022 (.037)	−.049 (.039)	−.045 (.032)	−.149 (.076)	−.108 (.064)	−.064 (.021)	−.056 (.021)
5. Years of education	.036 (.002)	.040 (.003)	.021 (.002)	.044 (.005)	.031 (.003)	.035 (.001)	.033 (.001)
6. Potential experience	.026 (.002)	.021 (.002)	.008 (.001)	.032 (.003)	.022 (.002)	.022 (.001)	.021 (.001)
7. Potential experience squared/1000	−.400 (.030)	−.382 (.039)	−.075 (.029)	−.476 (.063)	−.329 (.043)	−.327 (.018)	−.323 (.018)

The Incidence of Mandated Employer-Provided Insurance   129

	(1)	(2)	(3)	(4)	(5)	(6)	(7)
8. Apprentice (1=yes)	-.075 (.039)	—	—	—	—	-.165 (.027)	-.188 (.027)
9. Part-time worker (1=yes)	-.199 (.021)	-.126 (.015)	-.092 (.015)	-.203 (.040)	-.081 (.029)	-.128 (.010)	-.122 (.010)
10. Metropolitan dummy (1=yes)	.113 (.012)	.087 (.014)	.068 (.014)	-.240 (.056)	.131 (.014)	.109 (.007)	.111 (.007)
11. Married (1=yes)	-.040 (.108)	.033 (.026)	-.004 (.013)	.123 (.022)	-.015 (.083)	-.017 (.015)	-.015 (.015)
12. Married × Male	.160 (.109)	.055 (.029)	.120 (.023)	.091 (.435)	.095 (.084)	.139 (.017)	.126 (.017)
				.035 (.435)			
13. 44 state dummies	Yes	Yes	Yes	Yes	Yes	Yes	Yes
14. 44 state dummies × 4 activity dummies	—	—	—	—	—	No	Yes
14. R^2	.395	.294	.332	.433	.213	.514	.532
15. Sample size	4,784	2,708	1,928	1,556	4,268	15,244	15,244

[1] Dependent variable: log usual hourly wage. Each equation also includes an intercept and 4 year dummies. Columns 6–7 also include five dummy variables for each activity. Data are from the 1988, 1987, 1981, 1980, and 1979 full-year CPS files; see the Data Appendix for additional details. Standard errors are in parentheses.

wage–costs trade-off is largest for truck drivers, with an estimated coefficient of $-.97$ (t-ratio $= -2.9$). The other results suggest that approximately half of workers' compensation costs are shifted to wages for carpenters and gasoline station workers, but these estimates are fairly imprecise. On the other hand, the estimated trade-off between wages and insurance costs for plumbers is positive (1.73), but the coefficient has a large standard error.

The other variables in the wage equation generally have their expected signs. In all of these activities more education is associated with higher earnings; there is a quadratic relationship between earnings and potential experience; part-time workers earn less per hour than full-time workers, and apprentices earn less than fully trained workers. In addition, the equations include but do not report year dummy variables. The estimated coefficients for the year dummies indicate that real wages fell by roughly 20% in these activities between 1979 and 1988.

Columns (6) and (7) of Table 5 contain estimates for the pooled sample of the five activities. These equations also include four activity dummy variables. In column (6) we include 44 state dummy variables. In column (7) we interact the state dummy variables with the activity dummy variables. The estimated trade-off between insurance costs and wages depends critically on the specification of the state effects. If each activity is constrained to have the same effect (column 6), about 20% of workers' compensation costs are estimated to be offset by lower wages. However, if the activity effect is freed-up by state (column 7), fully 86.5% of workers' compensation costs are shifted to employees. Furthermore, an F-test indicates that state-by-activity effects explain a significant fraction of wage variability over the constrained state effects.

Evidently, the fixed state wage effects are also related to the level of workers' compensation costs. This relationship would occur, for example, if in some states unions have traditionally been influential in raising wages in some industry/occupation groups but not in others, and if influential unions are able to lobby for relatively more generous benefits for the types of injuries experienced by their members (e.g., back sprains vs. carpal tunnel syndrome). In this scenario, the less-restrictive model in column (7) would provide a more appropriate estimate of the trade-off between wages and the employers' cost of workers' compensation insurance.

A. The Importance of State Effects

The discussion above emphasizes the importance of the specification of the state effects in the pooled sample. It should further be noted that if the wage equations in Table 5 are estimated with the state effects omitted from the equation, the estimated wage–cost relationship is positive rather than negative in each of the five activities, as well as in the pooled sample of activities. For example, the coefficient on costs in the wage equation for truck drivers is positive .34 with a standard error of .16 when state effects are omitted.

There are several reasons to include state effects in the wage equations. First, state effects will pick up permanent cost of living differences between areas. Second, and perhaps more important, omitted state factors that traditionally have determined the generosity of workers' compensation benefits are likely to be correlated with the wage level of a state. As mentioned previously, benefits are likely to be greater in states that have a more powerful union movement, and strong union's are also likely to raise wages for nonunion as well as union members in the state. Another potential state-by-activity fixed effect is the risk of injury: Insurance rates will be especially high for an activity in states where that activity has an unusually high injury rate. Moreover, if there are compensating wage differentials for injury risk, we would also expect to find a positive association between insurance costs and wages.[26]

To the extent that injury risk is permanently greater in some states than in others (e.g., roads are always icier in Minnesota than in Florida, which affects truck drivers but not plumbers), including state-by-activity effects will control for within-industry state-level injury rate differences. Furthermore, the recent growth in workers' compensation costs is not likely to be due to union power, since union's influence has waned considerably in the 1980s. Instead, recent growth in insurance costs is likely to be due exogenous changes in medical costs, and to changes in benefit levels in response to the National Commission on Workmen's Compensation Laws' recommendations. In view of these considerations, the within-state variation in costs is probably a more appropriate source of identifying information.

B. Analysis of BLS Industry-Level Wage and Employment Data

In addition to the CPS, we analyze state-level, employer-reported data collected by the Bureau of Labor Statistics. This data set is based on employers' quarterly ES-202 reports, which are filed by all establishments covered by unemployment insurance laws. In 1988, these data contained

---

[26] We tried to assess directly the importance of this explanation by including the car accident rate in the wage equations for the truck drivers, as a measure of injury risk. Without including state effects, the car accident rate has a positive and statistically significant effect, but its inclusion only slightly reduces the positive wage–cost relationship. Because the vast majority of truck drivers' injuries are unrelated to driving accidents, the car accident rate may be a poor measure of injury risk for these workers.

information on 87.4 million private sector workers in 5.6 million establishments nationwide, or 99 percent of the private sector workforce.[27] The Bureau of Labor Statistics (BLS) compiles state-level averages of employment and wages by four-digit Standard Industrial Classification (SIC) from the ES-202 reports. Thus, we can use the BLS data to examine *both* wage and employment effects of workers' compensation insurance.

In comparison to the CPS, the BLS data have the advantage of being based on a virtual census of employers in the state. A disadvantage of the BLS data, however, is that the NCCI activity definitions do not match as well with the BLS data as they do with the CPS data because the BLS data are classified by industry alone. Therefore, to some extent the BLS data blur the occupational distinctions in the NCCI activity classifications.

We matched the state-level data for 1979 and 1988 to workers' compensation rates in the preceding year for four of the five activities in the sample. Unfortunately, it was necessary to exclude nonprofessional hospital employees because the SIC classification system does not distinguish between professional and nonprofessional employees. However, another six high-cost industries that can be matched between the NCCI and SIC classifications were added to the sample. The additional industries are agricultural machinery, excavation, gas and oil dealerships, lumber yards, masonry, and road and street construction.[28]

Figure 2 presents a scatter plot of the change in log average wage versus the change in insurance rates from 1978 to 1987 based on the BLS state-level data. The size of each observation in the plot is proportional to the number of truck drivers employed in the state. The graph also displays the fitted line from an employment-weighted regression of change in log wage on change in costs. A strong negative relationship is apparent. The slope of the regression line is -1, which is very close to the estimated extent of shifting in the trucking industry based on CPS data. Furthermore, most of the states (especially the large ones) tend to cluster fairly close around the regression line.

Table 6 reports estimates of regressions of the 10-year change (1979–1988) in the log of the average wage on the change in insurance rates for the pooled sample of activities. In levels, this specification is analogous to the within-state-by-activity specification shown in column 7 of Table

---

[27] The ES-202 data and the publicly available state-level data are described in BLS (1988). We are grateful to Michael Buso of the BLS for creating an extract of these data for us.

[28] These activities were excluded from the microanalysis either because they do not match well with the three-digit census classifications and/or because the CPS sample sizes are too small to give precise estimates.

The Incidence of Mandated Employer-Provided Insurance 133

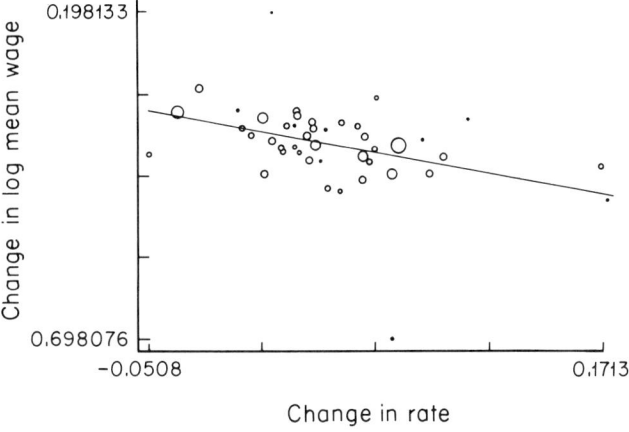

FIGURE 2. *Trucking industry, 1979–1988.*

5, only we do not have controls for individual characteristics in the state-level analysis. We estimate a similar equation with the change in log employment as the dependent variable. In the first two columns we limited the sample to the original sample of activities (excluding nonprofessional hospital workers), and in the last two columns we use the expanded set of 10 activities. The regressions are weighted by the number of reporting establishments in 1988.

TABLE 6
Aggregate Wage/Employment Data Coefficients with Standard Errors in Parentheses[1]

	Sample and Dependent Variable			
	4 Industries		10 Industries	
Variable	(1) Wage change	(2) Employment change	(3) Wage change	(4) Employment change
Intercept	−0.065	0.182	−0.062	0.163
	(0.011)	(0.025)	(0.008)	(0.019)
Change in rate	−0.863	−0.112	−0.561	−0.248
	(0.289)	(0.664)	(0.209)	(0.503)
R^2	0.05	0.0002	0.018	0.001
Sample size	176	176	388	388

[1] Equations are estimated by weighted least squares, where the weights are the number of reporting units in 1988.

For the original sample, the wage regression yields virtually the same coefficient on the workers' compensation cost variable as was found in the CPS microdata (compare column 7 of Table 5 with column 1 of Table 6). The results indicate that 86% of increases in workers' compensation costs are shifted to workers. The results for the expanded set of activities indicate a smaller trade-off between wages and insurance costs ($-.56$), but the estimate is still statistically significant and sizable. The similarity between the aggregate results based on BLS data and the microlevel wage regressions based on CPS data is reassuring, especially in light of their different unit of observation and industry definitions.

Columns 2 and 4 report results of regressing the change in log employment on the change in insurance rates. Because insurance costs appear to be only partially offset by lower wages, one would expect a negative coefficient on insurance rates in these regressions. The results provide some evidence of a negative effect of higher workers' compensation rates on employment growth, but the estimated coefficient is less than half its standard error in each sample.[29] If one assumes that 85% of workers' compensation costs are shifted to wages and that the remaining 15% are borne by employers, then the coefficient estimate in column 2 suggests that the elasticity of labor demand is $-.75$. On the other hand, if we assume that employers bear 44% of workers' compensation costs ($1-.56$), then the estimate in column 4 implies an elasticity of labor demand of $-.56$. Although these estimates are extremely imprecise, they are within the range of typical estimates of the elasticity of labor demand (Card, 1990; Clark and Freeman, 1980).

The following calculation gives an indication of the magnitude of the effect on employment of recent increases in workers' compensation insurance costs. Between 1972 and 1987, nationwide workers' compensation costs increased by about 1% of payroll, from .722 to 1.785% (Burton and Schmidle, 1989). If 85% of this increase was borne by labor and .15% by employers, and if we assume an elasticity of labor demand of $-.75$, then this increase in program costs would have reduced employment by .11%. Since approximately 90 million workers are covered by workers' compensation insurance, this means a loss of a little over 100,000 covered jobs.[30]

---

[29] We note, however, that the estimated wage trade-off and employment trade-off for the sample of 10 activities is sensitive to the weight used. The estimated wage–cost coefficient ranges from $-.50$ to $-.89$ depending on whether the equation is weighted by number of reporting units in 1979, employment in 1980, or average employment in 1979 and 1988. The coefficient on costs in the employment equation ranges from $-.03$ to $-.50$, depending on the weight used.

[30] According to Nelson (1990), in 1987 approximately 88.4 million workers were covered by workers' compensation insurance.

IV. APPLICATION: HEALTH INSURANCE

What can we infer about the likely consequences of mandatory employer-provided health insurance from the estimated incidence of the workers' compensation insurance program? Because employers who already provide health insurance are unlikely to be affected by such a mandate it is useful to consider the sectors of the workforce that have a low rate of coverage by healthy insurance. Table 7 reports the percent of various subgroups of the population that was covered by some form of health insurance in 1988. The relatively low rates of coverage for workers in the construction and agricultural industries, in small firms, and in low-wage jobs have been documented previously (e.g., Chollet, 1987).

The low rate of health insurance coverage in low-wage jobs is potentially important for our purposes because the floor established by the minimum wage may impede wage offsets that would otherwise result from mandating health insurance. The jobs we have examined in the workers' compensation program typically have wage rates well above the minimum wage. If an uninsured worker's wage is at or slightly above the minimum wage, the minimum wage may prevent wage offsets from occurring in response to benefit mandates. The existence of this kind of an institutional impediment would cause a greater employment reduction than suggested from our analysis of workers' compensation insurance.[31] Several authors have noted that the minimum wage may inhibit wage offsets in response to mandated health insurance (see Reinhardt, 1987; Monheit, Hagan, Berk, and Farley, 1985; Chollet, 1987). An important question is: How large is the share of uninsured workers that is potentially constrained by the minimum wage?

In an influential study based on the 1986 March CPS, Chollet (1987) claims that as many as 50% of uninsured workers earn less than 125% of the minimum wage, and that 35% of uninsured workers earn the minimum wage or less. Although we will present evidence suggesting these figures exaggerate the impact of the minimum wage, if a great many of the uninsured earn the minimum wage it is hard to imagine that important wage offsets would occur in response to mandated benefits.

To explore the impact of the minimum wage on health insurance shifting, we use the March 1989 CPS to estimate the earnings distribution of uninsured workers. We restrict the sample to non-self-employed individuals between age 16 and 65 who worked for pay in 1988. For each

---

[31] We note, of course, that insurance costs could be shifted by means of nonwage elements of the compensation package for minimum wage workers. Holzer, Katz, and Krueger's (1990) analysis of application rates suggests incomplete rent dissipation in minimum wage jobs, however.

TABLE 7
Percent of Various Groups Covered by Health Insurance

	Percent covered by			
Characteristics	Health insurance	Private health insurance	Insurance through own or dependent's job	Insurance through own job
Sex				
Male	84	83	76	65
Female	87	84	75	50
Age				
16–24	78	75	59	31
25–35	85	82	77	64
35–45	90	88	83	67
45–55	90	90	83	70
55–65	92	91	80	68
Race				
White	87	86	77	58
Black	78	72	64	53
Other	82	79	69	54
Hours				
>35 hours, 48 weeks	90	90	85	77
>18 hours, 26 weeks	87	86	80	67
Wages				
$W < \$3.35$/hour	71	62	45	11
$\$3.35 \leq W < \$5$/hour	73	68	55	26
$\$5 \leq W < \$10$/hour	86	85	76	58
$W \geq \$10$/hour	95	95	91	81
Education				
Less than HS	73	68	60	36
Finished HS	85	83	75	58
Some college	89	88	76	58
Post-college or more	94	94	87	75
Employer size				
<25 employees	74	71	56	30
25–100 employees	83	80	72	54
100 + employees	91	89	83	70
Industry				
Agriculture, mining	69	65	52	37
Construction	74	73	65	50
Manufacturing	90	89	85	77
Transportation	91	90	86	77
Trade	81	78	66	39
Services	87	85	75	55

Source: Authors' calculations from the March 1989 Current Population Survey.

TABLE 8
Percentage of Uninsured Workers Falling into Various Wage Intervals[1]

	Wage ≤ 3.35	Wage between $3.00 and $3.70	Wage between $2.75 and $3.95
A. All Workers			
Uncovered	19.4	10.5	18.6
Uncovered by employer plan	19.5	6.4	17.1
B. Full Time, Full Year Workers			
Uncovered	16.8	9.0	16.9
Uncovered by employer plan	15.2	8.3	14.8

[1] Sample excludes self-employed workers, and those who earn less than $1.00 per hour or more than $100 per hour. Sample size is 8506 for Part A and 6482 for Part B.

Source: authors' calculations from the March 1989 CPS.

worker in the sample, an average hourly wage rate is calculated by dividing annual earnings by the product of annual weeks worked and usual weekly hours. To trim outliers, we exclude observations on individuals whose derived hourly earnings are below $1 per hour, or greater than $100 per hour.[32] This sample is used to calculate the share of uninsured workers that is likely to be affected by the minimum wage.

The first row of Table 8 gives the fraction of *all* uninsured workers who fall into various wage intervals.[33] The second row gives the fraction of workers who are not covered by an employer-sponsored insurance plan who fall into each wage interval. Part B contains the same set of estimates for full-time, full-year workers (i.e., those who worked at least 26 weeks in the year and usually worked 18 hours or more per week). The results indicate that 19.4% of all uninsured workers in 1988 earned the minimum wage or less. The estimate is 16.8% when we limit the sample to full-time, full-year workers, which is the group most likely to be covered by a mandated health insurance law.

For several reasons, we prefer estimates that place a window around the minimum wage, rather than the open-interval estimates in column 1. First, the annual average hourly wage rate is likely to be measured with

---

[32] Eliminating outliers in this fashion does not qualitatively affect the results once the self-employed are excluded from the sample.

[33] The various sources of health insurance coverage are Medicare, Medicaid, CHAMPUS/VA care, employment-based insurance, and private health insurance. Coverage may be in one's own name or as a dependent.

considerable noise because it is based on self-reported annual hours of work, which is notoriously poorly measured (Duncan and Hill, 1985). Second, some workers who earn more than the minimum wage may be constrained by the minimum wage because their earnings are prevented from falling below the wage floor in response to mandated health insurance. Finally, we wish to put a lower bound below the minimum wage because there is a tremendous amount of noncompliance with the minimum wage.[34] If some individuals are paid less than the minimum—either legally or illegally—there is no reason to suspect that their wages will not be reduced if their employers are required to provide them with health insurance.

Column (2) places a 35¢ window around the minimum wage, and column (3) places a 60¢ window around the minimum wage. Since the estimated hourly cost of meeting the Federal health insurance mandate is 55¢ for a full-time, full-year worker (U.S. Congress, 1989), the wider interval in column (3) is probably a slight overstatement of the percent of uninsured workers who are constrained by the minimum wage. No matter how the wage intervals are defined, however, the results in Table 8 are quite different from Chollett's estimate that 50% of uninsured workers will be constrained by the minimum wage. According to our estimates, less than 20% of uninsured workers earn within 60¢ of the minimum wage. Although this is a nontrivial share of the uninsured, it suggests that for the majority of uninsured workers there is scope for wage offsets engendered by mandated employer-provided health insurance.

Why are our estimates considerably lower than Chollett's, even though both are based on March CPS data? The discrepancy is mainly due to the fact that we exclude self-employed workers. For example, including the self-employed raises the estimate of the number of uninsured workers below the minimum wage by nearly 10 percentage points. However, we believe that three reasons justify excluding the self-employed from these tabulations. First, the proposals outlined in Table 1 do not apply to self-employed workers. Second, self-employed workers are typically exempted from State and Federal minimum wage laws. Third, the earnings of the self-employed reflect returns and losses to capital investments.

Finally, we note that Table 8 may give an overestimate of the impact of the minimum wage for mandated benefits because many of the proposed mandated health insurance laws provide subsidies to small employers. Since relatively many low-wage workers are employed by small

---

[34] The extent of noncompliance with minimum wage was first documented by Ashenfelter and Smith (1979).

establishments, these subsidies would reduce the employers' costs of providing health care to low-wage workers. Tabulations from the March 1989 CPS indicate that 42% of uninsured individuals who earn less than the minimum wage are in firms with 25 employees or fewer.

On the other hand, the real minimum wage has increased since March 1989, and thus may be more of a constraint. Nevertheless, our results suggest that the minimum wage may not be as much of an impediment to wage adjustments in response to mandated benefits as previously believed.

V. CONCLUSION

This paper has analyzed the impact of cost shifting in response to increases in mandated workers' compensation insurance costs. The results suggests that a substantial portion of the cost to employers of providing workers' compensation benefits is shifted to employees in the form of lower wages. Given the similarity between workers' compensation insurance and many proposed employer-mandated health insurance plans, our findings suggest that a large share of the employers' cost of meeting health insurance mandates may be borne by employees. Furthermore, our tabulations of the share of uninsured workers whose earnings are near the minimum wage suggest that in 1988 less than one-fifth of uninsured workers were likely to be constrained by the minimum wage. Although the nominal burden of mandated employment-based health insurance will be borne by firms, if the experience of health insurance is similar to that of workers' compensation insurance, our estimates suggest that employees will ultimately bear a large fraction of the burden of financing mandated health insurance through lower wages.

In spite of our main conclusion that a sizable portion of the cost of mandated benefits is likely to be shifted to employees, we should also stress that the shifting of workers' compensation costs is incomplete. Employers bear at least some additional cost because of mandated work-injury insurance. As a consequence, we find that increases in workers' compensation costs are associated with reduced employment growth. Although extremely imprecise, our estimates suggest that every one percentage point increase in workers' compensation rates is associated with an employment decline of .11%. The adverse employment effects of mandated health insurance may well be larger than those in workers' compensation insurance because the minimum wage is likely to be more of a constraint for uninsured workers, especially in view of recent increases in the real minimum.

VI. DATA APPENDIX

A. Workers' Compensation Insurance Rates

The workers' compensation insurance rates used in Table 3-6 and Figure 2 are state manual rates, collected from each state's rate pages. Manual rates are expressed as a proportion of payroll. Manual rate data were generously provided to us by John F. Burton, Jr. In some cases, if manual rates were not available for a state we used the rate for the assigned risk pool, less 10%. The rate for the Minnesota trucking industry in 1987 is from Lewis, Myers, and Senese (1988), and is based on insurance industry data. Data are available for a maximum of 44 states and the District of Columbia in both 1978 and 1987. The states in the sample use the NCCI rating classification system, or a comparable system. The NCCI codes for the five activities used in the analysis are truck drivers (NCCI 7219), plumbers (NCCI 5183), gasoline service station employees (NCCI 8387), nonprofessional hospital employees (NCCI 9040), and carpenters (weighted average of NCCI 5403 and 5645).

B. CPS Data

The CPS data used in Table 5 are from the outgoing rotation group files for 1979, 1980, 1981, 1987, and 1988. The sample was limited to individuals between age 18 and 65 who were privately employed. The sample only includes individuals from the 45 jurisdictions that have manual rate data in 1978 and 1987. The 1978 manual rate was merged to observations in the 1979, 1980, and 1981 CPS samples; the 1987 manual rate was merged to observations in the 1987 and 1988 CPS samples. The "usual hourly wage" is the ratio of usual weekly earnings to usual weekly hours. Individuals with allocated weekly earnings were deleted from the sample, as were those who earned less than $1.67 per hour or more than $150.00 per hour in 1988 dollars.

The "married" dummy variable equals one if the worker is married with his or her spouse present. The "part-time" dummy variable equals one if the worker usually works less than 35 hours per week. "Potential experience" is age minus education minus 6. The "apprentice" dummy variable equals one if the worker's occupation code is an apprentice.

The following 1970 Census industry (CIC) and occupation (COC) codes were used to define the activities: truck drivers (CIC 417; COC 715), plumbers (CIC 67-78, COC 522 or 523), gasoline station employees (CIC 648), nonprofessional hospital employees (CIC 838; COC 630, 690, 694, 762, 901-903, 912-916, or 950), and carpenters (CIC 67-78, COC 415 or 416). The following 1980 Census industry (CIC) and occupation

(COC) codes were used to define the activities: truck drivers (CIC 410; COC 804 or 805), plumbers (CIC 60, COC 585 or 587), gasoline station employees (CIC 621), nonprofessional hospital employees (CIC 831; COC 435–437, 439, 443–444, 449, 453, 748, 777, 883), and carpenters (CIC 60, COC 567 or 569).

C. BLS Data

The BLS data are annual totals derived from quarterly ES-202 reports. The BLS data consist of state-level averages for 3- and 4-digit Standard Industrial Classification (SIC) groups. The dependent variable in columns (1) and (3) of Table 6 is the change in the log of the arithmetic average annual wage in each industry. The annual wage is in 1988 dollars. The dependent variable in columns (2) and (4) is the change in log employment. The SIC codes for the four activities in the basic sample in Table 6 are truckers (SIC 421), plumbers (1711), gas stations (SIC 5541), and carpenters (SIC 1751).

REFERENCES

Abowd, John M., and Orley Ashenfelter. (1981). "Anticipated Unemployment, Temporary Layoffs, and Compensating Wage Differentials." In *Studies in Labor Markets*. Sherwin Rosen, ed., Chicago: University of Chicago Press.
Ashenfelter, Orley, and Robert S. Smith. (1979). "Compliance with the Minimum Wage Law." *Journal of Politics Economy* 87, 333–350.
Boden, Leslie, and Charles Fleishman. 1989. *Medical Costs in Workers' Compensation*. Cambridge, MA: Workers' Compensation Research Institute.
Brittain, John A. (1972). *The Payroll Tax for Social Security*. Washington, D.C.: Brookings Institution.
Bureau of Labor Statistics. (1988). *Employment and Wages: Annual Averages*. Washington, D.C.: BLS.
Butler, Richard, and John Worrall. (1990). "Claims Reporting and Risk Bearing Moral Hazard in Workers' Compensation." Mimeo., Brigham Young University (July).
Burton, John F., Jr., H. Allan Hunt, and Alan B. Krueger. (1985). "Inter-state Variations in the Employers' Costs of Workers' Compensation, with Particular Reference to Michigan ad the Other Great Lakes States." Mimeo., Cornell University.
Burton, John F., and Timothy Schmidle. (1989). "Inter-state Variations in Workers' Compensation Costs." *John Burton's Workers' Compensation Monitor* 2, 1–15.
Brown, Charles. (1980). "Equalizing Differences in the Labor Market." *Quarterly Journal of Economics* 94, 133–134.
Card, David. (1990). "Unexpected Inflation, Real Wages, and Employment Determination in Union Contracts." *American Economic Review*, 80(4), 669–688.
Chollet, Deborah. (1987). "Public Policy Options to Expand Health Insurance Coverage among the Nonelderly Population." In *Government Mandating of Employee Benefits*. Washington, D.C.: Employee Benefits Research Institute.

Clark, Kim, and Richard B. Freeman. (1980). "How Elastic is the Demand for Labor?" *Review of Economics and Statistics* 62(4), 509–519.

Danzon, Patricia. (1989). "Mandated Employment-Based Health Insurance: Incidence and Efficiency Effects." Mimeo, University of Pennsylvania.

Dorsey, Stuart, and Norman Walzer. (1983). "Workers' Compensation, Job Hazards, and Wages." *Industrial and Labor Relations Review* 36(4), 642–654.

Duncan, Greg, and Daniel Hill. (1985). "An Investigation of the Extent and Consequences of Measurement Error in Labor-Economic Survey Data." *Journal of Labor Economics* 3(4), 508–532.

Feldstein, Martin. (1972). "Comment on Brittain." *American Economic Review* 62(4) 735–738.

Hamermesh, Daniel S. (1979). "New Estimates of the Incidence of Payroll Tax." *Southern Economic Journal* 45(4), 1208–1219.

Holmlund, Bertil. (1983). "Payroll Taxes and Wage Inflation: The Swedish Experience." *Scandinavian Journal of Economics* 85(1), 1–15.

Holzer, Harry, Lawrence Katz, and Alan Krueger. (1990). "Job Queues and Wages." *Quarterly Journal of Economics*, in press.

Krueger, Alan B., and John F. Burton, Jr. (1990). "The Employers' Costs of Workers' Compensation Insurance: Magnitudes, Determinants, and Public Policy." *Review of Economics and Statistics* 72(2) (May), 228–240.

Leibowitz, Arleen. (1983). "Fringe Benefits in Employee Compensation." In *The Measurement of Labor Cost*. Jack E. Triplett, ed., Chicago: University of Chicago Press.

Lewis, John Myers, and Michael Senese. (1988). "The Minnesota Trucking Industry and Workers' Compensation." *Report to the Legislature on Workers' Compensation in Minnesota: Background Research Studies* Minneapolis, MN: Minnesota Department of Labor and Industry.

Monheit, Alan, Michael Hagan, Marc Berk, and Pamela Farley. (1985). "The Employed Uninsured and the Role of Public Policy." *Inquiry* 22 (Winter), 348–364.

Moore, Michael, and W. Kip Viscusi. (1990). *Compensation Mechanisms for Job Risks*. Princeton, NJ: Princeton University Press.

Nelson, William J. (1990). "Workers' Compensation: Coverage, Benefits, and Costs, 1987." *Social Security Bulletin* 53 (April), 2–11.

Reinhardt, Uwe E. (1987). "Should All Employers Be Required by Law to Provide Basic Health Insurance Coverage for Their Employees and Dependents?" In *Government Mandating of Employee Benefits*. Washington D.C. Employee Benefits Research Institute.

Rosen, Sherwin (1987). "The Theory of Equalizing Differences," in *The Handbook of Labor Economics*, Orley Ashenfelter and Richard Layard, eds. Amsterdam: North-Holland.

Smith, Robert. (1979). "Compensating Wage Differentials and Public Policy." *Industrial and Labor Relations Review* (April), 339–352.

Smith, Robert S., and Ronald G. Ehrenberg. (1983). "Estimating Wage-Fringe Trade-Offs: Some Data Problems." In *Measurement of Labor Cost*. Jack E. Triplett, ed., Chicago: University of Chicago Press.

Summers, Lawrence H. (1989). "Some Simple Economics of Mandated Benefits." *American Economic Association, Papers and Proceedings* 79(2); 177–183.

Triplett, Jack E. (1983). "An Essay on Labor Cost." In *The Measurement of Labor Cost*. Jack E. Triplett, ed., Chicago: University of Chicago Press.

U.S. Chamber of Commerce. (1990). *1990 Analysis of Workers' Compensation Laws.* Washington, D.C.: U.S. Chamber of Commerce.

U.S. Congress. (1989). *Basic Health Benefits for All Americans Act: Report Together with Minority Views.* Washington, D.C.: U.S. GPO.

IS THE GASOLINE TAX REGRESSIVE?

James M. Poterba
MIT and NBER

EXECUTIVE SUMMARY

Claims of the regressivity of gasoline taxes typically rely on annual surveys of consumer income and expenditures, which show that gasoline expenditures are a larger fraction of income for very low-income households than for middle- or high-income households. This paper argues that annual *expenditure* provides a more reliable indicator of household well-being than annual income. It uses data from the Consumer Expenditure Survey to reassess the claim that gasoline taxes are regressive by computing the share of total expenditures that high-spending and low-spending households devote to retail gasoline purchases. This alternative approach shows that low-expenditure households devote a *smaller* share of their budget to gasoline than do their counterparts in the middle of the expenditure distribution. Although households in the top 5% of the total spending distribution spend less on gasoline than those who are less well off, the share of expenditure devoted to gasoline is much more stable across the population than the ratio of gasoline outlays to current income. The gasoline tax thus appears far less regressive than conventional analyses suggest.

The long-standing view that excise taxes such as the gasoline tax are regressive, imposing a heavier burden on low-income households than

---

I am grateful to the National Science Foundation, the MIT Center for Energy Policy Research, and the John M. Olin Foundation for research support. I received helpful comments from David Bradford, Alan Krueger, Marc Robinson, Daniel Slesnick, Robert Stavins, and David Wilcox. I am especially grateful to Hilary Sigman for outstanding research assistance and helpful discussions.

on their higher-income counterparts, played a central role in shaping the 1990 budget compromise. This issue is certain to be debated again, since these taxes are frequently considered as a means to achieve environmental, budgetary, and national security objectives (see Congressional Budget Office, 1986). Claims of the regressivity of excise taxes typically rely on annual surveys of consumer income and expenditures, which show that gasoline expenditures are a larger fraction of income for very low-income households than for middle- or high-income households (see for example KPMG Peat Marwick, 1990). Several recent studies, however, notably Kasten and Sammartino (1988) and Poterba (1989), suggest that year-to-year fluctuations in income among households at the bottom of the annual income distribution may exaggerate the regressivity of excise taxes. From a life-cycle perspective, these taxes, particularly the gasoline tax, are much less regressive than is commonly believed.

This paper argues that annual *expenditure* provides a more reliable indicator of household well-being than annual income. Whether a given tax is regressive should therefore be analyzed by testing whether it places higher burden on low-expenditure households than on their high-expenditure counterparts. My empirical analysis uses data from the Consumer Expenditure Survey to compute the share of total expenditures that high-spending and low-spending households devote to retail gasoline purchases. This alternative approach to measuring the distributional burden of gasoline taxes yields results that are strikingly different from those using the traditional approach based on annual income.

Low-expenditure households devote a *smaller* share of their budget to gasoline than do their counterparts in the middle of the expenditure distribution. Although households in the top 5% of the total spending distribution spend significantly less on gasoline (as a share of expenditures) than those who are less well off, gasoline's expenditure share is much more stable across the population than the ratio of gasoline outlays to current income. The reduced estimate of gasoline tax regressivity is not an inherent feature of using expenditures rather than income as a basis for assessing incidence. Some other energy expenditures, such as electricity, exhibit different cross-sectional patterns with much higher expenditure shares for low- rather than high-income households.

This study underscores a conclusion of the recent Congressional Budget Office (1990) excise tax study: "measured as a percentage of total expenditures, . . . outlays on these goods [subject to excise taxes] tend to be more equal [than outlays as a share of income] across family income classes.(p.xviii)." However, this paper moves beyond the CBO study, which focuses on gasoline's share of total outlays for households in different *income* categories. If lifetime income is better proxied by total expenditures than by current income, a more complete procedure involves ranking households by expenditures rather than income, and considering the resulting distribution of budget shares.

This paper is divided into five sections. The first presents summary statistics on the patterns of gasoline expenditure as a share of income and total expenditure, motivating subsequent analysis of what explains the differences between these incidence measures. It also considers the variation in expenditure patterns within income or expenditure categories, to provide some evidence on the horizontal equity of gasoline tax changes. This study focuses exclusively on household gasoline consumption, assuming that neither deisel fuel nor intermediate uses of gasoline are taxed.

Section II explores the characteristics of households who fare relatively better in the expenditure than in the income distribution. Nearly 40% of these households are either elderly or very young, suggesting that divergence between income and outlays may reflect long-term economic planning. Another significant group is experiencing economic hardship, such as unemployment or disability; in some cases these circumstances may be short term.

Section III examines the role of indexed transfer payments in offsetting tax-induced increases in gasoline prices for some households, particularly those near the bottom of the income and expenditure distributions. Low-income and low-expenditure households are much more likely to receive indexed transfers than are better off households; nearly two-thirds of the income received by households in the lowest expenditure decile is indexed. These programs blunt the regressivity of excise taxes by automatically increasing household receipts in response to consumer price increases.

Section IV considers the efficiency cost of the gasoline tax in light of other government policies such as Corporate Average Fuel Economy (CAFE) standards, which affect the complexion of the U.S. auto fleet. If the CAFE standards bind both before and after a gasoline tax increase, the efficiency cost of such a change is significantly smaller than estimates that ignore this constraint would suggest. Finally, a brief conclusion suggests several extensions of this work, both for analyzing the burden of motor fuel taxes and for examining excise taxes more generally.

I. WHO BUYS GASOLINE? INCOME VERSUS EXPENDITURE INCIDENCE RESULTS

The annual income distribution is unstable from year to year. In the Panel Survey of Income Dynamics, for example, a randomly chosen individual had only a 41% chance of being in the same income quintile in 1971 and 1978.[1] There was somewhat less mobility out of the bottom quintile, where 54% remained in both surveys, than other quintiles. Since households move across income categories, categorizing them as well-to-do or poor based on annual income data provides a noisy measure of long-term economic status.[2] Even modest mobility is sufficient to alter basic results on the distributional burden of taxes, particularly excise taxes. In Canadian data, Davies, St. Hilaire, and Whalley (1984) find that the average burden of sales and excise taxes for the lowest income decile, while 27% of annual income, is only 15% of lifetime income.[3] In their study, the average burden of excise taxes across all income groups is 13%, so the lifetime income calculation suggests much less excise tax regressivity than annual income data. For the highest income decile, the burden of excise taxes *rises* from 8.5% of annual income to 12.4% of lifetime income.

Focusing on lifetime income introduces two considerations that are absent in incidence computations based on annual income. First, there are predictable life-cycle patterns in earnings, asset accumulation, and consumption. Elderly households, for example, may spend more than their current income by drawing down assets. Their low annual income may provide a poor indicator of their economic status. Second, lifetime income is effectively a multiyear average of annual income. It is less sensitive to variation in a given year's earnings due to unemployment, changes in family status, or other transitory circumstances.

The notion that households behave on the basis of long-term income underlies the life-cycle and permanent-income theories of consumption. These theories, which are the foundation for most modern analyses of household consumption behavior, imply that a household's total expenditures may be a more reliable indicator of economic well-being than the same household's annual income.[4] This insight provides the theoretical

---

[1] Poterba (1989) reports further details on income mobility in the PSID, as well as other data sets that permit some analysis of income fluctuations.

[2] Some earlier incidence studies (for example, Pechman, 1985) exclude very low-income households precisely because their annual income may be a noisy measure of permanent income.

[3] Lifetime income is the present discounted value of a household's income throughout the lifetime. It is difficult to measure *ex ante*, but can be estimated using data on the stochastic properties of household income from year to year.

[4] A recent study by Carroll and Summers (1989) shows that within cohorts, occupations, and other broad groups, average consumption tracks average income over the life cycle. This casts doubt on the broad proposition that households save for retirement, but does not imply that for a *given* household, current income and current consumption move in tandem.

rationale for the empirical analysis that follows. Even if consumption is not set precisely in accordance with the permanent income hypothesis, for most households it is likely to reflect at least some forward- and backward-looking behavior, therefore offsetting some of the transitory noise in annual income.[5]

Similar arguments play an important part in the ongoing debate on whether income or consumption is a more appropriate tax base. If consumption is a better measure of a household's taxable capacity than its current income, then studies of the tax burden—regardless of whether that burden is comprised of income or consumption taxes—should use a measure of consumption to estimate a household's ability to pay. At a minimum, consumption outlays provide an interesting alternative perspective on the distribution of the tax burden across households.

A. Data and Sample

Data on income and expenditure patterns are drawn from the 1985 Consumer Expenditure Survey, a stratified national sample of approximately 2000 households. Households are interviewed four times during their CES experience, and at any moment, nearly 5000 households are taking part in the Consumer Expenditure Survey. My data sample includes only 1582 households—all those whose first expenditure interview occurred during the first or second quarter of 1985 (a total of 2608 households), who reported four consecutive quarterly expenditure interviews (a subsample of 1889 households), and with complete data on household income (a subset of 1582 households).[6]

Household income is defined as the average of pretax income reported in the first and last quarterly interview. In each of these interviews, households are asked about their income over the previous 12 months. This income measure, although a standard basis for assessing household economic status, is imperfect for two reasons. First, although it includes cash transfer payments such as Social Security or welfare, it excludes in-kind transfers such as Food Stamps or Medicaid. Valuing such transfers is difficult, but assuming a value of zero systematically understates the income of some poverty households. Second, the income measure does

---

[5] The KPMG Peat Marwick (1990) study of excise tax regressivity acknowledges the potential limitations of basing regressivity calculations on annual income data, but argues that solving this problem requires many years of income data to compute permanent income. However, total consumption can provide information on long-run income *even in a single cross section*.

[6] Households with incomplete income data failed to respond completely to income questions in at least one interview. This nonresponse pattern may be correlated with household economic status, and might bias the distributional estimates in later sections.

not reflect tax payments. This is due to data difficulties: the incomplete reporting of tax payments and the asynchronous nature of the tax data (last calendar year) and income data (current calendar year) in the Consumer Expenditure Survey.[7]

Total expenditures are the sum of total expenditures in each of the four interview quarters, excluding any outlays for new or used automobiles. The expenditure total includes the CES estimate of the rental equivalent value of owner-occupied housing services for homeowners, as well as rental outlays for households who do not own homes.[8] Auto purchases are excluded to avoid spurious volatility in the expenditures measure, since this purchase can be a large fraction of all other outlays in a given year. The robustness of the findings to this assumption is explored in later sections.

Using both income and expenditure measures, households are assigned to deciles of the income or spending distribution.[9] Summary statistics, principally averages of expenditure shares or expenditure-to-income ratios within each decile, are then computed to illustrate the distribution of gasoline expenditure patterns. Throughout the analysis, gasoline expenditures are the sum of household outlays for gasoline and motor oil. This study does not attempt to analyze the distribution of *indirect* gasoline tax expenditures, i.e., the taxes that may be collected from the retail distribution sector but eventually passed on to consumers.

B. Income- versus Expenditure-Based Incidence

Table 1 presents information on the usual measure of the distribution of gasoline expenditures: the ratio of these expenditures to income for households in different deciles of the pretax income distribution.[10] The table shows that low-income households display markedly higher expenditure-to-income ratios than higher-income households. For the entire bottom income decile, this ratio is more than 11%; even for households between the fifth and tenth percentile of the income distribution, gasoline outlays average 6.7% of pretax income. The table shows a relatively

---

[7] The sample includes some households with negative incomes, some due to business losses and some to other factors.

[8] In tabulations of expenditure ranking published by the Bureau of Labor Statistics, expenditures are defined to include outlays for cars and only the mortgage interest component of homeowner costs. Some of the rankings in this paper may therefore differ from other published reports based on the same data.

[9] The ranking does not correct for household size using an equivalence scale from applied demand analysis. Future work should explore this issue.

[10] Each entry shows the average ratio of gasoline outlays to pretax income for households in the decile.

TABLE 1
Gasoline and Motor Oil Expenditure/Income, by Income Decile, 1986

Income decile	Gasoline expenditure/income (%)
1	11.44
1 (excluding 0–5%)	6.74
2	6.54
3	6.36
4	6.08
5	4.97
6	4.69
7	4.38
8	3.75
9	3.56
10	2.40

Source: Author's tabulations using 1985 Consumer Expenditure Survey. See text for further details.

smooth decline in the share of income devoted to gasoline, to 4.7% at the sixth decline and only 2.4% in the highest income decile. Evidence such as that in Table 1 is frequently invoked to support the regressivity of excise taxes on gasoline.[11] Even ignoring the very bottom of the reported income distribution as noise, the results suggest that low-income households spend between two and three times as much of their income on gasoline as higher-income households.

An alternative perspective is provided in Table 2, which shows the fraction of expenditures devoted to gasoline for households grouped by total expenditures. When total expenditures exclude auto purchases and include imputed homeowner rent, consumers in the lowest expenditure decile devote 3.9% of their budgets to gasoline, compared with 5.6% for those in the fifth and sixth deciles. The highest expenditure decile devotes 3.4% of total outlays to gasoline, and if one focuses on the very top of the expenditure distribution, outlays are an even smaller budget share. For households with very high expenditure, those in the top 2.5% of the expenditure distribution, the budget share for gasoline is 3.0%, not significantly lower than the average for households in the highest decile.

The second and third columns of Table 2 consider alternative definitions of household expenditures, but yield similar conclusions on gaso-

---

[11] The recent Congressional Budget Office (1990) study focuses primarily on tax burdens relative to household income. It does present, however, some results using the total expenditure ranking employed in Table 2. Sammartino (1987) also presents results in the spirit of the current paper. Slesnick (1990) reports an intriguing related application in using total consumption outlays to measure poverty status.

line expenditure patterns. The second column includes outlays for automobiles in the expenditure total; this does not alter the pattern of higher gasoline shares in the middle than at either extreme of the outlay distribution. Because the expenditure total is larger, however, the gasoline share declines in all outlay categories. The average share across all households falls from 5.1 to 4.8%. The last column excludes both imputed homeowner rent and auto purchases from the expenditure. In this case the expenditure shares for the top and bottom expenditure deciles are identical. The average gasoline share in this case rises to 6.2%.

Figure 1 graphs the income and expenditure shares for gasoline, combining the information in Tables 1 and 2. The figure highlights two findings. First, the distributional pattern of gasoline expenditures is distinctly different in the two cases. Households in the middle of the expenditure distribution devote the largest budget share to gasoline, with levels nearly twice that of households with very high or very low expenditures. Rather than suggesting that gasoline taxes are regressive, the expenditure-based calculations suggest that gasoline excise taxes fall most heavily on middle-class households. Second, the figure shows that the variation in expenditure shares across deciles is much smaller than the variation in gasoline outlays as a share of income. The intergroup inequities associated with the gasoline excise tax are thus much smaller when the calibration is based on expenditure rather than pre-tax income.

The average income and expenditure shares presented above do not

TABLE 2
Gasoline and Motor Oil Expenditure/Total Expenditure, 1986

Expenditure decile	Including imputed rent, excluding autos	Expenditure definition including imputed rent and autos	Excluding imputed rent and autos
1	3.88	3.70	4.25
2	5.67	5.34	6.52
3	5.83	5.53	6.84
4	6.12	5.67	7.55
5	5.55	5.17	6.62
6	5.64	5.20	7.04
7	5.42	4.94	6.72
8	4.85	4.43	5.99
9	4.82	4.47	6.09
10	3.42	3.20	4.25
Average	5.12	4.76	6.19

Source: Author's tabulations using 1985 Consumer Expenditure Survey. See text for further details.

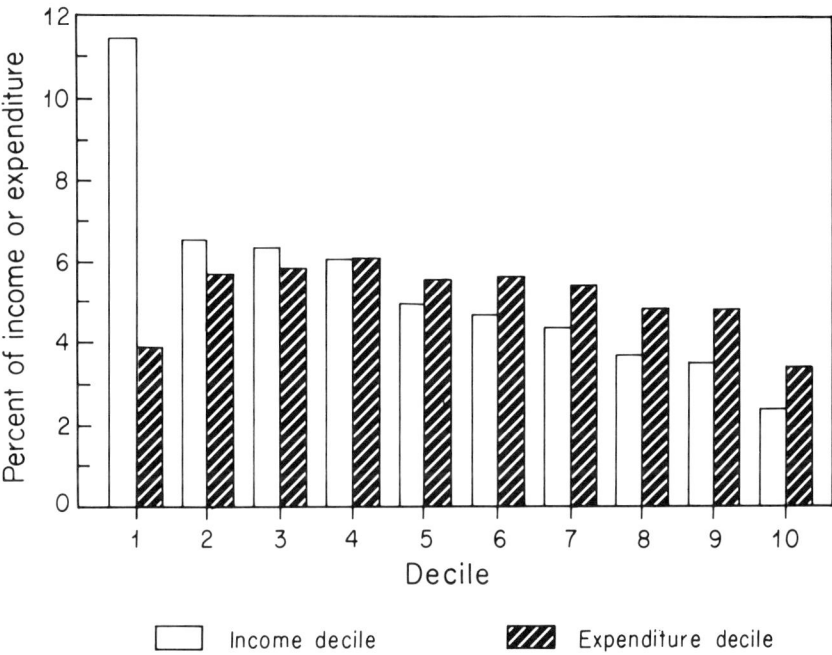

FIGURE 1. *Gasoline share of income or expenditure.*

address the heterogeneity of households *within* each decile. Some argue that excise taxes fall unequally on different households with similar tax-paying capacity because of differences in their expenditure patterns. Table 3 presents data on the fraction of households in each expenditure decile with no gasoline expenditures, as well as the share with expenditures that make up more than 10% of the household budget (roughly twice the average expenditure share). Only 14% of the households in the lowest expenditure decile devote more than 10% of their budget to gasoline, while more than one-third do not report *any* direct gasoline purchases. The share of households with either type of outlying expenditure pattern declines as one moves up the expenditure distribution. By the sixth decile, for example, fewer than 2% of the households report no gasoline purchases; 9.4% report outlays equal to more than 10% of their budget. None of the households in the top expenditure decile reported either type of extreme outlay pattern.

Households with no gasoline outlays, presumably city-dwellers who use public transportation, are heavily concentrated at the bottom of the expenditure distribution. Many of these households would actually be

TABLE 3
Dispersion of Gasoline and Motor Oil Expenditure Shares

Expenditure decile	Percent of consumers with gasoline expenditure share	
	Zero	>10%
1	36.5	14.2
2	11.3	15.6
3	8.4	15.5
4	0.7	16.0
5	4.3	11.1
6	1.9	9.4
7	1.2	6.7
8	0.6	5.1
9	0.6	5.7
10	0	0

Source: Author's tabulation using 1985 Consumer Expenditure Survey. Households are grouped into expenditure deciles based on total expenditures including rental equivalent value of owner-occupied housing, but excluding automobile purchases.

made better off by a gasoline tax, since they would not face higher outlays but would receive higher benefits as a result of cost-of-living increases in transfer payments.

The households who would be most heavily burdened by the tax are those who spend more than 10% of their budget on gasoline. This group is also concentrated in the lower expenditure deciles; in the five lowest deciles, nearly one household in six has a high expenditure share. These high-outlay households typically live in rural areas and are more likely to be in the south than in other regions. Holmes (1976) provides a more detailed analysis of the characteristics of high-gasoline-outlay households, along with an analysis of their burdens following the 1974 oil price shock.[12]

II. WHY DO INCOME AND EXPENDITURE RANKINGS DIFFER?

The dramatic differences between income and expenditure-based incidence measures suggest the need to analyze why income and outlay rankings diverge. This section considers two aspects of this question. First, it reports the joint distribution of household income and expenditure ranks, to determine whether differences between the income and

---

[12] Hill (1980) examines the same households 5 years later to investigate various responses—mobility, care purchase, etc.—to higher gasoline prices.

expenditure incidence results are due to relatively few households whose income and outlays differ. Second, I present a more detailed analysis of the households whose expenditure ranks exceed their income ranks, since the characteristics of these households could affect the interpretation of the results.

Table 4 reports the joint distribution of income and expenditure decile ranks across households. The upper panel shows how households in a given income decile, corresponding to each row, are allocated to expenditure deciles. The lower panel reports the reverse calculation, indicating how the households in a given expenditure decile are distributed across income deciles. In each case (but for rounding) the row entries should sum to 100.

TABLE 4
Joint Distribution of Expenditure and Income Deciles[1]

Income decile	Expenditure decile									
	1	2	3	4	5	6	7	8	9	10
1	61	16	9	4	3	3	1	0	1	3
2	22	34	17	13	7	5	1	1	0	1
3	8	25	19	17	12	7	6	2	2	1
4	4	14	21	14	21	8	8	6	3	1
5	1	10	19	16	18	15	10	7	4	2
6	1	3	10	18	20	17	11	14	4	1
7	1	1	2	8	10	19	24	20	9	7
8	0	0	1	3	7	21	22	20	17	8
9	0	1	1	1	2	5	13	20	32	25
10	0	0	0	1	2	3	8	9	26	51

Expenditure decile	Income decile									
	1	2	3	4	5	6	7	8	9	10
1	63	23	8	4	1	1	1	0	0	0
2	15	33	34	14	10	3	1	0	1	0
3	8	17	19	21	20	10	2	1	1	0
4	4	13	18	15	17	19	8	3	1	1
5	2	7	12	21	18	20	9	7	2	2
6	3	5	7	8	15	17	18	21	5	3
7	1	1	6	8	10	10	2	21	13	8
8	0	1	2	6	7	14	19	20	21	10
9	1	0	2	3	4	4	9	16	34	27
10	3	1	1	1	2	1	6	8	26	51

[1] Entries in each panel denote the probability that a person in the income or expenditure decile listed in the row margin would be found in the income or expenditure decile for each column. Calculations are based on 1985 Consumer Expenditure Survey.

Several features of the table are noteworthy. First, just over 60% of the households in the bottom income decile are also in the bottom expenditure decile.[13] Only 15% of the households in the bottom expenditure decile are ranked above the second income decile. This suggests a substantial group of households who fare poorly on *either* incidence measure. For this group, gasoline expenditures average 5.0% of income and 3.0% of total expenditures.

Second, the association between income and expenditure rank is similar at the upper and lower ends of the distribution. Seventy-six percent of the households in the bottom expenditure decile have pretax incomes in the first or second income deciles; 77% of the households in the top expenditure deciles have incomes in the top two deciles. These tables suggest that differences between the income and expenditure incidence results, although not due to a very small set of households, are due to approximately one-sixth of the sample for whom the income and expenditure rankings differ substantially.

The results in Table 4 do not provide any information on the identity of households who are in the bottom income decile, spend heavily on gasoline, yet do not appear in the bottom expenditure decile. Finding that a significant fraction of these households are experiencing transitory low income, or have expenditure in excess of income as part of a lifetime plan, would strengthen the argument for using expenditure rather than income measures of incidence.

Table 5 presents data on the households whose expenditure ranking exceeds their income ranking.[14] The elderly are the single most important group, accounting for nearly one-quarter of those whose expenditure rank exceeds their income rank. Another significant group, 7% of those with income ranks below their expenditure ranks, consists of young households. These households may face heavy expenditure needs and rely on loans or transfers from family members to finance this consumption. For both the young and old households, total expenditures may provide a much more reliable measure of long-run economic well-being than current annual income. A similar argument might apply to the house-

---

[13] This should equal the percentage of the households in the lowest expenditure decile who are also in the lowest income decile. In Table 4, however, these numbers are not identical (61 vs. 63%). The disparity arises because the households in the CES sample are *weighted* by sampling weights. Although each decile is defined to include approximately 10% of the total sampling weight of the CES data set, there can be differences in the effective size of the deciles owing to the nontrivial sampling weight of some households.

[14] The table does not describe the relationship between income and expenditure. Most households whose expenditure rank exceeds their income rank spend more than their income, but so do some households with expenditure ranks equal to their income rank.

TABLE 5
Who Spends More Than They Make?

Expenditure decile − income decile	> Age 65 (%)	< Age 30 (%)	Share of nonelderly who are		
			Unemployed (%)	Sick (%)	> 2 Children (%)
1	25	9	1	4	18
2	30	5	2	6	10
3	35	3	2	2	18
4 or more	22	5	0	7	9

Source: Author's tabulations based on 1985 Consumer Expenditure Survey.

holds that are isolated in the last column of the table: those with more than two children currently at home. For these households, current expenditures may be high relative to their average lifetime outlays.[15]

Table 5 also presents information on the significance of households who may be experiencing transitory income reductions. Two percent of all households with expenditure ranks above their income ranks are unemployed; another 5% report illness of some type. For the latter group, medical needs may raise current expenditures at precisely the time when the household's earning capacity is reduced. Nevertheless, these categories account for a relatively small part of the high spending/low income group, suggesting that lifecycle factors are more important than year-to-year income fluctuations in explaining divergences between income and expenditure rankings.

One feature of the Consumer Expenditure Survey data which should be noted is the relatively substantial difference between consumption and income for some nonelderly households, with consumption greater than income. The source of these disparities warrants further exploration, but two possibilities should be considered. One is that both consumption and income are measured with error. This suggests using a weighted average of consumption and income rankings to estimate a household's ability to pay, with weights depending on the relative measurement error variances. A second possibility is that income is systematically underreported, with many households working part-time in the "underground economy." This explanation implies a strong rationale for focusing on consumption, rather than income, in the incidence analysis.

---

[15] An alternative approach to analyzing expenditure versus income-based incidence measures would divide each household's outlays by an "equivalent scale" based on its demographic characteristics. This would avoid spurious findings of high expenditure ranks among some large households.

III. INDEXED TRANSFER INCOME AND GASOLINE TAX BURDENS

The standard analysis of excise tax burdens assumes that a household's income is unaffected by changes in consumer prices. This assumption is significantly in error, however, for low-income households who receive indexed transfer payments. For these households, as Browning and Johnson (1979) noted, tax-induced changes in consumer prices are offset, perhaps with a time lag, by higher payments. This important institutional feature of current transfer programs affects the incidence of excise taxes, and also implies that the revenue yield from higher taxes is smaller than partial equilibrium calculations would suggest.

Table 6 presents information on the role of indexed transfers at different points in the expenditure distribution. The results are striking. Two-thirds of the income received by households in the lowest expenditure decile is indexed. This reflects the importance of elderly families who receive Social Security, as well as other transfer recipients, in this group. Such indexed transfers are also important for households in the second expenditure decile, where they constitute 46% of income, but decline at higher expenditure levels. Only 3% of the income of households in the highest expenditure quintile is indexed for inflation.

TABLE 6
Income Indexing and Gasoline Tax Burdens[1]

Expenditure decile	Average share of income indexed (%)	Gasoline expenditure/ income	Unindexed gasoline spending/income
1	64.9	4.18	0.70
2	45.7	5.24	2.79
3	29.4	6.23	4.65
4	20.0	5.78	4.70
5	16.5	5.92	5.03
6	11.6	4.94	4.32
7	6.4	5.51	5.16
8	4.1	4.72	4.50
9	3.1	5.85	5.68
10	3.0	5.17	5.01
Average	18.0	5.38	4.41

[1] Column three is computed by averaging, for all households within a decile, gasoline expenditure/ income − indexed income share × 5.38, where 5.38 is the population average ratio of gasoline spending to income as shown in column 2. This implicitly assumes that population average spending patterns are reflected in cost-of-living adjustments to transfer income.

Indexation implies that a gasoline tax increase that drives up consumer prices will be partly offset by higher transfer income. The extent of compensation is based on the average expenditure patterns of all households, as reflected in the budget surveys that underlie the Consumer Price Index. For households with large gasoline expenditure, this offset will therefore be incomplete; for other households with little or no spending on gasoline and motor oil, the tax increase will yield an income increase with no offsetting change in the cost of living.

The last two columns of Table 6 provide information on how indexation affects the burden of the gasoline tax. Because the natural metric is the fraction of a household's income that is indexed, the second column in Table 6 reports gasoline expenditures as a share of income for households ranked by total outlays. These data show that even the standard incidence measure, outlays as a percentage of income, does not decline sharply as one moves from low to high expenditure deciles. In this case, the lowest expenditure decile devotes a lower share of its income to gasoline expenditures than any higher decile.

The last column in Table 6 reports households' "unindexed exposure" to gasoline tax changes. This is defined as (gasoline spending/income) − indexed share of income × β, where β is the average ratio of gasoline expenditure to income in the population. The parameter β measures the extent to which indexed transfer programs will increase in response to higher consumer prices for gasoline. For a household with only indexed income and with a gasoline-to-income ratio equal to the national average, higher gasoline have small distributional effects.[16] For a household with no indexed income, unindexed exposure equals its current spending as a fraction of income.

Table 6 demonstrates that allowing for indexed transfers substantially alters the estimated burden of higher gasoline taxes. For households in the bottom expenditure decile, unindexed exposure averages 0.7% of income. In the second decile, this exposure is 2.8% of income, rising to 4.7% of income for expenditure decile three. Gasoline outlays as a share of income range between 4.3 and 5.7% of income for the highest seven expenditure deciles. For the households in these deciles, however, the gasoline tax burden is *significantly greater* than that for low-expenditure households. This casts serious doubt on claims that the gasoline tax burdens "poor" households. Although the burden on very well off households is no greater than that on the middle class, the middle class

---

[16] Even in this case, there is a deadweight burden from the tax as the consumer price is higher. The increased income from transfers should be viewed as a lump-sum independent of the household's gasoline purchases.

burdens in turn are significantly greater than those at the bottom of the welfare distribution.

Many policies could be combined with a gasoline tax to alter the net distributional burden of a fiscal reform. Expansion of the Earned Income Tax Credit, the Food Stamp Program, or explicit income tax credits for fuel expenditures are all possibilities, which are addressed using microsimulation methods in CBO (1990) or KPMG Peat Marwick (1990). None of these "offset policies" reaches all of the households affected by higher gasoline taxes, but all could be used to partly blunt the distributional effects.

IV. CAFE STANDARDS AND THE DEADWEIGHT BURDEN OF GASOLINE TAXES

The foregoing analysis focused on the distributional effects of gasoline taxes with no consideration of their efficiency costs. Assessing the efficiency effects of higher gasoline taxes is complex for two reasons. First, gasoline consumption produces externalities including pollution and highway fatalities. Whether higher gasoline taxes are efficiency-enhancing or efficiency-reducing is consequently an open question.[17] Second, some of the margins along which households might adjust to higher gasoline prices, notably the purchase of more fuel-efficient autos, are subject to other government regulation. Corporate Average Fuel Economy (CAFE) standards specify target fleet fuel economy levels for U.S. and foreign auto producers, along with corporate fines for failure to meet the targets.[18] This section argues that these standards are currently binding, and consequently restrict the degree of consumer response to higher gasoline prices.

Studies of gasoline demand find significant differences between long- and short-run price elasticities. This is because short-run adjustment to higher prices consists mainly of reduced driving, while the long-run adjustment involves changes in the auto fleet and possible relocation of some households. Dahl's (1986) survey concludes that the short-run elasticity of miles driven with respect to gasoline prices is -0.3, while the long-run value is -0.55. A number of studies, however, suggest that the ratio of long- to short-run elasticities is greater. With respect to the miles per gallon of new autos, Dahl reports a short-run elasticity of

---

[17] Cordes, Nicholson, and Sammartino (1990) and CBO (1990) discuss the external effects of gasoline consumption in some detail.

[18] These regulations are distinct from "gas guzzler" taxes, which are levied on particular auto models.

+0.17 and a long-run value of +0.57. Crandall et al. (1987) use a quite different methodology, calibrating optimal producer response to changing gasoline prices, and estimate that a 1% increase in real gasoline prices will raise average fuel economy by .72%. The net effect of higher gasoline prices on gasoline consumption is the elasticity of miles driven *minus* the elasticity of miles per gallon with respect to prices. At least half of the long-run adjustment thus takes the form of changing fuel economy demands.

Higher gasoline prices beginning from current levels, however, might not produce any change in fuel economy levels. Table 7 shows the real price of gasoline (in $1989/gallon) for the last 20 years, along with the fuel economy of new cars sold in the United States. The table shows that in 1989, the fuel economy of new cars sold in the United States averaged 28.3 mpg when the CAFE standard was 26.5 mpg.

The table masks important heterogeneity in the relationship between

TABLE 7
Gasoline Prices and Corporate Average Fuel Economy Standards

Year	Gasoline price/gallon		Average fuel economy	
	Nominal	Real (June 1990$)	Actual	CAFE standard
1970	0.36	1.19	14.9	—
1971	0.36	1.15	14.4	—
1972	0.36	1.13	14.5	—
1973	0.40	1.16	14.2	—
1974	0.54	1.41	14.2	—
1975	0.57	1.38	15.8	—
1976	0.60	1.36	17.5	—
1977	0.63	1.35	18.3	—
1978	0.66	1.31	19.9	18.0
1979	0.88	1.58	20.3	19.0
1980	1.22	1.93	24.3	20.0
1981	1.35	1.93	25.9	22.0
1982	1.28	1.73	26.6	24.0
1983	1.23	1.60	26.4	26.0
1984	1.20	1.50	26.9	27.0
1985	1.20	1.45	27.6	27.5
1986	0.93	1.10	28.1	26.0
1987	0.96	1.10	28.4	26.0
1988	0.96	1.06	28.7	26.0
1989	1.06	1.11	28.3	26.5
1990(June)	1.14	1.14	—	—
1990(Sept)	1.35	1.32	—	—

Source: Gasoline price data from Data Resources, Incorporated. Data on fuel economy is drawn from *Motor Vehicle Facts and Figures* (1989 edition).

fleet fuel economy and the CAFE standards across manufacturers, however. Greene (1990) notes that several manufacturers, notably the Japanese, currently exceed the CAFE standards by a substantial margin. The link between fuel prices and auto design characteristics thus seems unaffected by CAFE standards for these producers. Other auto firms, such as BMW and Mercedes, currently violate the CAFE standards and pay significant fines; their behavior in response to higher fuel prices is likely to be mediated by the shape of the CAFE penalty function. Finally, for the three large U.S. auto manufacturers, fleet fuel economy has moved in tandem with the CAFE standards. Leone and Parkinson (1990) calculate that GM was constrained in two years, and probably constrained in four more years, between 1979 and 1989. They estimate Ford to have been constrained in 1985 and possibly 1982, while they find no evidence of binding constraints on Chrysler.

The net effect of fuel price changes on long-run gasoline demand depends on the relative market shares of these manufacturers. An accurate analysis of the efficiency cost of higher gasoline excises, however, clearly requires a careful analysis of the interaction between prices and standards.

V. CONCLUSIONS

One of the central shortcomings of this paper is its partial equilibrium approach, particularly with respect to two issues. First, higher gasoline taxes would probably result both in higher consumer prices and somewhat lower producer prices for gasoline; some of the burden would therefore be shifted to the owners of current oil reserves. These owners are largely the equity holders in U.S. oil companies, who are relatively well-off households in the expenditure metric, and foreigners. The ability of the United States to export part of the burden of higher gasoline taxes is an intriguing issue that demands further study. Part of the burden of higher gasoline prices might also fall on owners of relatively low-mile per gallon autos. Kahn (1986) provides clear evidence that used car prices respond to gasoline prices. Because autos are the second most important asset in many households' portfolios, significant price changes could have important distributional consequences.

The second general-equilibrium issue that deserves analysis concerns the use of gasoline as an intermediate input. This paper has focused only on households' direct consumption of gasoline, neglecting the implicit consumption in many goods that have been transported via gasoline-intensive means. A more complete analysis recognizing indirect consumption could be performed using input–output tables and a computational general equilibrium model.

This paper also raises more general issues about the relative merits of income and consumption for measuring household well-being. The long-standing debate about the relative merits of taxing income and consumption provides a familiar base from which to argue for modifications in standard incidence analyses. However, despite the efforts reported in this paper, the source of differences between consumption- and income-based expenditure analyses remains unclear. Further research is needed to resolve these differences.

REFERENCES

Browning, Edgar K., and William R. Johnson, (1979). *The Distribution of the Tax Burden.* Washington: American Enterprise Institute.

Carroll, Christopher, and Lawrence H. Summers. (1990). "Consumption Growth Parallels Income Growth: Some New Evidence." In B. Bernheim and J. Shoven, eds., *The Economics of Saving.* Chicago: University of Chicago Press, in press.

Congressional Budget Office. (1986). *The Budgetary and Economic Effects of Oil Taxes.* Washington, DC: Government Printing Office.

Congressional Budget Office. (1990). *Federal Taxation of Tobacco, Alcoholic Beverages, and Motor Fuels.* Washington, DC.

Cordes, Joseph, Eric Nicholson, and Frank Sammartino. (1990). "Raising Revenue by Taxing Activities with Social Costs." *National Tax Journal* 43, 343–356.

Crandall, Robert W., Howard Gruenspecht, Theodore Keeler, and Lester Lave. (1987). *Regulating the Automobile.* Washington, DC: Brookings.

Dahl, Carol A. (1986). "Gasoline Demand Survey." *Energy Journal* 7, 67–82.

Davies, James, France St. Hilaire, and John Whalley. (1984). "Some Calculations of Lifetime Tax Incidence." *American Economic Review* 74, 633–649.

Greene, David L. (1990). "CAFE or Price? An Analysis of the Effects of Federal Fuel Economy Regulations and the Gasoline Price on New Car MPG, 1978–89." *Energy Journal* 11, 37–57.

Hill, Daniel. (1980). "The Relative Burden of Higher Gasoline Prices." In Greg J. Duncan and James N. Morgan, eds., *Five Thousand American Families: Patterns of Economic Progress,* Vol. VIII. Ann Arbor: Institute for Social Research.

Kahn, James, (1986). "Gasoline Prices and the Used Car Market: A Rational Expectations Asset Price Approach." *Quarterly Journal of Economics* 101, 323–341.

Kasten, Richard, and Frank Sammartino. (1988). "The Distribution of Possible Federal Excise Tax Increases." Congressional Budget Office.

KPMG Peat Marwick, (1990). "Changes in the Progressivity of the Federal Tax System, 1980 to 1990." Prepared for the Coalition Against Regressive Taxation, Washington, DC.

Leone, Robert A., and Thomas W. Parkinson. (1990) *Conserving Energy: Is There a Better Way? A Study of CAFE Regulation* (Arlington, Virginia: Association of International Automobile Manufacturers).

Pechman, Joseph A. (1985). *Who Paid the Taxes: 1966–1985.* Washington, DC: Brookings Institution.
Poterba, James M. (1989). "Lifetime Incidence and the Distributional Burden of Excise Taxes." *American Economic Review* 79, 325–330.
Sammartino, Frank. (1987). "The Distributional Effect of an Increase in Selected Federal Excise Taxes." Congressional Budget Office Staff Paper.
Slesnick, Daniel T. (1990). "Gaining Ground: Poverty in the Post-War United States." Mimeo, Kennedy School of Government, Harvard University.